# Feminism with Men

# Feminism with Men

*Bridging the Gender Gap*

Steven P. Schacht and Doris W. Ewing

ROWMAN & LITTLEFIELD PUBLISHERS, INC.
Lanham • Boulder • New York • Toronto • Oxford

ROWMAN & LITTLEFIELD PUBLISHERS, INC.

Published in the United States of America
by Rowman & Littlefield Publishers, Inc.
A wholly owned subsidiary of The Rowman & Littlefield Publishing Group, Inc.
4501 Forbes Boulevard, Suite 200, Lanham, Maryland 20706
www.rowmanlittlefield.com

PO Box 317, Oxford OX2 9RU, UK

British Library Cataloguing in Publication Information Available

**Library of Congress Cataloging-in-Publication Data**

Schacht, Steven P.
  Feminism with men : bridging the gender gap / Steven P. Schacht and Doris W.
Ewing.
    p. cm.
  Includes bibliographical references and index.
  ISBN 0-7425-4169-X (cloth: alk. paper) — ISBN 0-7425-4170-3 (pbk.: alk. paper)
    1. Feminism—United States. 2. Male feminists—United States. 3. Sex role—United
States. 4. Man-woman relationships—United States. I. Ewing, Doris W., 1939– II.
Title.
HQ1426.S32 2004
305.42'0973—dc22

2004009863

Printed in the United States of America

∞™ The paper used in this publication meets the minimum requirements of
American National Standard for Information Sciences—Permanence of Paper for
Printed Library Materials, ANSI/NISO Z39.48-1992.

To my father, E. P. (Phil) Schacht, who has far more feminist potential than I ever gave him credit for, and my younger "brothers," stepsons Andrew Merrick and Nikolas Crichton, in hopes that they and other young men will bring about a feminist future

—SPS

To my son, Quintin, in hopes that he and other young men of his generation will bring about a feminist future

—DWE

# Contents

| | | |
|---|---|---|
| | Foreword by Michael Kimmel | ix |
| | Preface | xiii |
| Chapter 1 | The Stalled Revolution | 1 |
| Chapter 2 | Why Men Should Be Feminists: Steve's Story | 23 |
| Chapter 3 | How Patriarchy Wounds Us All: Doris's Story | 41 |
| Chapter 4 | The Crumbling of Patriarchy: Equality as the Wave of the Future | 59 |
| Chapter 5 | Envisioning Alternatives to the Contemporary Manhood-Making Machine | 75 |
| Chapter 6 | Becoming a (Pro)Feminist | 95 |
| Chapter 7 | Being a (Pro)Feminist | 119 |
| Chapter 8 | (Pro)Feminist Parenting: Learning How to Mother and Be a Positive Feminist Role Model | 135 |
| Chapter 9 | Feminist Women and (Pro)Feminist Men: Moving from Uneasy to Radical Alliance | 151 |

| | | |
|---|---|---|
| Chapter 10 | Undoing the Original Phallic Sin: Envisioning a Fourth Wave of Feminism | 165 |
| | Afterword by Lisa Underwood | 183 |
| | References | 185 |
| | Index | 193 |
| | About the Authors | 203 |

~

# About Steve Schacht
## By Way of a Foreword

Steve Schacht was one of my role models. I'm sure it would have surprised him to hear me say that, especially since I was more than a decade his elder, and he often credited my books as among the major influences on his own work.

But Steve was a role model because he was so damned courageous. There's no other way to put it. He constantly put himself out there—way out there, in fact, beyond formal respectability, on the margins, where the people he studied and admired lived. He didn't have to be marginal: he chose it. Steve was a middle class straight white guy who hung out with, and even partially identified with, working class black gay drag queens. He was a hunky blond jock who played with students' projections in the classroom only to demolish stereotypes. He was a north-midwestern small town boy, raised on Wonder Bread and Minnesota-churned butter, who jumped off a cliff into the netherworlds of gender and sexual nonconformity.

No one would have expected this of the mid-80s graduate of University of North Dakota, who went off to graduate school at Colorado State well versed in quantitative sociology and statistics. But even there, he chose a somewhat unconventional topic for a dissertation: a study of how men use obscene phone calls to intimidate and harass women. His teaching, even in graduate school, was unconventional, and he broke barriers between teacher and student because of political commitment, not for personal gain. He identified as much with his students as he did as a sociologist.

Such choices had their costs. For a decade, Steve bounced from temporary position to temporary position, unable to secure a full-time tenure track job. Montana State, Gonzaga, Western Washington, Southwest Missouri State, Weber State—hardly the circuit for an aspiring drag queen or their student! Yet everywhere Steve went, he galvanized students, pushing them to think beyond any preconceived boxes they had expected. It's hardly an overstatement to say he rocked their world.

Aside from his engaged teaching, perhaps the only other constant in those years was that everywhere he went, Steve developed a strong collegial relationship with one uncompromising feminist woman colleague—a relationship that was politically engaged and probably somewhat maternal. These colleagues were his mentors, his feminist sounding boards, his academic support system. And two of them, Jill Bystydzienski and Doris Ewing, became his co-authors, co-editors, and among his dearest friends. And one of them, Lisa Underwood, whom he met while at Montana State, was colleague, companion, collaborator—and the love of his life.

When he finally landed a tenured job, at SUNY Plattsburgh in 1998, he landed in a department that knew what it was getting itself into—and welcomed it. In these last 5 years, Steve was his most productive as a writer, teacher, and scholar. Several books, guest editorships of journals and anthologies, and about a dozen articles explored the worlds of drag queens, feminist theory, and masculinity.

Perhaps that productivity was also spurred by a confrontation with mortality, as his job at Plattsburgh coincided with his diagnosis with colon cancer, which he battled with courage and humor for five years.

Steve's research and teaching centered on two themes: First, he sought to expose and thereby contribute to the demolition of the myths men live by. From obscene phone calls to "harmless" homophobic and sexist sporting activities, Steve was determined to make men "see" the costs of their behaviors, both to others as well as to themselves. In "Teaching about Being an Oppressor," a paper I published, first in *Men and Masculinities* and later anthologized in *Privilege* (a book I edited with Abby Ferber), Steve used Peggy McIntosh's "invisible knapsack" model to enumerate all the ways in which he benefited from being a man in our society. By exposing these benefits, he hoped to nullify them, to render them impotent. He was less interested in renouncing manhood, and more interested in renouncing its unearned privileges.

It was in his second arena that he truly found his calling: the compassionate engagement with the world of those men who have already begun that demolition of traditional stereotypes of masculinity: drag queens. Drag queens played with gender in a way that captured Steve's imagination and loosened his ties with essentialist notions of masculinity. If masculinity were no longer a fixed category, nor an inherently oppressive worldview, then perhaps dismantling patriarchy would be a little less difficult and a lot more fun.

Steve also served as my personal guide into that world, a world in which he felt so comfortable (and I felt so uncomfortable). After we had presented papers together at the National Women's Studies Association meetings and the ASA meetings, he took me to drag clubs he knew. The shows were fun, often hilarious, and even more often over the top.

And Steve understood the politics of my discomfort: that drag queens both embraced and celebrated the most traditional caricatures of femininity, and thereby offered simultaneous critique of traditional gender norms and a seemingly uncritical embrace of them. Had I been with anyone less politically astute or emotionally understanding, I would have had a truly terrible evening. But Steve understood, but did not privilege, my discomfort. Instead, he revealed, in person and in his writings, both the "absolutely fabulous" and the "flawlessly customary" world of drag.

I was really honored when Steve asked me to write the foreword to this book. I'll leave it to the reader to sort out the political and sociological arguments that he and Doris Ewing make. Steve was often hyperbolic to make a point—perhaps that partly explains his attraction to the drag world—and many, including myself, would question whether we need a "fourth wave" of feminism to fully incorporate men and masculinities, when one of the signal features of third wave feminism is its willingness to engage with men in working together in building gender equality. As a dialogue between Doris and Steve, it serves as a model for engaged and respectful communication between women and men, between mentor and mentee, and between, in that sense, second and third wave feminisms.

Steve knew he was dying of cancer for a long time, and maintained his teaching and his loving family life until the end. He lovingly reconnected with his father, and grew closer to Lisa, as he drew his family close. He maintained constant email contact with a far-flung group of friends, students, and colleagues, and, as always blurred the differences among them.

Steve and I also stayed in pretty regular email contact, though sometimes he was in too much pain to write much. In his last months, I sent him the CD of Warren Zevon's last album, *The Wind*, which was released in August 2003.

Zevon had long been one of my musical heroes, who masked his fearless optimism in some of the darkest and most cynical cloaks, writing seemingly sympathetic songs about mercenaries, spies, mass murderers, and, of course, werewolves of London. As he was dying of incurable lung cancer, Zevon gathered his family and friends for one last hurrah, and produced a hauntingly beautiful album that was long on compassion but mercifully short on maudlin self-absorption. In the album's final cut, Zevon asks the listener only to "keep me in your heart for awhile."

Steven Schacht died on November 21, 2003, surrounded by his friends and loved ones. He died as courageously as he had lived. Ah-oo.

Michael Kimmel
New York City
May 2004

# Preface

We met over a dozen years ago, in 1991, at Southwest Missouri State University. Doris was an associate professor and had been teaching at SMSU for nearly twenty years, while Steve was an assistant professor in his second visiting position since graduating in 1990. Age was only one of many significant differences between us, including our gender and sexuality. Yet we both also strongly self-identified as feminists. This one shared, vitally important commonality between us became the basis of creating an ongoing dialogue across difference and forging a working alliance to explore what sort of role men might play in the creation of a feminist future.[1] *Feminism with Men* represents our efforts to date to envision how women and men—together—might work toward creating a nonoppressive future.

*Feminism with Men* is a blend of our disparate personal experiences grounded in an academic feminist framework that loosely guides our discussion and analysis. While the primary focus of our book is feminism and gender in the United States, where appropriate, we also utilize cross-cultural examples and make note of the global implications of contemporary gender relations. The targeted readership of our book includes men with simply a beginning interest in feminism, men presently trying to live a feminist reality, and both men and women in academia theoretically exploring ways to combat oppression. In hopes of reaching the broadest audience possible, we have attempted to write this book with a primary focus on accessibility, but we have also provided extensive endnotes for those more interested in the various academic observations and arguments we make. Recognizing that some male readers of our book may already have a feminist self-identity—in our experience, most typically expressed as profeminism or male feminism—we have adopted the term *(pro)feminist* in an effort to inclusively describe and appeal to both of these diverse groups and all men who aspire to realize a feminist world view.[2]

*Feminism with Men* begins by noting the general beliefs in both the public mind and in many feminist circles that being a feminist means experiencing the world as a woman, that only women can be feminists, and that the social category of "men" is the enemy to women seeking gender equality. Such an outlook was of vital importance in the founding of the contemporary feminist movement. Unfortunately, however, much of feminism has continued to focus on gender exclusivity and to have an implied sometimes explicitly stated conceptualization of men as the enemy, and this has kept many men and women from identifying as feminists. We argue that the continued exclusion of men may explain why feminism is at present a stalled revolution.

Of course, the foremost reason for limits on feminist successes is the misogynist policies and practices of a male-dominated society. The conservative backlash that began in the early 1980s, often grounded in religious fundamentalism, has also served to dampen the feminist message.[3] We also recognize that problems have arisen when feminist women have tried to join forces with some self-identified (pro)feminist men.[4] The fact nevertheless remains that, as long as the feminist movement continues to be viewed by the general public as just one more narrow special interest group, seen as largely promoting the needs of just women, few men or women involved with men will embrace its cause. As we consistently argue throughout this book, the only way feminism will be able to bring about the widespread changes in society it envisions is to find fruitful ways to enter into partnership with men in the pursuit of an oppression-free future. We end chapter 1 arguing that feminist values are neither female nor male in focus and benefit but are ultimately part of a broader ethical outlook that would enable all people to live and truly prosper in a world without the harms of present forms of oppression.

In chapters 2 (Steve) and 3 (Doris), we separately offer our disparate personal journeys for coming to feminism and why we believe both women *and men* should embrace a feminist outlook. In both of our chapters, strong note is made of the unnecessary harms that result from oppressive masculine practices. Although coming from different perspectives, we both agree that women *and men* suffer from the harms of misogyny and male dominance. We also individually explore the numerous ways we have personally benefited from embracing a feminist worldview and why we believe feminism is a necessary ideology for survival in the future.

Chapter 4 explores ways in which our society is at a crossroads and why old patriarchal prescriptions and solutions are no longer adequate to address the pressing problems of the present. We note that today many Americans feel a general sense of "dis-ease" in that their lives are out of control, and they believe that much of what they do has little meaning beyond survival, immediate pleasures, and fleeting satisfactions. Similarly, many people feel alienated from their work, families, communities, and even themselves. We end the chapter by arguing that feminism has much to offer women *and men* who are interested in creating and pursuing a more meaningful and life-affirming way of being in the world.

Chapter 5 explores the superficial but all-powerful aspects of the modern manhood-making machine. The four pillars of masculinity and manhood—sex, money, power, and violence—are explored in terms of their unrealistic expectations and how, on the surface, most men would be considered huge manhood failures. We then explore some of the more prominent masculine venues that late capitalist patriarchy has created so that men who would otherwise be losers can also experience, often vicariously, manhood "successes": pornography, televised sports, gambling, video games, and alcohol. The chapter ends by arguing that men hoping to realize a feminist way of being must acknowledge the empty, often harmful promises and demands of the manhood-making machine, and then journey within to discover exactly what sort of life they really want to live.

Much has been written about the process women follow to become feminists. Since much of a feminist consciousness has been conceptualized as ultimately grounded in women's experiences of being oppressed, we argue in chapter 6 that men must travel a different path to feminism wherein they acknowledge that their role in contemporary gender relations is that of the oppressor. Writing specifically for the man who is just beginning a feminist journey, we then outline what we believe are several important trailheads for men on the way to becoming a (pro)feminist. All of these paths are fundamentally based on recognizing how many of men's conscious and unconscious actions are often quite oppressive to women and learning new, equalitarian ways of being in relation with both women and men.

Noting that there is a difference between *becoming* and *being* something, chapter 7 explores some additional considerations that men who make a long-term commitment to feminism often have to address. Particular attention is paid to how homophobia and misogyny often keep men from expressing a feminist outlook or acting accordingly, especially in the presence of other men. Suggestions are then made for effective, albeit often different, ways in which men can consistently "be" feminists in relation to women and men. Recognizing the power of socialization in gendering people and creating a sexist society, chapter 8 explores ways in which men could learn to be effective (pro)feminist parents. As in the previous chapter (7), we emphasize that children learn most from the congruity and integrity of the actions of a (pro)feminist man. Also building on some of the ideas initially put forth in the chapter 7 on "being" a (pro)feminist in the presence of women, chapter 9 explores how truly radical alliances between men and women might be forged and maintained in the pursuit of an oppression-free future.

The final chapter (10) of the text explores how the oppressively harmful masculine practices of the United States have in many ways become a global phenomenon. Under this lens, the 9/11 terrorist attacks are examined as both predictable and inevitable outcomes of present masculine politics on a world scale. We then argue that the time has come to end the insanity of the exploitive and oppressive practices that harm us all and that jeopardize the continued survival of Mother Earth. The text ends with an argument for the creation of a fourth wave of feminism wherein both the oppressed and the oppressor would forge partnerships across difference to reverse the destructive direction in which we are now headed as a species and as a planet.

We began work on *Feminism with Men* in 1997. Writing this text has been an ongoing, long-term endeavor. Because of the disparate social categories we belong to, our experiential backgrounds are obviously quite different. Except for our personal chapters (3 and 4),[5] each chapter, paragraph, sentence, and sometimes even word represents a negotiated inclusive outlook that was made possible through labor-intensive dialogue. *Feminism with Men* very much represents our struggle to take our differences and make them strengths for realizing a feminist future for both women and men.

At present there are no clear road maps for creating a feminist future. There is no golden age of gender equality or any nonoppressive models of cooperation from the past to draw on that are relevant to the modern world.[6] Like ourselves, however, many feminists and people opposed to oppression yearn for a day when equality will become the norm instead of some utopian dream. We hope that by word and example we have taken yet one more small step in realizing a world wherein everyone may become truly equally vested partners in enjoying all that life has to offer.

# Notes

1. Schacht and Ewing 1997a, 1997b; Schacht and Ewing 1998; Ewing and Schacht 2000.

2. See Messner 1997 for a more detailed discussion of differences in self-identity between (pro)feminist men.

3. Faludi 1991.

4. See Canaan and Griffin 1990 and Friedman and Sarah 1992.

5. Nevertheless, each of us also gave the other extensive feedback for revision of the "personal" chapters.

6. See Eisler 1987 and her argument that male dominance is more a historical anomaly of the past five thousand years of patriarchy than the norm of our species' existence.

# CHAPTER ONE

# The Stalled Revolution

Recognizing the irreconcilable tension between the search for a secure place from which to speak, within which to act, and the awareness of the exclusions, the denials, the blindness on which they are predicated.

—Biddy Martin and Chandra Talpade Mohanty[1]

During the 1970s, there was great excitement about feminism and a sense that realizing what it called for—gender equality—would change the world. Many of those who participated in the movement at this time felt that, if women united together in sufficiently large numbers, male dominance would crumble and gender equality would fill the resulting void. "Sisterhood is powerful," "I am woman, hear me roar, in numbers too large to ignore," and "Women unite, stand up and fight, abortion is a women's right" became rallying cries for the women's movement. After congressional passage of the Equal Rights Amendment and acts such as Title IX (both in 1972), and the legalization of abortion in 1973 through the Supreme Court's *Roe v. Wade* ruling, victory seemed imminent. Yet, as time would tell, ten years later the Equal Rights Amendment would fail to win confirmation (falling short by two states) and the right to an abortion would increasingly come under attack. While Title IX would increase the number of women athletes, female athletic program directors and coaching positions, once the almost exclusive province of women, would increasingly be filled by men. By the 1990s, the term *feminism* itself was increasingly becoming an F-word of sorts to many women, as it has always been in the public mind, with anyone claiming such an identity often being written off as nothing more than a man-hater and probable lesbian. What was once a vital social movement with no limits was now viewed by feminists themselves as entering into a period of abeyance.[2] What had gone so wrong in such a short period of time?

After the failure of states to ratify the ERA, feminism started to fragment into many small groups, each with their own agenda and ideological perspectives. While the second wave of feminism in the 1970s was, at least in the public mind, largely unified under a "one size fits all" vision, the third wave of feminism most visibly emerging in the early 1980s contained many obviously different, sometimes competing ideologies. As a result, today there is no one feminism but rather an extensive assortment of feminisms. To mention some of the more prominent feminist perspectives an individual can draw from and/or claim identity with, there is liberal feminism, cultural feminism, radical women of color, radical feminism, lesbian separatist feminism, postmodern feminism, socialist feminism, multiracial feminism, standpoint feminism, psychoanalytical feminism, eco-feminism, and womanism.[3]

As evidenced in this far from exhaustive list of feminisms, and very much like most post-modern social movements, third-wave feminism is explicitly sensitive to experiential differences that result from one's race, class, sexual orientation, and nationality. Since most women experience other forms of inequality beyond just gender, this new outlook recognizes that there must be "different strokes for different folks" and a flexibility of possible solutions to perceived issues. Even before the failure of the Equal Rights Amendment in 1982, mainstream feminist organizations like the National Organization for Women (NOW) and the National Women's Studies Association (NWSA) were already being criticized for primarily representing only the interests of white, middle-class, heterosexual American women. This failure to include minority women, and a general embarrassment about lesbians in their midst, resulted in questions about whether groups such as NOW and the NWSA could even speak for the majority of American women. Voices previously silenced in the 1970s by a call for a united political front were, in the 1980s, demanding not only that they be heard but that their issues be given equal standing to the concerns of their white, straight, often economically better-off sisters.[4]

All of this occurred precisely at a time when the nation was entering a conservative period that involved a significant backlash against all civil rights movements.[5] Claims of oppression and reverse discrimination by white males undermined efforts for any progressive change. Feminism was often portrayed by the media as an attempt to put women's rights ahead of other people's, as being antiman and antifamily, and basically a movement of dykes

and weirdos. Like special interest groups, small feminist groups began competing with each other for members and resources while rejecting those with
whom they had ideological differences. Lesbian separatists, always present,
became more vocal in calling for alternative culture rather than reforming
the existing one.

Other groups, such as women of color and Third World women, often
formed alliances with men in order to combat more broadly defined socioeconomic oppression. Sadly, most young women of today largely define feminism as a movement of their mother's generation and something that has little relevance to them. Shifting from a seemingly unified outlook to one that
is splintered, *feminism* has become a confusing term that means many things
to different people.

Unfortunately, many contemporary feminist groups seem to have a strong
focus on maintaining ideological purity, however that might be defined in
the given setting, and aggressively attack any insiders who might dare offer
criticisms of their chosen definition of feminism.[6] Any serious criticism of
feminist thought by inside members is frequently met with harsh response,
often being silenced by the claim that any serious questioning of widely accepted feminist ideals or "facts" ultimately benefits patriarchy. Even well-
recognized feminists receive negative sanctions in the form of cutting comments and derogatory labels if they are seen as defectors from the group's
"party line." Some of this rigidity is understandably necessary to present a
united front to combat outsider attacks from the media and right-wing politicians; nevertheless, such a stance not only silences insider dissension but it
grievously stifles any thoughtful self-examination within feminism.

We believe, however, an equally valid argument can be made that the silencing of serious criticism about present feminist practices actually supports
patriarchy. This is a form of oppression called cultural imperialism, the rendering of "other" perspectives as invisible or deviant, and very much one of
the master's tools.[7] Moreover, when a movement is unresponsive to the needs
of the social group it claims to be speak for—all women—and often fails to
validate members' very real experiences, commitment is weakened and many
drift away. Today, many women and men who are making very feminist
choices in their personal lives refuse to self-identify with the women's movement. Feminism will continue to be marginalized in the larger culture as long
as mainstream women and men feel alienated from the movement.

In the section that follows, we argue that imbedded in the very success
and politics of the feminist movement in the 1970s were also seeds of its
seemingly inevitable downfall. We believe, however, that the same seeds
that caused the women's movement to become a stalled revolution can be

fruitfully reenvisioned to finally make the far-reaching feminist goal of gender equality a more realistic possibility.

## The Seeds of Failure

> And whereas this can appear as the necessary and founding violence of any truth-regime, it is important to resist that theoretical gesture of pathos, in which exclusions are simply affirmed as sad necessities of signification. The task is to refigure this necessary "outside" as a future horizon, one in which the violence of exclusion is perpetually in the process of being overcome.
>
> —Judith Butler[8]

Seemingly inherent in any truth-regime—old or new—is a defined outside, an "other," an enemy, and a signifier to validate the necessity of the ideology being exercised or proposed.[9] This seems to hold true regardless of whether the given ideology is well established, with a long tradition, or is a newly emerging outlook in opposition to an ideology already in place. In fact, most ideologies, old or new, seem to be predicated on some exclusion that comes to signify the importance of, and to give seeming inherent meaning to, the chosen worldview. Thus, most ideologies appear to be based on some dialectical stance, always in direct opposition to some real or constructed "other."

Almost all of the many emerging social movements of the past thirty years have been based on some form of identity politics, such as one's gender, race/ethnicity, sexual orientation, social class, religion, nationality, or age.[10] These identities selected for movement building have been single, fixed, and rigid—albeit still socially constructed—such as the Black movement, the gay movement, or the women's movement. Moreover, each of these identity movements have been born out of the very real oppression such individuals experienced in the larger society. And as one would expect, each of these emerging social movements has proposed an ideology that has an inherent enemy as its basis. In all these cases, the enemy logically and quite understandably has been the given oppressor group. The emergent identity is both juxtaposed, yet still in dichotomous objection to, the identity of the given dominant group; thus, a form of binary rejection is seemingly the inherent basis of all oppositional identity politics.

Nevertheless, one must also conclude that this is a quite necessary first step to challenge any of the many preexisting inequalities. Not only is there strength in numbers, but for any subordinate group to truly understand its own experience of oppression, people must share experiences with others in a group made up exclusively of members from the oppressed group. This is requisite for individual empowerment and the creation of a group identity sufficiently large to confront the inequalities experienced by individual members of the emerging collective. Consciousness-raising and empowerment are obviously unlikely outcomes if members of the given dominant group—the enemy—are in one's midst. Thus, the maintenance of an outside, replete with an "other" as its occupant, is necessary at the inception of any newly founded identity that sets out to politically contest the oppression of its individual members.

For feminists, the obvious and quite legitimate ideological "other" and enemy has been the quintessential dominant class itself—men. Especially during the late 1960s and early 1970s, a time during which the second wave of feminism occurred, this ideological recognition lead to the formation of exclusive women's groups to raise awareness about patriarchy and to empower individual participants.[11] Women in these groups shared experiences of oppression with each other that enabled them to name men as their common enemy. Categorically denouncing male dominance and all the oppression that accompanies it was without question a necessary first step in forming a sustainable feminist movement.

Unfortunately, however, once feminism had so successfully identified a common enemy—men—it had also planted the inherent seeds of its own limits and downfalls. While few feminists envision a future in which women would be the dominant gender, men have been rigidly cast into the role of "other," always the potential enemy who can never be fully trusted. Even in feminist groups that have accepted a few token "good guys" as members, these men are still often viewed as "the 'other' in our midst." What began as a political strategy for organizing took on so much anger in feminist rhetoric that it became very difficult for many women to identify any meaningful and equal role for men in the women's movement. Not only is it impossible to achieve gender equality by excluding men, but such an outlook ironically promotes essentializing notions of gender that have long been used to support and sustain existing gender inequalities.

## Undoing Sexism in Feminism

> As long as females take up the banner of feminist politics without addressing and transforming their own sexism, ultimately the movement will be undermined.
>
> —bell hooks[12]

Men in patriarchal societies are said to use women's "otherness" as a symbolic signifier to attest to the power of the phallic and male dominance. In a strange twist of fate, the women's movement in so fashioning men to be their "other" has, in an inverse manner, created its own phallic signifier of sorts. This is not to say that women are now more powerful than men, or even desire to be; however, it is to say that much of women's empowerment and resulting oppositional identity has been the result of a process that has featured the ideological rejection and exclusion of men—feminism's operational "other." While, as we have already noted, this was necessary for the creation of the women's movement, it has also led feminists to continue to exclude men. It is difficult to imagine how the continued omission of men will ultimately result in gender equality.

Most feminists today, especially those in academic settings, use more politically astute language and identify "patriarchy" as the enemy. However, such a seemingly neutral naming practice is largely an abstraction, like blaming "the system" or "society" for all your ills. It is all so persuasive that, short of totally withdrawing from mainstream society, no solutions seem possible. Ranting and raving about patriarchy conjures up images of Don Quixote tilting at windmills. This image does not speak to most people on a personal level that would "get the juices flowing." Although patriarchy is a politically correct target, on an emotional level it is still the men who are seen as ultimately the enemy by many feminist women.

Obviously, it is unrealistic to expect men to join a social movement that defines them as the enemy. Moreover, the vast majority of women have significant men in their lives whom they deeply care for, such as fathers, spouses, sons, and friends. Thus, this underlying principle of feminism has made it nearly impossible for all but a very small handful of men to embrace this worldview.[13] It has led to the rejection of feminism by women who otherwise could agree with many of the specific concerns and ideas that feminism proposes.

Some feminist theorists insightfully argue that the social institution of heterosexuality provides the ideological bedrock upon which all gender inequality is based.[14] Unfortunately, this has lead some lesbian separatists to implicitly and explicitly accuse heterosexual feminist women of sleeping with the enemy, of not being truly woman identified, and, ultimately, of being traitors to the cause.[15] As a result, many heterosexually identified feminists take a defensive posture, lest their intimate association with men call into question their ability to make truly feminist choices in their lives.[16]

Assuredly, there often are very real costs associated with heterosexual relationships for women, but these are the result of social expectations of what are considered gender-appropriate behaviors, not inherent biological aspects of being a woman or a man. Merely being a man or a women is not sufficient grounds to incur gender oppression. Rather, it is institutional structures and values reflected in individual attitudes and behaviors in *both men and women* that cause and make alive gender inequality. Moreover, while lesbian separatism is a valuable choice and life-line for many women, the fact is that this is a meaningful option for only a small number of women (presently perhaps 10 percent at best). The majority of women will continue to be in sexual relationships with men and, of course, not all lesbians are feminist.

Even for many women actively embracing a feminist stance, simply and categorically defining men as the enemy has caused divisiveness between feminists. Most women of color and Third World women refuse to identify with feminism because of its rejection of men and largely see it as the domain of privileged white middle-class women in the West. These women experience multiple forms of oppression beyond sexism (e.g., racism and classism), and the men in their communities also share these experiences. Such women are fighting a revolution on several separate but intersecting fronts and understandably are resistant to embrace what are perceived as notions of man-hating and the exclusion of men just to fight for women's rights. Many, if pressed, are more likely to join with men against white oppression, and the corresponding classism that often accompanies it, than to join with white women against their own men. Not surprisingly, feminist women of color have been far more likely to envision meaningful roles for men in the struggle against oppression than have their white sisters.[17]

Although feminism is presently a stalled revolution of sorts, real progress has nevertheless been made during the past thirty years. Liberal feminist groups such as NOW and the NWSA have brought about many sociopolitical changes; the glass ceiling for women has moved up to a higher level, and there assuredly is increased awareness about sexism in our society. More minority women's voices are being heard, and there is increasing tolerance of gay and lesbian individuals in our society. Thus, obviously a great deal has been accomplished, but much remains to be done. Realistically, all people of goodwill—regardless of their gender, sexual orientation, ethnicity, or religion—will be needed to envision and create a feminist reality. If truly given the choice, we honestly believe that most people would rather live in a world based on empathy, peace, and equality than in one based on hatred, warfare, and oppression. For this to occur, each of us must acknowledge the role that we play in the continuance of gender and other forms of inequality, as women and men, oppressor and oppressed.

While the exclusion of men, categorically defined as the enemy, has played a vital role in the creation of a contemporary feminist identity, it has also caused almost all men and the majority of women to reject the feminist ideology as a design for change. Their rejection has severely limited feminism from reaching its ultimate goal of gender equality. If a truly feminist future is ever to be realized, who and what the enemy is must be redefined. We believe the time has come for feminism to redefine what is to be considered the enemy—ultimately, the sexist thoughts and behaviors of men *and women*—and what sorts of outlooks will be necessary to bring about a nonoppressive future. In short, for feminism to move from a presently stalled to a once again vital revolution efficacious enough to bring about true gender equality, a significant paradigm shift will have to occur in feminism.

## Envisioning a Paradigm Shift

Some historians have noted that civilizations seem to go through a cyclical process. In the formative period, new ideas and ways of doing things are mixed with the traditional, change is in the air, and large numbers of people are passionately committed to bringing about called-for changes. The classical period is one of great energy and achievement, a time when earlier visions are translated into action and all adherents prosper. Gradually, strong leaders utilizing despotic power emerge and the populace becomes less involved; the focus is more on empire building than improving the daily lives of the common people. The post-classical period is characterized by an increasingly formal style that stifles creativity and new ideas, leaving little or no room for experimentation. External opposition and internal divisiveness, coupled with competition for resources, undermine any shared vision or purpose. The civilization falls into decline. Unfortunately, feminism appears to be going through a similar process.[18]

We now know that organic models of history, such as the one just offered, are more descriptive than predictive, as not all civilizations follow these same series of stages in some lockstep order. When the descriptions fit, however, they can provide meaningful questions for consideration. People caught up in the process may fail to see the bigger story, as it often is told over many lifetimes and sometimes even centuries. Typically, the "post" period is one of increasing rigidity and declining vitality. This period is also marked by confusion and disillusionment until something new comes along—a paradigm shift—that can incorporate the old into a larger vision. We believe it is time for a paradigm shift in feminism.

Any new feminist paradigm will have to be flexible and truly inclusive, a broad-based coalition of interest groups with respect for differences. All genders, racial and ethnic backgrounds, sexual orientations, socioeconomic levels, ages, and nationalities must be welcomed and included in this coalition.

Ideological purity and rigid standards for inclusion are counterproductive to building such a coalition. Tolerance, acceptance, and ultimately respect for all who are challenging existing inequalities and trying to adopt nonoppressive ways are needed to unify people into such an alliance. For this to occur in feminism, explicit and implicit categorical outlooks of who is the enemy— now seemingly all men/patriarchy—will have to be reconceptualized to view the enemy as sexist and oppressive thoughts and behaviors undertaken by both men and women. Whether exploited by the media or insinuated in feminist theory and practice, the ever-popular war between the genders will have to be replaced with radically new outlooks and ways of doing things that will enable both women and men, the oppressed and the oppressor, to enter into a partnership to end oppression.[19]

While men have a long history of involvement in feminist issues, much of their activity has been opposed to feminism or, when supportive, has been at best an auxiliary and peripheral allegiance to the larger women's movement.[20] Perhaps part of this limiting outcome is that in our society "human concerns" have traditionally been narrowly defined as "women's issues." Thus, what we are calling for is not just men's participation in what are often seen as women's issues, but for men to eventually become equal partners in the building and sharing of a feminist reality. We believe herein is found the vision and the promise of a nonoppressive, egalitarian future for all people.

Inequalities found in contemporary gender relations are complex issues with no simple solutions. How we conceptualize these issues clearly influences the outcome. Scarcity models that view gains for women only at the expense of men in some zero-sum competition for resources promote resistance to change. Blame and accusations, such as slogans of "unearned male privilege" and "reverse discrimination," have often generated a lot more heat than light. A truly inclusive feminist theory and practice is needed that accepts sympathetic men as comrades in struggle and equal partners in the building and sharing of a feminist reality. Or as bell hooks argues, "A male who has divested of male privilege, who has embraced feminist politics, is a worthy comrade in struggle, whereas a female who remains wedded to sexist thinking and behavior infiltrating feminist movement is a dangerous threat."[21]

Change is difficult when it is widely believed that current structures are not only normal but inevitable. Five thousand years of patriarchy have left people convinced that it is the natural form of human organization. Yet alternatives to patriarchy and male domination do exist. What little is known about ancient societies strongly suggests that partnership models for living were once the norm instead of the exception.[22] Our ethnocentrism often leads us to discount the egalitarian ways of Native Americans and other contemporary tribal societies as backward, with little to offer us.[23] Despite all the examples of gender equality one might draw upon, it is still a formidable task to see them as real possibilities

Anthropologists have documented that certain forms of social organization are associated with specific means of production and technology levels. Patriarchy is typical of agricultural and pastoral societies, but the apparent necessity of this social structure seems to break down when societies modernize and industrialize. Today both men and women increasingly work in jobs where physical strength is irrelevant. Reliable birth control and day-care centers have given women the opportunity to plan and control reproduction, slowly eroding the traditional basis for a gendered division of labor. With most women now receiving their own paychecks, women do have real economic power and businesses cannot survive without taking them into account. As we enter the postindustrial age of technology and cyberspace, the "usefulness" of patriarchy would appear to be coming to an end. Sociocultural evolution would seem to be on the side of the egalitarian future rather than working against it.

Gender roles are slowly changing, but time alone will not solve existing problems. Historically, male dominance/patriarchy has adapted to new circumstances by changing form—things often have to change an awful lot to remain the same—and some of these modifications have actually made it, like a retrovirus, stronger and more resistant to change. People, both men and women, are also reluctant to change their own behavior or deeply examine their own gendered assumptions, as change is always uncomfortable and frequently frightening. People seem more interested in simple solutions and ways to dismiss the true complexities of the issues, saying that we are all "just people" and basically the same. Such a position minimizes how deeply sexism and oppression are ingrained in our societal structures and the very real differences in experience and perception of women and men, which make it difficult to critically examine all the gender inequalities that do exist.

The goals and assumptions of major social institutions in American society are increasingly being challenged on all fronts. The high cost of dominance and oppression, of exploiting the environment for demands of ever-increasing productivity, and the turning away from basic human needs has resulted in widespread cynicism and dissatisfaction. People want to work less and spend more time with their family and friends. They seek relief from the constant stress of competition and materialism, the control of their lives by large corporations, and the filling of their lives with meaningless responsibilities. Both men and women are ready for a change.

Ending ideological sexism is a necessary first step but insufficient to bring about significant change. It alone will not end exclusionary practices or bring people together. If equality is ever to have real meaning, it must occur in both public and private arenas, in formal institutions, and in our personal lives. Rather than exclusively focusing on those who oppose change, time and energy must also be spent on welcoming those seeking a feminist future and building coalitions with them. All those open to feminist ideals must be encouraged to participate regardless of their specific views or depth of commitment. Real dialogue between feminist women and (pro)feminist men and cooperative efforts in our communities to bring about change are the only things that will promote greater understanding. It is only through the process of working together in partnership and as equals that barriers between men and women will ever be eliminated. For this to actually occur, radically new forms of gender relations will have to be envisioned and acted upon.

## Reconstructing Gender Relations

Virtually all people understand gender as two very discrete categories, male and female. As a society we use dichotomous characteristics, based on sex, psychological states, and interpersonal ways of being, to illustrate polarized differences.[24] At birth, each of us is given one of only two possible labels, girl or boy, which subsequently determines how others treat us and how we are expected to act. When we initially meet someone, this label is the first and, perhaps, most important assessment, conscious or unconscious, that we will make, and it directly determines our expectations and treatment of the other person. Individuals who fail or refuse to live up to these two essentially prescribed social states of being are met with "ostracism, punishment, and violence."[25] Social forces demand that we accept one of only two possible states of being, and both men and women's attitudes and actions reflect and sustain dichotomous gender designation.

The binary basis of male and female also provides an important ontological blueprint for all preexisting hierarchical inequalities. To many, the values, characteristics, and ways of being associated with men and the masculine are seen as dominant and inherently superior to those associated with women and the feminine. Accordingly, men are seen as the rightful leaders of society while women are seen as natural subordinates. These beliefs are strongly reinforced by the teachings of patriarchal religions and supported by the practices of all major social institutions.

Although in recent years people have paid lip service to equally valued and complementary gender traits, many people still react in emotional ways that strongly suggest that these traits are not viewed as equal. This either/or societal design is found in an array of other social categorizations such as white/black, rich/poor, and straight/gay, which also call for the sorting of all people into corresponding dominant and subordinate statuses. When woven together, these intersecting matrices of existence simultaneously enable, constrain, and almost entirely determine one's life choices and experiences.

Postmodern research has attempted to deconstruct this dichotomous notion of gender, demonstrating that there are few if any absolute gendered behaviors.[26] This theoretical perspective convincingly argues that gender is a socially created concept that significantly varies by time, culture, and social status in the given social structure. Through face-to-face social interaction, people come to understand what attitudes and behaviors are expected as "normal" for men and women. An elaborate system of conspicuous and insidious social control is established to enforce these norms, rewarding those who conform and punishing those who fail to do so. Children are taught to feel bad about themselves if they do not conform, as failure to do so results in ridicule and exclusion by peers.[27] Pressures for a child to conform to gendered expectations are so overwhelming that by adulthood she/he seldom questions the "absolute reality" of these socially created assumptions. Behavioral conformity to the vast majority to gendered norms, in turn, is used as evidence of the seeming innateness of being male or female, while those who refuse or are unable to live up to these standards are conceptualized as abnormal, freaks of nature, and less than human.

Yet in patriarchal societies the given behavior undertaken is often of far less importance than the gender of the individual that undertakes it. For instance, in a society where only men make baskets or pottery, it is a task that requires great artistic talent, but if women do these same things, it is a craft that anyone can learn to do with a little practice. In Western societies a man who prepares food is a chef, while a woman who does so is a cook. In all male-dominated societies, men's work always receives higher economic rewards, supposedly because it requires greater physical strength and/or skill. In Third World countries it is common to see women climbing rickety ladders, balancing a load of bricks on their heads, while a male bricklayer sits quietly cementing each brick in place. In many cultures women carry heavier loads and do more physical labor than men.

In the West, men are considered more rational and objective, while women are emotional creatures who lack the stability and logic to be trusted with important decisions. Women are seen as being moody and controlled by their biological cycles and base instincts, whereas men are viewed as reasonable, rational, and closer to God. Because of these mythical views of gender, men are expected to assume major leadership positions, to be responsible for long-range planning, and to set the basic goals and objectives of society. These sexist views are so built into our social institutions that they continue to have social influence long after the majority of people may have rejected them intellectually.

Gender expectations also vary by race and class, reinforcing other indicators of status. Victorian "ladies" had delicate sensibilities and "swooned" easily (mostly because of the corset and other restrictive undergarments), while immigrant women worked long hours in factories and black slave women bore the lash in field labor alongside their men. In such cultural models of gender, the answer to Sojourner Truth's "Ain't I a Woman?" is obviously no. Only white women of means could be true women—the seemingly rightful heirs of the "natural" characteristics of womanhood—while women of color and those in the lower classes were denied this claim. Such sexist, racist, and classist assumptions make it clear that gender is socially constructed.

Moreover, the very notion of what gender is becomes quite complicated when one considers transgendered individuals.[28] If individuals can simply change their gendered attire and mannerisms, and then successfully pass in public as a member of the opposite sex, is the resultant behavior really impersonation or more imitation of a gendered script for which there is no original? Transgendered individuals have perhaps always existed, but during this past century, through technology and surgery, we have witnessed the creation of the transsexual individual who can biologically and often legally become a member of the opposite sex. People can choose the outward manifestations of who they feel they really are inside. While most transgendered individuals still focus on dichotomous notions of gender, the relative ease with which they cross these either/or gender barriers clearly demonstrates that gender is a learned behavior. What we call male and female is actually far more complex and capricious than the discrete, binary categories we try to force upon all individuals.

While deconstructing the seeming innateness of gender is obviously an important first step in understanding how gender inequalities are created and maintained, postmodernism has rightfully been criticized for breaking social reality into ever-smaller pieces while offering little to take its place. Taking postmodernism to its logical extremes, identity as we know it is so stripped from the individual that it leaves no basis for social action or movements like feminism. Recognizing the social basis of gender identity and other social identities (i.e., race, class, sexual orientation, and so forth) is a necessary but insufficient step for bringing about equality. Once something is dismantled, such as the oppressive "nature" of gender, something must be offered in its place. Otherwise, at best, old forms will manifest themselves in new ways to fill these voids, or at worst, chaos will reign. Since the creation of nonoppressive realities will require all people—women and men—to join together in cooperative partnership, we will have to envision a new social order, new identities, and new ways of interacting with others.

## Envisioning a Truly Inclusive Feminist Future for Everyone

Two models for reconstructing gender and socially creating new gender expectations predominate in feminist thought today. Much of Western feminism encourages androgyny, a belief that people of both genders should be free to develop their own potential by incorporating both male and female traits. Differences between the genders should disappear as opportunities and resources become equally available to persons of both genders. On the other hand, Third World women and minority women in this country, tend to embrace a model of complementary gender roles. Men and women are seen as different, each having their own areas of interest and expertise. As such, both genders must work together because they complement each other, each gender supplying things the other lacks. Many of the divisions in contemporary feminism revolve around issues raised by these two models.

In theory androgyny offers freedom from oppressive gender expectations, which is quite appealing. Unfortunately, however, under the mantle of sameness, Western feminists have often pitted men and women against each other in direct competition. This outlook creates a zero-sum game where any women's gains are seen as being purchased at the expense of men, and any women's losses are seen as the result of male oppression. Antagonism between the genders and some degree of "man-hating" seem to be inherent in the Western feminist model. The media have played on this perception, leading many women to reject feminism rather than embrace a movement that seems to be in direct opposition to men they love.[29] Despite the rhetoric of some feminists that men need to be included, there has been real resistance by *women and men* to doing so, a resistance that has contributed to the "stalled revolution."

The complementary model emphasizes cooperative efforts between the genders to achieve change beneficial to both. Often combined with strands of socialist feminism, this outlook argues that both men and women are oppressed by the larger socioeconomic, political and/or racist system. Because women have been taught to have more finely developed human relation skills and are perceived as "natural" nurturers, this model holds, that women should be given greater power and authority for making family and community decisions. Such arguments have empowered poor women to take control of vital human services such as health, education, and community welfare. In the end, however, men's characteristics and women's characteristics are seldom equally valued, and women are still restricted to subordinate roles.

Clearly, both of these models have advantages and limitations. Can a model of feminism be constructed that is neither oppositional nor subordinate to men? Obviously, the first and foremost goal of feminism is to establish gender equality and oppose all forms of oppression, but what other outlooks would be necessary for this to occur? We believe the criteria for such a model are clear:

1. The very different and real experiences of individuals based on the social classifications of gender, race, class, sexual orientation, and so forth must be recognized, honored, and seen strengths, not as impediments to bringing about an equalitarian future.
2. There must be maximum encouragement for the freedom of all individuals and groups to develop their own potential, talents, and interests.
3. Cooperative efforts among all people of goodwill must be advanced regardless of gender, race, class, or sexual orientation.
4. The well-being of families and communities everywhere must be promoted.

This, then, is the task of our book: to socially construct a new model of gender relations and to suggest ways in which this may be achieved. Such an effort will require a commitment to the cooperative involvement of both women *and men*, as feminism can no longer afford to exclude men if it has any hope of bringing about the significant social change envisioned by early feminists. For this to occur, feminist values and ways of acting for men will have to be envisioned and promoted.

## Feminist Values and Ways of Acting for Men and All People

The creation of an equalitarian future will require a radical reconstruction of gender relations. On the surface, this may sound like an overwhelming, perhaps even impossible, task. However, since feminist values are ultimately human values, such ideals and ways of acting are perhaps commonsensical and not all that unconventional even for men. In fact, we suggest that to varying degrees, all of us as young children were taught the following "traditional values," values that are also quite feminist in meaning and potential application:

- It is better to help than hurt people, especially those less fortunate, such as the poor, the elderly, the sick, and children.
- People are more important than things. Everyone should be treated with respect and never as a thing or an object.
- Violence is never an acceptable way to solve problems.
- Getting along with others, cooperatively working together, and sharing are better than competition, conflict, and trying to get and keep everything for yourself.
- Everybody should get a turn, equally have a say in decisions, and get their fair share.
- We should try to make the community where we live and the world in general a better place to live for everyone.
- We should treat the land with reverence and act kindly toward nature.
- Equality, fairness, and justice for all are morally right, while dominance, exploitation, and oppression are morally wrong.

Unfortunately, as young boys grow older they are taught that traditional feminist values do not apply to the real world; long before puberty they are forced to learn what are seen as more practical, instrumental ways of being. On the other hand, girls and other apparently lesser beings (the poor and people of color) are expected to continue holding these admirable traditional/feminist values into adulthood. Their presumed naïveté is seen as charming, attractive, entertaining, and necessary for applying the healing bandages to the damage wrought by men's rational actions.

The second wave of feminism correctly identified how these insidious beliefs were used to maintain women's subordination and oppression. The truly powerless have always been taught to focus on relationships, to emphasize emotional and intuitive qualities of being, and to have lower career aspirations. Women formed consciousness-raising groups, rejected their childhood socialization, and took assertiveness training to learn to think and act more like men. The hope was that if women—especially white, educated, middle-class ones—could learn to successfully operate in the competitive male world, they would equally share in the privileges and benefits categorically but differentially afforded to men. A few women have individually benefited as a result of these strategies, but there has been little change in the social structure. Women who advance by learning to think and act like men are unlikely to be strong proponents for feminist change.

Clearly, what is required is that men (and some women) give up oppressive forms of male privilege and ways of being in relation to others and instead learn to think and act in ways that are typically expected of and associated with women. Men must reaffirm those traditional values we were all taught as children. They must demand that institutions be more responsive to human needs and use their power and privilege to bring about structural change to this end. What is needed is coalition politics: the coming together and joining of men and women who share traditional values so that each can contribute to constructing and living such a worldview, in which they can individually make a difference in a manner that benefits everyone. We then become fellow travelers in the search for social justice and more humane, life-affirming ways of living.

Already we can see examples of this happening. The appeal of the Green movement in Europe and the environmental movement in the United States indicates that large numbers of people are recognizing that unlimited growth and technological advancement in the search for ever greater profits lead to environmental destruction. Many men are no longer willing to sell their souls to the corporation for material gain.[30] The destructiveness of modern warfare makes it an unacceptable solution to most international problems. Voices in the media across the United States protest the violence and chaos in our cities, the moral decay and loss of meaning, and the social isolation we feel in our communities. People are ready for a change.

However, we cannot genuinely change society by using the same old patriarchal strategies and ways of doing things. As Audre Lorde insightfully stated nearly twenty years ago, "the master's tools will never dismantle the master's house."[31] Feminism is much more than just an awareness of injustice and the affirmation of humanistic values. It is a style of working together where cooperation replaces competition, a way of being that welcomes and respects a diversity of nonoppressive perspectives, and a value system that rewards efforts for the common good over individual self-interest. Since most people shape their behaviors to the expectations of the existing reward system, there must be real change in how benefits are distributed. It is not enough to recognize the shrinking rewards given for conformity in the present patriarchal system. Men and other dominant members of society will stop using oppressive forms of privilege and power only when they see that dominance, control, and exploitation are no longer viable options and that more equitable ways of being are positively rewarded.

It is for this reason that existing (and yet to be founded) (pro)feminist groups of men are so vitally important.[32] Here men can talk with other men about the negative consequences of patriarchal assumptions and behaviors and, in their place, offer positive, feminist-based alternatives. The truth is that feminist/traditional styles of thinking and acting simply work better for self and community. These groups provide resocialization and teach men to think and act in ways more traditionally associated with women—not to be passive and powerless, but to be compassionate and to use the personal power each of us has for the general good of all people.

To borrow some insightful words from Paulo Freire:

> This volume will probably arouse negative reactions in a number of readers. Some will regard [our] position vis-à-vis the problem of human liberation as purely idealistic, or may even consider discussions of ontological vocation, love, dialogue, hope, humility, and sympathy as so much reactionary "blah."[33]

Feminists, especially those in academia who have worked long to establish feminism as n intellectually rigorous pursuit, may object to the seeming "sloppy sentimentality" of our thoughts here. Our position may be seen as supporting some nostalgic, essentially Victorian notion that women are "the gentle sex" and ultimately responsible for upholding moral values and civilized sensibilities in an otherwise competitive and brutal male world. This, of course, is the core of the complementary gender model, one that many critics argue locks women forever in a state of "separate but unequal." Nevertheless, it is true that we are valorizing the values most often associated with women, such as nurturing, love, and compassion for others, and believe it is a sad commentary on patriarchy (and some feminist women in practice) that the basic goodness associated with these ways of being is so identified with inferiority. In this ultimately misogynist outlook, any group truly exposing and living basic humanistic values can never escape a subordinated status, while only those women who learn to reject these values can ever become successes in patriarchy.

When rational/instrumental values are not balanced with more traditional/feminist values, then materialism, competitive individualism, run-away technology, and exploitation for narrow definitions of profit that benefit the few will eat away at and destroy the social fabric of our families, communities, society, and world. The new feminism we are suggesting, inclusive of men and all people, seeks to bring about a balance and to return to traditional values, which most people were taught as young children but which many of us have sadly forgotten as we have grown older. This will ultimately require us all, but especially men, to relearn how to view and relate to others and the world.

This new social order must be based on the recognition that it is not possible to reap the benefits of dominance and privilege without also being a potential victim. Winners are only made possible by losers and, in hierarchical social orders where almost all are marginalized on some criteria, we inevitably share in the losing. Men must recognize that their pain, both physical and mental, is the result of patriarchal values and that they too would benefit from change.

Social institutions reward aggressive/competitive behavior, and men fear being discounted and "treated like women" if they fail to successfully compete.[34] Most implicitly know that it is a patriarchal lie that wealth and power inherently bring happiness, but they also recognize that as long as oppression exists, it is better to exploit than to be exploited. Active steps to change the values and rewards on which our basic institutions operate are obviously required.

A famous feminist slogan is "the personal is political." Today, in this time of political disillusionment and apathy, perhaps a better slogan would be "the political is personal." No longer can we hide from the pain of patriarchy and pretend that what happens outside our immediate social networks is irrelevant. We must work together to bring about systemic change. We passionately believe that traditional/feminist values and ways of being are the only ones that can reverse the cataclysmic course we are now following as we advance into the new millennium.

## Realizing a Feminist Future

It is urgent that men take up the banner of feminism and challenge patriarchy. The safety and continuation of life on this planet require conversion of men.[35]

Any meaningful feminist agenda of the future will have to be rooted in an awareness of the hitherto invisible ways in which patriarchal and corresponding gender assumptions have dominated our thinking and prevented us from recognizing viable choices for social change. This work will have to be done by both women and men, separately and together, if we are to move beyond the narrow range of options that can be seen through patriarchal lenses. We believe that the time has come for us to reject these priggish patriarchal boundaries and to begin to rethink old problems in new ways.

The creation of nonoppressive realities will ultimately involve all people cooperatively joining together in new partnerships to seek radically new ways of envisioning and acting in relationships. This will require a belief that things can be different, a vision of what this should be, and a commitment to making these changes happen. It also requires a change in what behavior is rewarded. Such positive social change will require each of us, but especially men, to relearn those traditional—perhaps ultimately feminist—values we were taught as children.

This book is very much like an aerial photograph of a largely uncharted territory. Each of its chapters attempts to map out small pieces of this vast landscape. We hope that *Feminism with Men* will contribute to illuminating this frontier and will lead others to join in this ongoing dialogue and exploration of the possibilities of what might be. Present ways of doing things must change before we destroy ourselves and the planet. The time has come for us to start working together instead of slowly but all too surely suffocating under the oppressive weight of divisive, individualistic patriarchal realities.

**Parable**

Spider knows
each strand of Her web

and when Her callers
break away
destroying her weaving as they go
She does not die
but spins again
the pattern
of her life

no fool is She
no more a fool than I
for traveling on
a single thread
because she knows
having often seen
what comes from the center
can never be
forever broken

—Jaci (1939–1980)[36]

Drawing on the strength of the individual threads that each of us travels on, when woven together in an all-encompassing, nonoppressive manner, a brilliant tapestry emerges that radiates with the potential beauty of everyone's center. In writing this book we have attempted to intertwine the individual threads we are each traveling on to offer a truly inclusive vision of feminism that is far more powerful than its separate parts.

# Notes

Portions of this chapter were adapted from Ewing and Schacht 1998.

1. Martin and Mohanty 1986, p. 191.
2. Taylor 1989.
3. Offen 1988; Lorber 2001.
4. Moraga and Anzaldua 1983; Walker 1983; Lorde 1984; Baca Zinn et al. 1986; Collins 1991.
5. Faludi 1991.
6. From our experience, on forums such as the electronic WMST-List and the MS Boards, there is often considerable condemnation and censure of anyone who is critical of feminism even if it be in a constructive manner.
7. Young 1988; Lorde 1984.
8. Butler 1993, p. 53.
9. Bystsydzienski and Schacht 2001.
10. Aronowitz 1992; Morris and McClurg Mueller 1992.
11. Morgan 1970; Deckard 1983; Newton 2000.
12. hooks 2000, p. 12.
13. Sharik 2000.
14. Dworkin 1987; MacKinnon 1989; Schacht and Atchison 1993.
15. Rich 1980.
16. Wilkinson and Kitzinger 1993.
17. hooks 1984, 2000; Lorde 1984.
18. Many historians and sociologists have advanced and described the cyclical nature of history and social change here. See Ashley and Orenstein 2000 for more detailed descriptions of the often cyclical basis of societal change.
19. Eisler 1987, 1995.
20. Kimmel and Mosmiller 1992.
21. hooks 2000.
22. Eisler 1987.
23. Herdt 1994.
24. Lorber 1994.
25. Butler 1991, p. 24.
26. Lorber 1994; Butler 1990, 1993; Fausto-Sterling 1985, 2000; Schacht 1998.
27. Lorber 1994.
28. Garber 1992; Lober 1994; Feinberg 1996; Bullough, Bullough, and Ellias 1997; Cromwell 1999.
29. Deckard 1983.
30. Gerson 1993; Connell 2000.
31. Lorde 1984.
32. See the Appendix of Schacht and Ewing 1998 for sampling of such groups.

33. Freire 2002, p. 37.
34. Faludi 1999.
35. hooks 2000.
36. Steven Schacht's mother.

~

# CHAPTER TWO

# Why Men Should Be Feminists:
# Steve's Story

Chapter 1 offered various reasons why both women and men should embrace a feminist worldview to bring about gender equality. Within this argument, however, was only a general discussion of why men should even want to be feminists. That is, what sort of specific benefits does feminism and its call for reconstructing gender relations offer to men? Answering this question from our two personal perspectives is the task of chapters 2 and 3.

In this chapter, I (Steve) offer my experiential reasons, as a man, for becoming a feminist and why I think other men would benefit from embracing a feminist world view (Doris will speak for herself in chapter 3). Implied in this discussion is my growing understanding that thinking and acting in traditionally masculine ways are oppressive and harmful to women. This recognition provides the basis of the second section of this chapter, wherein I argue that, despite the many social forces that make most men ignorant of the costs of women's subordination, some men have become aware of women's oppression, typically through significant women in their lives (as I did), and that this provides a wonderful opening for these men to adopt a feminist outlook and way of being in the world.

Also found in my discussion of becoming a feminist is my eventual recognition that "doing masculinity" is also often very costly to men, especially those subordinated in the process, and that feminism should be about ending not only women's oppression, but all forms of oppression. Accordingly, the third section explores the costs of present gender relations for men. Men would appear to be the winners of the present "battle of the sexes," but the

harms far exceed any realistic benefits associated with such oppressive practices. My chapter ends by noting the significant costs of contemporary gender relations for both women and men and the promise of a feminist future
for all people.

## Growing Up

Perhaps, like many other men who claim a feminist identity, the path I traveled to grasp such an outlook has been meandering, often painful, and not
well marked. The seeds of this very divergent course of personal being were
initially planted by a woman who was, among many other beautiful things, an
artist, a poet, a radical feminist, and my mother. She spent untold hours trying to share with me the anguish and the hope of her feminist vision. In my
preadolescent years I accompanied my mother on numerous pre–*Roe v. Wade*
protest rallies (the chant "women unite, stand up and fight, abortion is a
women's right" still clearly rings in my ears), often helping her paint banners
and signs to carry as we marched. She took me with her to anti–Vietnam War
protests at the University of Minnesota campus (1968–1970), several rallies
for George McGovern (on election day I was sent home from school for wear-
ing a McGovern T-shirt, as my school also served as a polling place, and she
thought it was great that I had the day off to spend with her), numerous NOW
meetings, and untold Women's Art Registry Movement (WARM) openings
for various feminist artists in the Twin Cities. Until my teen years, my mother
was my best friend and most trusted confidant even though I had many close
same-age playmates, both male and female, at this time.

The presence of strong, independent women like my mother was by far
the rule rather than the exception in my childhood. Both my grandmothers
left their physically abusive husbands during a time when divorce, regarded
as a social stigma, was also difficult to obtain. My maternal grandmother was
one of the first female bank tellers in Chicago in the 1930s, when only men
were seen as responsible enough to handle money. Meg Lake, a woman the
family met while living in England and whom I grew up fondly calling Nan,
taught me a great deal about what it means to be a strong, caring individual.
Nan was a widow in her sixties who had lived as a pensioner for years. Without ever appearing judgmental, Nan never hesitated to offer her sage advice
to me when she thought I was doing something wrong (what I can now see
as being oppressive toward others) yet was just as quick to give her support
and approval when she thought I was doing the right thing (treating others
equitably). Many of these lessons were taught with fascinating stories of her
growing up in Scotland and living through World War II. As one would ex-

pect, almost all of my mother's friends were strong feminist women themselves. My mother's feminist values in raising me were very much reflective of, and consistent with, other important women in my childhood.

In a somewhat ironic twist of fate, I was also raised by an equally involved and caring—albeit in a very masculine way—father who was in many ways my mother's antithesis. Until I was six years old, he was in the Air Force and a navigator on F-4 fighter planes. In 1967 he became a pilot at Northwest Airlines and our family moved to Minneapolis. As one might expect from a former fighter jock (in his late-sixties and retired, he still flies high performance acrobatic airplanes competitively and teaches others how to fly these planes), the activities I undertook with him were very different. Model rockets, innumerable fishing trips and plane rides, racing sailboats, and ski trips (both locally and out West) were all ways I would share significant time with my father growing up. When I was old enough (ten), he took me on hunting trips, and often thereafter guns and hunting trips to places like Iowa and South Dakota were birthday and Christmas presents asked for and given. Replete with significant class privilege, I was afforded limitless opportunities for doing masculinity. Like many boys growing up, I knew my father as my first teacher of the intricacies of manhood and all the privilege it had to offer.

Although the entire family often did do enjoyable things together, like vacations to visit relatives and friends in Arizona, Florida, California, and Europe, in a very real sense, my mother and father individually, quite visibly but perhaps unconsciously, competed for my attention, as if in a contest to see whose values I would most embrace and accordingly call my own. Moreover, both very much adopted a parent-as-pal approach to child-rearing in this family competition of sorts, and in hindsight, I must admit I was very much the stereotypical overindulged, spoiled child growing up. In many ways, their conflicting values became scripts for the disparate ideals I would embrace and the behaviors I would undertake as I grew older.

For better or worse, both of them separately did a wonderful job of indoctrinating me into two very different worlds and ways of being—feminism and masculinity—but the personal costs were significant. My brother Jim, three years younger, often seemed to be treated as an afterthought as my parents showered their attention on me. Attempts were made to keep things even between us, especially monetarily, but perhaps because he was younger, and/or the fact that he was not the daughter my mother always hoped for as a second child, he always seemed to be unfairly treated as a second-string player in our family contest.

As probably both a reflection and result of this ideological competition, my parents separated for several years during my mid-teen years, each taking turns living in the family home with the other maintaining an apartment. Since my father was a pilot and away for many days of the month, in a sense, their separation had probably already occurred years before their formal breakup. Both dated; my mother even publicly became a lesbian, openly stating and showing her affection for her female partners, while my father pursued flight attendants and other younger women. Although my parents eventually did reunite, this was largely the result of my mother's becoming critically ill, and their personal differences remained quite apparent.

It is perhaps not so surprising, given societal expectations of "successful" young men, that my father's ways of being—and all the masculine privilege it had to offer—once I reached my teenage years seemed far more valuable, and I increasingly rejected the wisdom of my mother's voice. Correspondingly, during this time I undertook nearly every imaginable "stupid men trick" there is, from playing hockey, to binge drinking, to driving a sports car (often far too fast and under the influence of alcohol and various other drugs), to starting fistfights with other men, to womanizing. This also meant that I increasingly spent more and more time in male-exclusive groups, and except for largely sexual purposes, sadly had little meaningful social interaction with women.

Being quite average in height and weight, but having an acumen that enabled me to almost always get in the last cutting remark, I often surrounded myself with young men who were often larger and/or older. I was often the "mouth" of masculinity in these groups, whereas they often provided the muscle to back up whatever I might say. Frequently, like a pack of wolves, almost always under the influence of alcohol and or/some other drug, we set out to see who could sleep with the most women—score—and sought out other men to verbally and physical subordinate, all in the quest to prove our seeming superiority, our manhood. Little stood in our way as we sadly cut a swath of wanton destruction wherever we went. Moreover, even though I was arrested numerous times between the ages of fourteen and twenty-one, my class privilege enabled me to hire a lawyer; combined with a racist criminal justice outlook that white "boys will be boys," that meant that I was never really held accountable for my illegal and destructive actions.

I could see the disappointment in my mother's eyes each time she became aware of my most recent masculine exploit, but in some sick sense, it almost seemed to validate the appropriateness and increase the value of my destructive, often misogynist behaviors. In something like a classic Freudian separation complex, much of what she stood for and what at one time I had shared with her, seemingly became the exact opposite of who I then sought to be. At a point in my life when I was most engrossed in these various masculine rituals, nineteen, my mother died, and perhaps as if to punish her for doing this, I would unfortunately remain lost in a masculine daze for years to come.

## My Return to Feminist Beginnings

Realistically, I did not revisit the values my mother so earnestly tried to instill in me until my mid-twenties when I was in graduate school. In my master's program, as a "budding" young sociologist (or perhaps more like a dormant flower coming to life again), I began to explore the many different theoretical explanations of what ills the world and the possible ways to fix it that sociology has to offer. While each of these perspectives seemed to provide some answers, none of them matched the clarity of my mother's voice that I increasingly now began to hear—that sexism is the root of all that ails society. By the time I was working on my Ph.D., her voice had become so insistent that I chose to do my dissertation on obscene telephone calls as instruments of male dominance, and almost all my work since then has been on gender-related issues grounded in some feminist theoretical perspective.

Perhaps even further attesting to the efficacy of my mother's voice is the fact that during both my master's and Ph.D. programs I was sorely lacking any real radical feminist role models. The few women that were found in either of these programs would have to be considered liberal feminists at best. While working on my dissertation, however, this strangely seemed to work very much to my advantage. That is, what do you do with a highly motivated young man—I was correctly perceived by my fellow graduate students as a rate-buster and understandably shunned—who is doing a radical feminist analysis of obscene telephone calls in a program that emphasizes rural sociology and Third World development? To counterbalance this, I undertook a program of study in which all the elective courses were in the statistics department, published an article with each of my sociology committee members (all purposely selected for their general sociological expertise and apathy toward the program's core focus), and, with the guidance of my committee chair, Patricia Atchison, wrote an entirely hassle-free dissertation that, beyond minor editorial suggestions, was entirely a creation of my own making. I completed my Ph.D. in a somewhat unheard-of three years.

Quite truthfully, the first radical feminist role model I would personally came in contact with in all those years since my mother's death in 1980 was Doris Ewing, whom I met in the fall of 1991 when teaching at Southwest Missouri State University. Initially standoffish to my being a little too enthusiastic and masculine in my approach, she slowly but surely showed me—

by words and example—what being a radical feminist with integrity is all about. Despite her understandable feelings toward men in general—avoidance and distrust—she nevertheless took the time to personally share with me the experiential world of her feminist outlook. Although I had read untold feminist works, she was the first individual to take the time to offer me her personal reading of all these various works from a woman's perspective. She patiently and literally opened a world to me that previously I had only read about. This is a gift for which I am forever indebted to Doris.

I would spend only two years teaching at SMSU. Like many positions to follow, in spite of having high teaching evaluations and a quite active publication record, I was basically fired for being too radical, too feminist, too queer, and an obvious gender traitor of sorts. Consistent with my SMSU experience, since leaving graduate school in 1990 I have held six different positions, spent a year unemployed, and been divorced twice.[1] Moreover, during the early years of my return to my mother's feminist ideals, I increasingly found myself being betrayed and rejected by men (especially those in academia). Conversely, many of my attempts for seeking acceptance from feminist women were met with a cool reception, often filled with indifference, mistrust, and even hostility. Having been disappointed so often, many women understandably distance themselves from self-proclaimed male feminists.

And yet as dire and bleak as these realities may initially appear, I also believe myself to be a quite privileged and fortunate individual. I partially use the term "privileged" so as to not confuse my various ordeals with the very real oppression so many women experience. After all, at any time I always had the *choice*—itself indicative of privilege and something seldom afforded women and other subordinated people—to embrace the tyranny of those passing judgment on me (in particular, many of my superiors in academia and men in general) and would have been quickly accepted as one of them.

More specifically, I consider myself quite fortunate to have been able to heal many of the wounds of my past, both inflicted on others and self-imposed, as I now believe I am becoming the son that my mother would have been proud of. It is in honor of her life, and all the important values that she taught me, that I now try to live my own life. I also use the terms "privilege" and "fortunate" to be reflective of the significant people who have supported and accompanied me on this largely unknown path I am presently traveling. Without these individuals always being there for me over the past few years, I am convinced that, for various reasons, I would not be here today to write this passage.

## Growing into a Feminist Understanding

I believe my first step toward realizing a feminist outlook was to recognize that many of my actions (and sometimes lack thereof) were harmful to significant women in my life. No longer wanting to participate in women's oppression or to collude through inaction, I actively set out to change my ways and share my newfound vision with others. Perhaps like many feminist women (as discussed in chapter 1), I had a feminist outlook that until very recently had an explicit misandrist bias. Male course participants and friends often called me a man-hater, said I must hate my penis, and asked me if I would rather have been born a woman. To a certain extent, there was some truth in their accusations, at least my explicit hatred of men, as I often used my feminist stance as an excuse to personally and publicly deride and belittle men. Moreover, if I had treated women in a similar manner, my behavior would have rightfully been seen as quite misogynist. Although I was actively working on breaking free from oppressing women, I was still maintaining a sexist outlook that falsely enabled and justified my now treating men as lesser and seemingly subordinate to my new feminist ideals.

To be honest, as a white heterosexual male from a privileged class background, I can lay no claim to having ever experienced oppression. Since most of my daily interaction with men is with other somewhat similarly situated individuals (i.e., male friends, academics, and participants of my courses), I found it really difficult to see any costs associated with being a man in our society. Moreover, my feminist outlook at the time made me largely oblivious of the very real oppression many men experience because of their race, class, or sexual orientation. I was far too busy repenting for my past sexist ways—a recovering misogynist, of sorts—and like some ranting, holier-than-thou televangelist, chastising other men for partaking in such behaviors.

Since 1994 I have been involved in an ongoing ethnography of gay drag queens. For over a year (1999–2000) I facilitated a violence intervention group with convicted batterers in which all of the men were from ethnic minorities and/or from working class backgrounds. Many of the gay men who have befriended me in various drag contexts have generously shared with me their experiences of being oppressed, as have the men in my batterers group. This led to an important and quite recent realization on my part. Not only was my mere existence and past behavior oppressive to women, but so are the attitudes and actions associated with my class background, race, and sexual orientation—to women *and many men*. That is, men do not experience any sort of gender oppression, but many men do experience class, race, and sexual orientation oppression.

Prior to my seeming epiphany, on a rational, apathetic academic level, I could acknowledge that men, too, could be oppressed, but on a gut level (based on my experiences with men largely similar to myself) this did not ring true. All I could emotionally and rather myopically see was men's oppression of women. Actually listening to men's experiences of being oppressed, becoming close friends with some of them, gay men in particular, I could finally viscerally appreciate the insidious and multifarious basis of oppression. Moreover, it is through my gay male friends, many of them drag queens, that I would first experience an emotionally based same-sex friendship. This forced me to deal with many of my own issues of homophobia and to grudgingly recognize how many of my attitudes and seemingly well-intended prior interactions with gay men had actually been based on their subordination to maintain my lofty heterosexual station.

Susan Faludi in *Stiffed* makes a powerful argument that perhaps one of the most significant wounds many men suffer in the pursuit of manhood, as either the "dutiful" or the "rebel" son, is never being able to experience the affection, love, and acceptance they felt as a child from their father (assuming they even had a father figure of this sort in their lives, growing up).[2] For many years I wrote my father off as unable to express these feelings and, from my feminist outlook, viewed myself as superior to him and his masculine ways of being. My recent and continued battle with colon cancer has forever changed our relationship in a positive way. I started to demand that he say to me "I love you" and to give me hugs and kisses, and while his discomfort at doing so was sometimes quite obvious (especially at the beginning), he has recently thanked me for teaching him how to do these things, something that his father never taught him.

The truth of the matter is that my father is actually an extremely caring individual who, like many men in our society, has never been taught how to express and share his emotions and affections with others. There is a real unfairness in simply writing these men off without offering them reasons and ways for changing. Perhaps, like my father, I think with a little guidance many manly men are quite capable of change and learning to be affectionate toward others. As I recently wrote him, "Dad, I want to thank you for your increased willingness to express affection and feelings of love to me. At least for me, a hug and a kiss from my father, whether in the hospital or not, age five or 41, feels quite comforting. I can finally not blame or resent you for not being able to do what you didn't know how to in the past, and now cherish your expressions of love and affection." As much as my own self-definition of feminism has limited me in terms of how I have viewed other men, it also has provided the roots for healing to occur in many areas of my life.

As a result of all of this recent feminist growth on my part, I am increasingly not so quick to write off other men in general as "misogynist scum bags," inevitably subordinating them in the process. Beyond my male feminist and gay male friendships, men I can now respectfully call friends (some of them students) are police officers, National Guard members, rugby players, and fraternity members. In groups of men such as these I most risk falling back into competitive, sexist ways, but it is also here that I have played an important role in spreading a feminist message to those least likely to ever hear it.

As reflected in the poem below, written by my mother (a true story about a woman in my neighborhood growing up), my present definition of feminism is about treating all people as valuable and potential equals, as I believe all forms of superiority—regardless of how overt or insidious they appear— are a disease that ultimately leads to oppression. I look to rid myself of the poison of feeling superior to anyone and to live in a healthy world of true equality for all. Using myself as an example of someone who was sadly very afflicted with the plague of superiority at one time, in perhaps some bizarre way I demonstrate that there is hope for even the most oppressive of us to recognize how harmful our attitudes and behaviors can be to others, and to change our destructive our ways.

**I Didn't Even Know Her Name**
She lived in the neighborhood,
not close enough to be a neighbor,
but in the neighborhood.
We never met,
I know her only as she was known
by others, a sloppy housewife,
who had "let herself go"
as they say.
A woman who displayed,
at the slightest opportunity,
the feminine weakness for
talking too much of too little,
her words like clutching fingers
keeping the efficient from their efficiency.

I saw her once,
from a distance,
just after three of an afternoon,
that time of day when neighbor women
tend to feel most acutely

the prick of significance
of their many roles.
She seemed so insignificant,
as she shuffled out to her doorstep
with disheveled hair and gesture,
an indecisive form in a torn bathrobe.

As I passed her by
I told myself a secret,
so softly I wouldn't
hear it myself,
that she made me feel so superior.
Her mere existence provided
the proper contrast
for appreciation of me.
Others, too, must have
shared my secret,
for they left her carefully alone,
as if fearing contamination.

One evening,
not long after I had seen her,
she got up from her bed,
where she had been spending
more and more of her time.
She must have heard the voices,
the laughter, the living sounds
of her children,
as she walked quietly across the room
to where the gun was kept,
loaded,
waiting,
for something to happen.
And for one moment, perhaps,
she realized her significance
as she thrust the gun between her lips
and put a period
to the endless sentence
without subject
which had been her life.

And I
when I knew it all

was sick
with the sweetness of my superiority.

— Jaci (1939–1980)

## Unveiling the Faces of Women's Oppression

We live in a society where ignorance truly is bliss, especially for those with unearned male privilege and status, which in turn often provides men with an excuse to deny the existence of the very real and harmful sexist hierarchical realities that surround us and the active role men must play in their maintenance. While some men are willing to admit that women are disadvantaged in our society, very few men are willing to acknowledge that they themselves are overprivileged.[3] After all, to actually do so would mean that men would not only have to admit the unearned and unjust basis of their advantage but perhaps even personally change and give up some of their privilege (especially oppressive forms). In the highly competitive world we live in, giving up any advantages—earned or unearned—one might have in the game of life would seem foolish, at best, to most men.

Intuitively, almost all men do believe themselves superior, and many even pay homage to this oppressive social reality, but few are willing to admit just how harmful such an outlook is to women in our society. Like myself growing up, one way many young men effectively dismiss women's oppression is through same-sex friendship groups where women are seen as the "other," objectified as sexual prey, in some ways even seen as the enemy, and ultimately used as the real estate upon which real men do masculinity. Accordingly, pornography, strip shows, and even prostitutes often play important roles in these settings, as they serve as a medium over which male bonding is accomplished, and both reflect and sustain the misogyny upon which they are based. Women, in pictorial form or in the flesh, merely provide the necessary but detested turf upon which many, if not all, masculine identities are misogynistically based. It is nearly impossible to see the pain or hear the screams of an object, let alone the enemy, unless it is to use these images or sounds as signs of superiority and for pathological enjoyment. To truly deaden any feelings of empathy—to be a "real man"—means that men must deny not only the feelings of those around them, men and especially women, but also repress their own feelings in the process.

As a result, men in these groups are expected to always guard against becoming too emotionally involved with any one woman. If they do, their friends will accuse them of being "pussywhipped," a "mush," and weak, and they potentially risk no longer being welcomed to partake in the group's activities as a full member. Terms such as "bitch," "fag," and "gay" are also frequently used in these settings as put-downs, suggesting that anything associated with the feminine, except for purely instrumental purposes (sex), should be avoided at all costs. Many young men will boastfully proclaim that they plan to remain single forever, as if thinking that true intimacy is somehow evil and something to be feared, and that being intimate might force them to view a woman as potential equal and give up their priggish, masculine outlook of the world.

Many women enter the dating battlefield looking for a man who will emotionally relate to them, or a man they think they can reform and teach this to, while men expend considerable energies seemingly trying to avoid intimate relationships. In the past, "getting caught" often meant getting a women pregnant, whereas today this often means seeing the same woman more than once for sexual purposes (i.e., in some men's groups you only get points for scoring the first time and sex thereafter is seen as suspect). Either way, "love 'em and leave 'em" is a motto that all men have heard and many prescribe to. Of course, the majority of men eventually do become emotionally involved with women, but when this happens, the group may view them as fallen comrades, captured by the enemy, and forced to give up their freedom to be with a woman. As the verses of the song declare, "another one bites the dust."

And yet most men have (or eventually will have) significant women in their lives—as partners, mothers, sisters, daughters, or just friends—whom they deeply care about, love, and sometimes even view as equals. I believe herein lies the beginning seeds of feminism for men. By making men aware of the unearned advantages that society confers upon them, and the misogynist attitudes necessary to maintain such outcomes, some men begin to see how such practices and attitudes are oppressive to the significant women in their lives. This leaves many men in an ideological bind: How can they personally express concern and respect for the welfare of these women all the while supporting realities that cause women's oppression in larger societal settings?

For me, this has obviously involved making (and continuing to make) many significant changes in my life. My life partner, Lisa Underwood, is an incredibly strong, independent woman who works as a crisis counselor with survivors of sexual and physical abuse. We are fortunate, as our respective jobs allow us to both support and complement each others' efforts in constructing and living a feminist worldview. Housework is not decided in terms of "his and her" jobs but in terms of what needs doing, and someone (often both of us) just does it. Attempting to live as equals has also meant that I have been able to experience a deep sense of intimacy previously unknown. Our personal energy typically seems to flow together, instead of in opposition to, or in spite of, as did many of my previous relationships.

The way I view and interact with women in general has also significantly changed. I have slowly learned ways to view women without inevitably objectifying them in the process. I have learned that listening is just as valuable as speaking and that I do not need to have the last word in every conversation. My learning to listen has led many women to generously share with me their experiences, feelings, and insightful visions of what a just world might look like, and as a result, I have increasingly found ways to appreciate and relate to women as equals. In short, I am increasingly coming to understand that feminism is both a public stand and a personal way of being, and that the two are really one and the same.

While often not under the guise of feminism, yet quite probably in response to feminist activism, increasing numbers of men in our society are starting to acknowledge women's oppression and trying to do things to promote gender equality. Men's involvement in the home and raising children has slowly but surely increased, with a few even opting to become house husbands while their wives actively pursue a career. Many men are becoming involved in traditional women's problems, such as rape and wife battering, starting programs and activities that confront men's misogynist attitudes. As reflected in Doris's son Quintin's and my growing-up experiences, increasing numbers of young men are being raised by feminist mothers. Sure, regressive, backlash agents of misogyny still exist, such as Howard Stern, but an emerging trend toward gender equality nevertheless continues.

Men of goodwill who have the courage to admit how unjust and harmful present gender relations are to the significant women in their lives can become vital change agents in undoing the resultant misery and pain inflicted on all women in order to maintain male dominance. For truly holistic healing to occur, however, men will also have to recognize that, in spite of all the seeming benefits male privilege has to confer on them, doing manhood often involves significant, sometimes deadly, costs to men themselves.

## Recognizing Costs of Maintaining Male Dominance for Men

Unlike me, many men grow up well aware of the costs of maintaining male dominance. While feminists have done a great job of illuminating male violence against women and how oppressively costly such behavior is to women, seemingly lost in this important societal recognition is the fact that perhaps most of men's violence is actually directed toward other men. Men make up 76 percent of all homicide victims and an estimated 80 percent of assault victims in the United States, with most being killed or assaulted by other men. Like the young gunmen in Columbine High School, some men who are victims of male violence so up the masculine ante that they respond in incredibly lethal ways. Tired of being "picked on" and "bullied" (rather imprecise terms that society uses to characterize boys and young men's bruised and bloodied bodies), some of these previously emasculated young men strike back with deadly force. The significant loss of life, sometimes even including their own, all seems worth it if they can for a fleeting moment feel like a real man. The dead bodies they leave in their wake serve to signify how powerful and masculine they really are.

Significant numbers of boys also grow up in households where they are sexually and physically abused. Of course, once again, the perpetrator of their victimization is most typically an adult man, but the fact remains that both women and significant numbers of men are forever scarred by abuse in childhood. Moreover, the bodies of subordinated women *and* men serve as the terrain upon which male abusers exert masculine superiority. In fact, in many male subcultures, beating a man into submission earns you many more points than doing the same to a woman. Regardless of who is victimized in the process, as in the first-blood rituals of deer hunters, masculinity demands that someone must be subordinate—a signifier of one's superiority—for manhood to be proven. Whether in wars or fights in a bar, the schoolyard, or the home, "to the victors go the spoils," with the trampled bodies of women, children, and men all attesting to how important the given exercise in masculinity must have been and how "sweet" it is to be a winner. While men, in their pursuit of proving their superiority, are almost exclusively responsible for such oppressive outcomes, both women and many men bear the costs of men doing masculinity.

Ironically, some of the costs associated with male dominance are borne by those actually exercising dominance. Men, in their pursuit of manhood, are far more likely than women to partake in high-risk behaviors that result in personal injury and sometimes death. Perhaps unsurprisingly, 75 percent of all binge drinkers are men, 86 percent of all careless driving accidents are caused by men, and men are more likely than women to be injured or killed in an accident. "Stupid men tricks," in all their various forms, combined with often dangerous traditional male workplaces and vocations, mean that men's own bodies often provide the fodder consumed in the doing of masculinity. Many men define such risks as acceptable costs in the pursuit of manhood, some even view them as an enjoyable thrill, but the fact remains that many men are needlessly injured and killed trying to prove their masculinity.

As already noted, men are far less likely than women to express empathy for others and often repress their own feelings. Being the tough guy—the man—has significant emotional costs. While women are far more likely to be diagnosed with depression, some psychologists argue that men may in fact experience much higher rates of depression, much of it undiagnosed because of many men's inability to admit emotional problems. Sharing one's feelings with others, let alone admitting emotional difficulties, is something many men are unwilling to do, as they are afraid it would suggest vulnerability and weakness. Combining an instrumental male outlook with an unwillingness to seek emotional help results in men having much higher rates of completed suicide. Through an objectifying male lens, one's own body becomes a means to end.

If survival and growth are seen as signs of a healthy organism, doing masculinity and maintaining male dominance appear to be a very costly enterprise for women, children, and men (both as oppressor and oppressed). Male dominance is perhaps the ultimate Pyrrhic victory—men win the battle between the genders, but the losses are so staggering that all involved are losers.

## Healing from Oppression

Perhaps one of the easiest ways to argue the benefits of feminism for all people is to start by clearly noting the costs of manhood. As discussed in this chapter, veiled by the "natural" and "normal" appearance and behavioral expectations of being the man in our contemporary society lies a gendered story grounded in subjugation, subordination, and oppression. Daily, untold numbers of people are harmed, wounded, and forever scarred in men's pursuit of doing masculinity. These seeming faceless individuals are in actuality our partners, children, parents, siblings, and friends, as well as ourselves. The truth is that present-day definitions and ways of doing masculinity could be viewed as the most destructive epidemic ever witnessed, and the number one health crisis facing all people on our planet.

I am so passionate about feminism because it not only holds the promise of eradicating all forms of exploitation and oppression, but it is the only ideology that can ensure the survival of planet earth. We have now had thousands of years of a patriarchal reality, and the "progress" of this "civilized" structural arrangement has put us at the brink of self-destruction. In contrast, radical feminism's life-affirming-giving-enhancing values are the only ones comprehensive enough to reverse the cataclysmic direction patriarchal societies are leading us. Quite simply, I believe feminist values and realities are the only ones that can ensure the survival of this planet. As such, I choose to direct my energies into feminism and life as opposed to patriarchy and death.

Ultimately, my attraction to feminism was brought about by and continues to be instilled by the significant women I have had the honor of knowing throughout my life. In the past, I have tacitly sat by and watched a misogynist, male-dominated society attempt (often with great success) to destroy these intelligent and beautiful women. My mother died over twenty years ago because a male physician misdiagnosed her abdominal pains as simple "female problems" when she had colon cancer. (For her cramps, the doctor told her to go home and take a hot bath, which caused the tumor in her colon to rupture. She nearly died from the internal hemorrhaging, spent six weeks in intensive care, and died five years later from the cancer that had spread to her liver.) I have watched nearly every academic woman who has befriended me struggle on a daily basis with a patriarchal system (the university) that structurally and often individually sets her up for failure. The vast majority of women I have known have been raped in one way or another.

The pain that these and other women have experienced has become mine. As such, I can no longer idly stand by and silently be part of the problem. To do so would mean that I would not only be assisting in the destruction of individual women who are very close to me and part of my referent, but each time I hesitate to act means that another part of me is potentially (and far too often actually) destroyed. The personal experiences of these women have became my political reality.

For the damage to be undone and real healing to begin, men must be made aware of just how harmful doing male dominance is for women, children, other men, and even themselves. I believe that feminism is about such awareness. Actually recognizing all the destruction wrought in the name of manhood takes far more courage and strength than any imaginable contemporary masculine attitude or behavior. The same must be done with other forms of inequality, such as that associated with class, race, and sexual orientation. Then, and only then will a nonoppressive future become possible.

I guess I have always tried to live my life without regrets. That may be easier for me than for some, given my class background and the advantages I had growing up. Nevertheless, there are many things I have done in the past that I would never do now, and by changing, I do believe the healing begins and many of my past misdeeds are forgiven. The truth is, when faced with colon cancer in 1998, I came to the conclusion that I could die today and would have *no* reason for complaint. I have done and seen so much, not just the tourist version, but as full participant of the big show. Thus, every day since has been the bonus round for me, one in which I look to give back all that I took and was given in the past. Thankfully, when I do die, it will be with a peace in my heart that feminism has made possible. Everyone dies, leaving the world as we enter it, with nothing more than ourselves, and ultimately as equals. I dream of the day when people can be equal not only when they enter and leave the world, but also while they are alive.

## Notes

1. My first marriage ended, through no fault of my spouse, when I finished graduate school. My newly rediscovered feminist values made it impossible for me to appreciate her primary focus on realizing feminine beauty, something I had found attractive and paid homage to when we first met. My second marriage to Anna Papageorge was firmly grounded in a feminist-based union and in many ways because of this, it ended on a far more difficult note. After postponing her own career aspirations for over five years, we made the painful decision that the only way Anna could realize personal happiness was for us to go our separate ways, and she has since gone on to successfully complete graduate school in library science.

2. Faludi 1999, p. 356.

3. McIntosh 2000.

CHAPTER THREE

~

# How Patriarchy Wounds Us All:
# Doris's Story

This chapter describes the path that I (Doris) followed in coming to a feminist consciousness. I am approximately the same age as Steve's mother, so there are probably many parallels in our journey. Much has been written about internalized oppression, but it is difficult to understand how one can be blind to surrounding realities without having experienced it. One is aware of many small injustices, but interprets them in the context of individual experiences without recognizing the big picture of patterns and underlying assumptions. We then try to navigate a course between cultural givens in order to advance our own options and interests. Of course, this strategy may help individuals, but it never challenges the system. That must wait until a new ideology, capable of explaining all of the small, personalized injustices, redefines the issues in a larger framework. Feminism in the late 1960s and early 1970s was that ideology for me and many others.

Men, especially during this time, were also trapped by stereotypical gender assumptions, programmed to fill expected roles in business, politics, the family, and other instrumental ways of being in the larger society. Together, male and female genders were taught to join in an Ozzie and Harriet dance of respectability, to subordinate their interests to the family and the workplace, and to never question the system. Ultimately feminism is about freeing both women and men from the straitjacket of an oppressive order, for men experience internalized oppression—albeit often as the oppressor—just as surely as do women.

## Coming of Age in the Conservative Fifties

I was born in 1939 and grew up in a traditional, middle-class family. My father was the provider and authoritarian decision maker, while my mother was a "housewife" (literally, married to the house). This pattern was repeated in the homes of my friends, so I had little exposure to alternatives. Men were powerful and did important things in the world, while women were loyal helpmates who seldom did anything exciting. As a child I play-acted male roles (e.g., cowboy, sea captain, adventurer) since women seemed to do nothing but care for children and the house. I fiercely resisted attempts to turn me into a "nice little girl." Being an only child, however, I was pampered, overprotected, and nevertheless taught the social graces of womanhood, and programmed to become a wife and mother. By early adolescence I knew that I was different and that I did not fit the mold my parents tried so hard to force on me. Yet, I assumed this difference was personal failure—I was weird—rather than there being anything wrong with the mold.

As a small child, I once asked my mother why we sang at Christmas about "peace on Earth, good will to men" and not to women also. Her answer was that, "When the men are happy everybody is happy." Although she meant it as a joke, this was her reality. My father was the center of her universe and she spent her whole life trying to please and placate him, with little identity of her own. My father's temper (he was the only one allowed to show anger) and his controlling behavior gave her few opportunities for independence. I was a senior in high school before he "gave her permission" to get a driver's license.

My mother survived by doing what Erving Goffman called "practicing the arts of shamelessness," small acts that provide some freedom from control at the cost of self-respect.[1] We had many secrets together of the "don't tell daddy" kind, in which she gave me permission or small amounts of money out of her household "allowance" to circumvent his rules. She also had jokes, small deceits, which proved how foolish men could be. My father came home from work in mid-afternoon and then wrote reports until about 5:00 P.M. in a special, off-limits room known as "his office." If my mother was not working when he came home, he would "growl" in disapproval. She kept a pan of water on the stove and, when she heard his car, she would be stirring it at the stove. Then he was happy and the evening would go well. As a child, I never understood why she was an alcoholic.

Adolescents can be very cruel to those who are different and do not conform. I never went through the stage of being preoccupied with boys, clothes, and pop culture expected of teenage girls. I did "drive my teachers crazy" (both school and church) with my incessant questioning about the why of things. The Girl Scouts was my only refuge during this time. There I was surrounded by strong women role models and was valued for my initiative and leadership abilities, my inquiring mind, and my love of adventure. Scouts was defined as special women's space that left unquestioned the nature of things in the larger society. Outside of my home, men were largely irrelevant to my social world unless they posed a direct threat or an obstacle. This early theme has been present in much of my adult life. Nevertheless, I remember being asked to vote for student government president during my first year in a large, urban high school. Not knowing either candidate, I voted for the boy because "men are better at running things." Of course, this was internalized oppression—women actively supporting male dominance and accepting our own inferiority.

## Free, Oh Free, Oh Free at Last

My personal Independence Day occurred in the fall of 1956 when I set off for college far from home. My father had carefully chosen a small private liberal arts college with great hopes that I would find a suitable husband. Instead, I immediately joined a group of campus radicals and "beatniks," foreign students and faculty, who were questioning the status quo. Rejecting my parent's conservative religious and political views, I joined the Unitarian Church and became a pacifist, socialist, and supporter of civil rights. (Both of my parents had been raised in the Deep South and were "anti-everybody.") My father was greatly displeased (most of my activities I kept secret), but simply discounted it as a phase of adolescent rebellion. In truth, my views had already changed in high school, but I knew it was not safe to share what I was thinking at home. My father was seriously concerned about my future when I made the Dean's List in my first year rather than joining a sorority.

During the six years I was in college (BS and MSW) I demonstrated for civil rights and for peace, circulated petitions to "ban the bomb" and marched across Manhattan to protest the first atomic submarines. I knew people who had been blacklisted by Joe McCarthy as communists and two who had fought against Franco in Spain. We read the beatnik poets and existentialists and discussed Buddhism far into the night. I was acutely aware of the injustice of French colonialism in Algeria, but still I did not have a clue about feminism. I had never even heard the words "feminist" or "patriarchy" (women who fought for the right to vote at the turn of the century were suffragettes). I fought against the oppression of those "less privileged," unaware of the subservient role women were playing in all these "progressive" social movements. All of the leaders of these movements were male, while women were expected to be the behind-the-scenes helpmates who did the more routine work. Even "radical" women viewed a career as supplementary to family and homemaking responsibilities. Of course, this was all before Betty Friedan published the *Feminine Mystique*.[2]

During my undergraduate education, except for those teaching women's physical education, I took only one course from a woman professor. Our daily lives on campus were rule-bound in an effort to protect us from ourselves. Even more amazing is the fact that these rules were voted into place by the women themselves. Most women students believed the message and took the rules quite seriously. I tried to challenge some of these rules (but not the underlying assumptions) and was met with hostility from many of the women, although a few secretly confided their agreement. Private doubts were never to be voiced in public. Perhaps the best measure of internalized oppression is the degree of consent by the women (or whatever subordinated group) involved.

People today will have difficulty imagining that college women could accept and actually promote such a restrictive environment. There were no dorm hours for men, but women had to be safely locked down: 10:00 P.M. on weeknights, midnight on Saturday, and 11:00 P.M. on Sundays. Parental permission was required to be out of the dorm overnight, and the dean of women held "fire drills" in the wee hours of the morning to catch rule-breakers, while attendance was taken by women elected to be monitors for each floor. Suspected lesbians suddenly disappeared without explanation. Undesirable behavior, such as interracial dating, was reported to parents by the dean of women. Girls were not allowed to wear pants on campus except for special occasions, and we were required to dress for dinner (stockings for girls and a coat and tie for men).

The deeply sexist assumptions underlying these arrangements were never questioned. The men would be tomorrow's leaders and the women would be their wives. Women needed to be sheltered from the harsher aspects of the outside world, as they were more "fragile" and different from men in temperament. It was just seen as "human nature" that men were more aggressive and competitive, that they would try to "score," while women had to ward off inappropriate advances and ultimately hold up the standards. An unmarried woman who got pregnant was "loose." Good women could not be raped. Aggressive or competitive women, like those involved in sports, were somehow unnatural. Being an old maid was proof of your failure as a woman. The status of women on campus was largely determined by dating and the status of the man they dated. As a result, I felt pushed to be dating somebody and did go out with some of the men in the radical groups in which I was involved, but often without much deep feeling.

After obtaining my BS degree I enrolled in a master's in social work program at a large, urban university. My parents considered this a respectable career for a woman until she married and had children, so they were supportive. Here I experienced real freedom in an environment of diversity and increased opportunity, all of which I found very exciting. However, casework was frustrating, as I learned that many of the problems were systemic in origin. Helping people "to adjust" to dehumanizing conditions did little to remedy the problems. Women were beaten, emotionally abused, and abandoned while "the system" tried to hold families together at any cost and negatively judged women who "could not hold their man." Fathers seldom paid child support, leaving women and their children to live in poverty. Marriage seemed like a 60–40 proposition, with 60 percent of the responsibility for its success and 60 percent of the blame for any failure going to women. I recognized all these oppressive realities of the social welfare system, yet I never questioned the gendered assumptions that so penalize women. The widespread support of sexist beliefs by everyone I knew—men and women, students and faculty, radicals and conservatives—kept me from questioning gender inequities.

I received my MSW in May, 1962, and dutifully married the same month. My husband was basically a kind and sensitive man who really cared about people, loved nature, and was less constricted by conventional ideals. He had a wonderful ability to relate to folks from all walks of life, to find something of value in people often discounted by others, and to take pleasures from simple things. We shared many of the same social values. Because he was from a "good family," my parents ignored the bushy beard and guitar, discounting it as more adolescent rebellion. Since my husband's mother had always worked, he expected to help with the housework and established a much more egalitarian style than that to which I was accustomed. I remember trying to push him into more of a leadership role, what I had been taught to consider normal, and I was surprised when he refused. He was quite supportive of my career and personal ambitions, actively encouraging me to return to school to earn a Ph.D. We had many personality differences, some of which were gendered, but I cannot say that I was oppressed as a woman until, after several years of marriage, we had a child. Previously, we had both had freedom to follow our own interests, but now things changed and child care would be almost entirely my responsibility. These changes coincided with my earliest exposure to feminism, and I discovered there were limits to his egalitarianism. In 1972, after ten years of marriage, we divorced when our son was eighteen months old. It was during this period that I first began to self-identify as a feminist.

During the mid-1960s my awareness about social justice issues began to change, first in discovering the poor in America, then to the atrocities of the Vietnam War, and finally to feminism. In each case, my opinions changed shortly after issues had been "discovered" by the liberal press. For the first time I realized the full extent to which my "independent thinking" was shaped by the media and powerful social institutions. It seems I was in a flock of radical sheep, obediently following the leadership (mostly male) each time it changed direction. Perhaps that realization has been the single greatest epiphany in my life. I returned to graduate school in 1966 with a strong interest in the sociology of knowledge, "how we know what we think we know." I read history and anthropology in order to "step outside" of my cultural time and place, focusing on power relationships (neo-Marxism) and the way that society shapes ideology. I cautiously affiliated with liberal causes but would no longer accept any "party line" without question.

## Finding Feminism

I have been fortunate in escaping much of the abuse and exploitation other women have experienced, yet I too bear the scars of patriarchy. I know that I have sometimes lowered my expectations and have accepted things I should not to have accepted. I think of the clothing I wore as a young adult, tight skirts and spike heels with pointed toes. It was not until I read Mary Daly's Gyn/Ecology and her description of the similarities between Chinese foot binding and women's fashions in the West that I realized the frightening truth.[3] Men feel sexually powerful (turned on) by restrictive clothing that makes women appear helpless, dependent, and vulnerable to attack. I still feel uneasy when out alone at night, even in a place that is entirely safe. Although I sometimes go to a movie alone or out for dinner with a woman friend on Saturday night, it does not feel right or comfortable. I know that my actions and choices are restricted and that I must always be aware of my vulnerability as a woman. If Andrea Dorkin can get raped just by sitting in a hotel lobby, no woman is ever truly safe.[4] The behavior of a few men puts all women at risk.

I did not learn feminism from books but, rather, from practical life experiences. Having a child, and recognizing that my marriage was disintegrating, led me to question many of my previous ideological assumptions about how things ought to be and to seek realistic alternatives for living. Being a single mother, I experienced many of the practical difficulties (from child care to obtaining credit) that had given rise to the women's movement. I actively sought, and found, many strong women role models in the community.

During the summer of 1974 I worked as a volunteer for a radical women's liberation group in Chicago and learned my feminist theory there. This group opposed all forms of oppression, including classism and racism, and fit well with my prior views. Although they worked primarily with poor and minority women, they were not antimen, as they recognized that the women they served were also highly identified with the class and/or racial oppression that the men in their lives experienced. The group reflected a combination of feminism and the New Left that promoted a broad social justice agenda. This made good sense to me. I returned home and began volunteering with female-dominated groups seeking to help women and girls. This is where I learned organizational and consensus building skills and began to take back my own power. I participated in consciousness raising groups, read the popular feminist literature, and became politically active.

I learned early that "women's rights" and "women's liberation" are two very different movements. Women's rights focuses on social and political issues, seeking a series of small adjustments in the system that will benefit women. Women's liberation is a radical challenging of assumptions which underlie five thousand years of patriarchy. The first focuses on "men of power" and ways to convince or force them to make changes—to allow some women to compete in the system or to serve as tokens—with the movement primarily defined by what they are against (i.e., men). The second sees patriarchy as a set of mental constructs that each of us, both women and men, carry in our own heads, notions that must be "evicted" in order to bring about a paradigm shift. Political changes (e.g., *Roe vs. Wade*) are important, but without altering the mental constructs, old abuses simply take new forms.

Women's rights organizations, such as NOW, seem willing to sacrifice deeper principles for political expediency. Since political power is often about image, focused objectives, and presenting a united front, the resulting demand for political correctness often leads to oppression itself. Issues that are considered divisive are ignored, leaving some groups feeling unheard. Thus, efforts in the 1970s were primarily directed toward issues affecting middle-class white women, largely ignoring their poor and minority sisters whose exploitation, in part, made their middle-class lifestyle possible. Anti-male sentiments were ironically combined with efforts to make women more like men (e.g., assertiveness training on how to climb the corporate ladder), and traditional women's work was further devalued. All this seemed too simplistic, a reduction of complex patterns of oppression to just a battle of the sexes, and it failed to challenge the underlying assumptions that trapped both women and men. Criticism of American imperialism (economic exploitation of developing nations) was rejected by these women's rights groups as too divisive, especially since Third World women identified with the oppression of their own men more than with Western feminism. Androgyny was in and then it was out. Like so many other movements, "freedom" required a litmus test that ultimately decided who could and could not be part of the group.

The problem, of course, is that decision making within the women's rights movement was still based on patriarchal ways of thinking. Thinking was binary (men vs. women), linear (logical steps to reach an objective), and hierarchical (a ranking of relative power and importance). Women sought to alter the societal means and ends in ways that would give women a better chance of "winning," while not really challenging the basis of either. Only after membership declined during the conservative backlash of the 1980s did these organizations explicitly adopt a more inclusive and broad-based philosophy. However, they remain primarily white and middle class in membership, and their underlying structure and agenda has changed little.

Challenging the assumptions of patriarchy is much more than women's liberation; it is the freeing of all people everywhere—and ultimately, the healing of the Earth. It does not produce dramatic victories but, rather, is a process of gradual change over several generations. Its goal is to alter how we see others and nature, not as objects or things to be manipulated and controlled, but as partners in establishing a new order based on cooperation and harmony. "Power over," the patriarchal values of dominance and control is the true source of our exploitation, dehumanization, and alienation. Rather than power over, we must shift to models of "power with" and the growth-supporting notion of "power under" (i.e., empowerment). Feminism, in this sense, sees men as allies in establishing a new world order. Of course, there is often a discrepancy between stated ideals of feminism and its practices. Unless men are accepted by feminists and allowed to be equal partners in this endeavor, few changes will take place.

## I've Looked at Clouds from Both Sides Now

My first lesbian relationship was with a very competent African American woman, older and more experienced and my superior in academic status, at the time of my separation from my husband. However, she had always played a feminine role and she pushed me into the dominant position. At this point (1971), I was just beginning to explore feminism and not yet fully committed. She was not really a feminist and even joked that my attempts to make her one were contrary to my own best interests. It was in this relationship that I first discovered male privilege, that exhilarating feeling that I was, in a sense, lord of the manor and that generous favors were mine to give.

This relationship ended when I changed jobs after my divorce. I was alone for a year with my son, now a toddler, who required constant attention. Homework and child-care responsibilities, along with working full time, took all of my energy and left me with little opportunity to do much beyond surviving day by day. I was feeling quite depressed and was grateful when I found a bright and strong woman, very independent and sure of her identity, who was willing to move in with me and share the responsibility. Once again, she chose to work part time and to be the primary homemaker, buying us matching coffee mugs—mine said "Housework's a Bitch" and hers said "I'm experienced." During the years we lived together we had a deep personal relationship, but the imbalance in money (and the resulting power) caused an underlying tension. I was ecstatic to be able to distance myself a little from the daily grind of housework and child care, to find a home-cooked meal waiting for me and clean clothes in my closet. I was very appreciative, "helped" with the chores, was generous financially, and was puzzled as I watched her gradually becoming more depressed. Somehow we had reestablished the traditional heterosexual marital patterns of my youth.

I was amazed to learn that femininity and masculinity are situational and not biological at all. These traits are a byproduct of unequal power and privilege or characteristics simply attached to dominant and subordinate roles. I saw the truth in the feminist saying that the only way a woman can be truly free of housework is to exploit another woman. It is the situation that is oppressive, even when the dominant person is not. I watched as our relationship gradually deteriorated into a series of small bickerings, conflicts without focus or solution. It's much harder to blame men when you have been there! I thought a lot about Joni Mitchell's song "Both Sides Now."

During the past twenty-five years I have had relationships with other women, always struggling to find ways to make them egalitarian. There is no easy formula, and I empathize with men trying to make that choice. I know that having small children puts a strain on all relationships and especially on the primary caregiver. When one person owns the house and has a larger income, that person has more power, whoever seems to be dominant in daily decisions. Traditional marriages, whether gay or heterosexual, have the same problems and breakdown in the same places. It is not about men versus women but about power versus powerlessness. I learned the hard way that I could not have the kind of relationship I wanted while holding on to the unequal power that comes with the provider/protector role. The pleasure associated with traditional male privilege often comes at the cost of true intimacy and trust.

For the past fifteen years I have been in a loving relationship with a strong and independent professional woman. It is very important to both of us that we "be there" for each other emotionally and for practical things but that neither of us be the dominator or the dominated. There seem to be no road maps for such a journey, so we have moved forward with caution. Each of us has a grown child or children, owns her own house, has her own income and bank account and fulfills her own financial responsibilities. Experience has taught us that "money is power" in a relationship. We have adopted a pattern that is more than "perpetual dating" yet somehow less than marriage, one that at present seems to offer the best of both worlds. After retirement we hope to sell our homes and relocate somewhere, perhaps on the West Coast. The relationship we have developed and nurtured in the past fifteen years has allowed us the time to establish new ways of sharing power, alternating being the one who is vulnerable and the one who is supportive, and a deep respect for our differences. It is our greatest hope that we will be able to continue to grow together in loving, equal ways, spending our older years together doing those things that we most value and that give us pleasure.

I think I initially turned to women because it felt safer and I was not required to give up my personal power (I needed a wife!). However, I also discovered that sameness, for me, made possible a much deeper understanding, closer bonding, and real intimacy. I experienced a depth of understanding I had never had with a man. Clarifying and acting upon my sexual orientation permitted me to have a new kind of relationship with men. Meaningful nonsexual friendship became possible, and I was less threatened by the view men had of me.

## Feminism and Academia

Academia, until recently, has had little to do with my feminist identity. It was almost as if I sought to keep them separate to avoid contamination of my feminist ideals. I am a feminist and a sociologist, but I am not sure I am a "feminist sociologist." When I attended graduate school in the late 1960s, there was little feminist consciousness and no mention of feminist issues in the classroom. All of the regular faculty in the department were men. Although I consistently made high grades, I was never included in the elite group (all male) who went out for beer with the professor after class. Faculty were pleasant and treated me fairly, trying to be helpful when I asked for assistance, yet none ever asked me to participate in their research or encouraged me to present a paper. Women students were appreciated as teaching assistants but were seldom asked to do anything else.

It is a commentary on the times that women graduate students accepted our lack of mentors as unfortunate but normal. There were seven or eight older, married women students in the department, thrown together by our similar experiences and marginalized status. Even our research interests and backgrounds counted against us; they were women's concerns, which were felt to more properly belong in social work or home economics. "Real sociology" consisted of theory and quantitative methods, the forte of bright male students. When it came time to write dissertations, we wandered the halls like orphans seeking some faculty member willing to be our advisor. Surprisingly, we all eventually earned our Ph.Ds.

My experiences with sociology beyond the graduate department were not much better. I accepted a teaching position in a large regional university where women were accepted as workhorses in the department but given little status and excluded from decision-making groups. I have watched my university circumvent affirmative action policies, stonewall sexual harassment complaints, and gut a proposed women's studies program through forced compromise, resulting in a gender studies program that is underfunded, understaffed, and unsupported by the administration. I have seen women colleagues used and exploited, only to be cut down by the revolving door of tenure.

At professional conferences, the liquor flowed freely at parties sponsored by textbook publishers where women had to constantly ward off unwanted sexual advances from senior professors. If "the personal is political," there was little, if any political feminism in sociology during the 1970s and 1980s. Today, people are more aware of demands for political correctness, but I am skeptical about how much has really changed. My personal experiences have taught me to see academia as dangerous territory for women.

Gradually, however, I also recognized that there were relatively few men in academia with significant power. A small handful actually had much power, some were wannabes, but a lot of my male colleagues were as discounted and marginalized as women. I learned that most attacks were not really personal but rather strategic—plans to manipulate or remove obstacles to some personal agenda. Men of conscience, who preferred to operate on principle rather than expediency, were often attacked viciously. I have found that genuine alliances with these men have been crucial to my career. Just as my primary threats have came from men, so men have been my primary source of salvation. These men had access to some power while, unfortunately, women colleagues were so marginalized that they could be of little assistance. I owe these men of honor and principle a large debt of gratitude. Most were not truly feminist, but they believed in fairness.

## Redefining My Relationship to Men

Throughout my life there have always been men I admired and respected, and women who triggered my deep anger. I have seen both men and women suffer under exploitive systems where they felt powerless. The simple formula of "men as aggressors and women as victims" has never worked for me. Because I have trusted women more and allowed them into deeper parts of myself, I have experienced more betrayal and pain from women than I have from men. As an adult, my relationships with men have been less complicated and sometimes even more rewarding.

I jokingly think of myself as more "anti-testosterone" than against men. My anger is triggered by aggressive competition, the drive for dominance and control (especially in the pursuit of sex, money, and power), and the one-upmanship that leads to defining everybody as objects to be manipulated and exploited. I despise the macho subculture of adolescent boys that values physical aggression, "scoring" with girls, heavy drinking, and risk-taking behavior to prove one's manhood. As adult men, the aggression and manipulation usually become more covert and verbal, but the drive for dominance and control is still there. All of this is what most feminists refer to as patriarchy.

Certainly, I am not suggesting that gender differences are hormonal, as studies of other cultures clearly demonstrate that these are learned behaviors. In American society there are many men who have rejected these ways of being, and some women who have adopted them. In our society we have internalized the John Wayne/frontier mentality, where the single individual, through force and will, shapes his own destiny and builds an empire in the process. In contrast, men in non-Western cultures, especially those in tribal societies, are frequently rewarded for being nurturing, cooperative, and egalitarian. I have met many men who were sensitive, intuitive, vulnerable, and caring (and, of course, many women who were not!). I think of these men as truly "gentle-men" and have valued their friendship over the years. Male teachers and visionary leaders have had a tremendous influence on my thinking.

Many of these "gentle-men" were aging hippies—husbands of my women friends, quiet thoughtful men at the university where I taught, or social activists in my community. Some played the guitar and wrote folk songs with a sensitive, personal focus. One of these men, whom I never knew well but who nevertheless had an enormous personal influence on me, was Ric Masten. He was a Unitarian Universalist Troubadour Minister, who wandered the country singing his songs of peace and love. Some were gay men, like my friend Jim, who was often there for me when I was struggling through my son's painful adolescent years. Then there was Bill, who wore large elf ears to parties, and works as an RN with AIDS patients. Others I have known at pagan gatherings, men who truly love the Earth and believe in social justice. Rejecting the materialism and impersonal competition of today and replacing them with values of a simpler time when peace and love were what really mattered Many of these men seem strangely out of place in the modern world, but often they have been an anchor for me when I lost my way.

When I first met Steve, he was a "testosterone-driven" feminist, an aggressive fighter against patriarchy but certainly not a "gentle-man." When in a group of women he was very sensitive and supportive, but with men he was an aggressor. He did not fit any of my existing categories, and I was at a loss to know how to relate to him. I watched Steve act and be heard in arenas where "gentle-men" were usually discounted (i.e., treated like women). This raised a new issue for me; to what extent could patriarchy be used to fight patriarchy? Steve could talk to football players, fraternity members, and men in ROTC about the harmful effects (to everybody) of exploiting women, and they would listen and learn from him. He was clearly a valuable ally, even when I felt skeptical about him personally.

However, when Steve was with women, or in women's space, his personal style became quite different. More than any other man I have known, Steve was willing to really listen to women. He sought to understand our life experiences and perspectives without judgment or interpretation. When in women's spaces he assumed the role of "respectful guest," a supportive listener who sought to empower others without assuming a position of expert. So often (pro)feminist men seek to intellectually structure the meaning of women's lives and then guide them toward doing feminism right. Instead, Steve sought to know and understand, asking how he could help. It was out of these interactions that our relationship grew.

I continued to be uncomfortable around Steve in mixed groups because it was here that the more aggressive aspects of his personality often came into play. I would become a silent observer in these situations, glad he was "on my side," for he was a formidable opponent. Had I not known of his gentle side, I would have walked away. I felt an internal conflict; what do you do with a testosterone-driven man who is fighting for the right cause? Often feminists use these men but never really relate to them or "let them in." Yet, when he was with women, all of his arrogance and competitiveness disappeared. Steve was a puzzlement.

Perhaps the lesson I learned from Steve in the early days of our friendship was that even men who had a very traditional masculine style might also have a gentle side. Over the years I had always had male friends whom I trusted and could confide in, but these were usually men who would have been considered "soft" by society's standards. I have long argued that feminists need to make room for these gentle-men in our movement, while maintaining distance from those who put out traditional male vibes. I watched Steve reach out to these more traditional men, to inspire them with a feminist vision, and change their way of being in the world.

My son, now in his early thirties, is traditionally male on the outside, but he has a gentle interior. In order to be okay in the eyes of society he has felt pushed into many masculine behaviors that were not always comfortable for him. I know that many men are seeking alternative ways of being a man, ways that will not bar them from societal rewards or punish them in the process, but will allow them to reclaim lost parts of themselves. I needed to expand the range of men who could potentially be included in feminism. Steve, and my son, showed me this truth, that potentially everyone can be a feminist.

Of course, the notion of inclusion always contains its binary opposite of exclusion. At least initially, it may not be wise to welcome every man regardless of his attitudes and values. Certainly, we do not want to put the fox in charge of guarding the hen house. But the risk of being overcautious is the lack of strength that comes from small numbers. Rather than imposing a litmus test on the intentions of others, I would prefer self-selection based on clearly articulated feminist goals and principles. For feminist ways of being to grow and flourish, women must be willing to take a chance on men who have positive intentions and a commitment to gender equality. Personal style is most likely to change with inclusion—the learning of a new style for a new social movement.

Over the years I have watched Steve change as he has become more embedded in feminism and more accepted by feminist women. Perhaps "style" is simply a way of adapting to the perceived expectations of the group in which you are a part. If so, feminists have much more to gain from inclusion than they do from exclusion. Accordingly, feminists must also change their style of relating. Feeling powerless and discounted by the system has generated deep anger and a porcupine defense against men. Determined never to be the victim, many women feel they must be compulsively strong and hesitate to let men in or to share their true feelings and vulnerability. Both men and women must change to bring about a real feminist coalition between the genders.

## The Need to Include Men

There are few men today who self-identify as feminists, although some state that they are supportive of the women's movement. Women have often excluded men, sometimes blatantly claiming that a man cannot be a feminist. Yet most women have many relationships with men, and change, especially on the interpersonal level, requires a cooperative effort. Even in political and economic arenas, women can gain little without men being actively involved. For too long feminists have marginalized sympathetic men and have ignored or devalued their contributions. Women simply cannot change the world alone.

As long as feminism is defined as being "against men" in the public mind, few men will ever choose to seriously consider embracing this perspective. Likewise, few will be willing to commit deeply to lifestyle changes that seem to only benefit women. There is a need to reframe feminist thinking and rhetoric away from what it is against and toward what it affirms, a better way of living for all people. Perhaps the term feminism has too much emotional baggage, too long a tradition of exclusiveness, to be a banner under which all people can unite. Both men and women have significant work to do to bring about the widespread changes envisioned in this new reality. The work is the important thing.

The beginning step for men is to come to truly respect women, to seek nonoppressive ways of being in the world, and to actively advocate for the fair and equal treatment of all. I believe there are many decent men with liberal attitudes who are already doing these things. The next step is for them to really listen to women, to come to value their intuitive and experiential ways of knowing, and to understand from an insider perspective the issues and problems women face. Too often men have an aggressive and competitive style of communication, based on dominance and control, that leads them to discount or undervalue what women are saying. Yet I have worked with some men in the university and the community, and have talked with the husbands of my feminist friends, enough to know that there are men who really do listen and who try to make changes in their interpersonal relationships, to put into practice what they have learned.

Usually, this is as far as men move in the direction of feminism. They consider themselves "pro-feminist" but feel unable to fully identify with the feminist movement because they are not a woman. The energies and contributions of these gentle-men are lost because there seem to be few meaningful roles for sympathetic men in the women's movement. The primary exception to this is that men have increasingly been involved in working with other men to end abusive behavior (rape, battering, community violence). For most men, social acceptance and their own self-image requires them to conform outwardly to the expectations of being a man and to meet the general criteria on the outside, even when they may think or feel something very different. Being a self-proclaimed feminist man is truly a no-man's land with many hazards and few rewards.

I suffered along with my son as he attempted to navigate the steep, rocky slopes of manhood. Taught by his pacifist mother not to fight, he attracted bullies and frequently came home crying. Finally, in about the fifth grade, I arranged for him to take martial arts. The fighting did not stop until high school when he soundly beat two of his tormentors. I learned an important lesson about young manhood; only the strong can afford to be gentle. Ironically, because he is perceived to be strong, he can be a gentle-man, and now, when he speaks out on equality and social justice issues, other men listen.

Women also have significant work to do. They must find ways to take back their power without blaming men for all of their ills. There is a real danger in portraying women as victims of male oppression, of suggesting that women can only gain power if men voluntarily agree to relinquish it. This simply affirms male superiority and men as the rightful gift-giver. Women are taught, primarily by other women, that to succeed they must give away their power. Of course, such behavior gains societal approval, but it has few rewards. Strong men are attracted to strong women, and they lose respect for women willing to be taken advantage of and exploited. Women who give in to men are often discounted and, rather than earning credit that can be collected later, they increase the chance of further exploitation; unused power evaporates while empowerment, reclaiming one's own personal power, decreases oppression. This is an internal change, which must begin with women. Men are often unaware of the sacrifices women make since they come automatically, so the contribution goes unrecognized. Empowerment does not mean withholding from men but rather establishing a balance of exchange by making what women do more visible.

bell hooks has said that "we are not asking for men to save us but to quit harming us, and this will happen through inclusion." I am not minimizing major injustices in the system; all people of goodwill have an obligation to work for constructive change. Both men and women have significant work they must do to rout out the patriarchy within. By identifying men as the sole cause of gender inequities, women continue to give away their power and may deny their own role in maintaining existing structures. Inclusion means that men and women must both do their own internal work, and that they will then work together to end all forms of oppression.

For many years I associated primarily with other women, read women authors, listened to women's music, and became absorbed in women's culture. Except for practical matters, men were largely irrelevant in my life. This was never because of a hatred of men but, rather, a need to find my own voice as a woman. It was my friendship with Steve that convinced me that men could be feminists and that men and women could work together toward shared feminist goals. Although separateness may be necessary for a time, meaningful change can only occur through inclusion and the efforts of a critical mass of committed persons. The problem, of course, is to find an accepting environment where this can take place, one which is not claimed as primarily men's or women's space.

I have been deeply involved in Earth-based spirituality for a long time. Some feminists have criticized honoring god/goddess traditions as reinforcing traditional gender expectations, but I have found it to be very healing. Women can reclaim their beauty and strength by identifying with a strong female image (Goddess) in a way not provided by compassionate male images (Jesus, Buddha). Likewise, men can seek to develop their intuitive, nurturing side by exploring the long tradition of peaceful nature gods. I now practice my spirituality in a group of men and women who honor both the female and the male principle in the universe, who are deeply committed to feminism, to life affirming values, to healing the earth, and to ending patriarchal oppression everywhere.

Spirit has always been viewed as male (the life-giving breath of the father), but the soul has been seen as female (the nurturing womb of the mother). Both men and women in America today are "soul-hungry," with a deep longing for meaning, connection, and personal spirituality. The soul is alive with feeling; the spontaneous joy of being alive, a passion for justice, a true caring for others, for finding meaning in the small things of daily existence. It is a quest for divine connection with all of nature and the cosmos, with humanity, and with the divine that dwells within each of us. Both the spirit and the soul are free and nongendered.

Many people try to self-medicate their alienation from life with TV, drugs and alcohol, cheap thrills and easy amusements, yet find all of these things unsatisfying. Masculine values and ways of being in the world cannot repair the damage done by patriarchy. We must reclaim those ways of being which have traditionally been viewed as feminine, creating a balance between male and female energies. This is the Tao in Chinese philosophy, yin and yang, male and female flowing together in perpetual intercourse.

Feminism, at its best, is about acceptance, harmony, and inclusiveness—a commitment to walk gently with the Earth and all her creatures—and to live in such a way that all have equal opportunities for self-fulfillment. There is no one true feminist path, but a multitude of paths that can be adapted to fit the diverse needs of many people. Feminist fundamentalism and exclusivity prevents the formation of a critical mass necessary for widespread social change. Significant change will occur when all people, both men and women, work together toward this shared vision: peace on earth, goodwill toward humanity.

# Notes

1. Goffman 1961.
2. Friedan 1963.
3. Daly 1978.
4. Dworkin 2000.

CHAPTER FOUR

⌘

# The Crumbling of Patriarchy: Equality as the Wave of the Future

Institutions and ideologies are forced to change when the everyday experiences of people become so different that the old solutions no longer work. Women have long recognized the detrimental affects of patriarchy as a system of male dominance that stifles opportunities and potential contributions of women. Men are also increasingly beginning to question patriarchal values as a system that, for them, leads to high stress and few of the promised rewards. Many continue in the "rat race" only because they cannot envision any workable alternative.

Cross-cultural anthropological research indicates that for most of human existence patriarchy has been the exception rather than the rule.[1] We now have some forty years of feminist scholarship in anthropology demonstrating how gender roles and gender inequality can vary considerably, depending on environment, type of economy and political system, likelihood of warfare, and numerous other social factors.[2] Societies at the lowest levels of technology often have the most egalitarian and democratic structures.[3] Survival in these cultures depended on voluntary cooperation, and, without police or a standing army, group leaders had limited abilities to force their will on others.[4] Work was divided by gender; men hunted while women gathered wild foods and/or tended to village gardens, but both made a valued contribution to the food supply.[5] Much of the work was cooperative, and men often were extensively involved in child care. In societies such as these women had considerable freedom and status.[6] A husband was dependent upon his wife's labor for food, and if he became too oppressive, she could return to her family of origin. Because of this high level of interdependency, decisions were made by consensus and accommodations were required since, if the group splits apart, the survival of all was threatened.

Patriarchy occurs when men control the means of production and are seen as the only true producers of food and family income.[7] Male dominance requires technological advances that make possible the accumulation of wealth and surplus food, thereby permitting some to take positions (i.e., as chiefs and clan leaders) of control over others. The subordination of women simultaneously emerges with the creation of social classes and often authoritarian political authority. Men shift from hunting to herding animals (pastoral cultures) and harnessing them to plow (intensive agriculture). Wealth and status are determined by men's property—the ownership of animals and land—and women come to have no significant role in food production. Women lose their status and freedom in pastoral societies, and are often forced to work only in the home at less valued tasks.

Cultural adaptations are shaped mostly by the economic subsistence strategy, the level of technology, and the environment in which the society is found. Thus, the Judeo-Christian (and Islamic) tradition began and developed in a context of intensive agriculture and pastoral societies firmly entrenched in male dominance. For five thousand years these patriarchal assumptions have formed the base for cultural development, leaving people to believe that this is the "normal," seemingly "natural," form of social organization. Is it any wonder that so many have difficulties envisioning any alternatives?

Patriarchy, however, is increasingly maladaptive to advanced industrial and post-industrial societies such as the United States and Western Europe.[8] Old institutions are rapidly changing in both form and function, and there is a general trend toward gender equality. Yet a cultural lag exists in which old ideals are often used to deal with pressing contemporary problems. Using these antiquated patriarchal strategies has led to rampant and disastrous consequences, primarily because of new technologies that allow for harm on such a greater scale. Some of our most pressing fears and social issues—war, the environment, the global economy, computer-related crimes, gun violence—are all the result of technology run amok within a framework of outdated laws, values, and social institutions.

Technology is not inherently evil or oppressive but simply the application of science to solving human problems. Today these problems are still largely framed in terms of dominance and subordination, and any solutions, moral and scientific, are often guided by patriarchal values and assumptions.[9] New ideals for the usage of technology need to be envisioned so that it can be used in the service of all, rather than benefiting the few who in turn use it to control the rest of us.

On an individual level, patriarchy creates a highly competitive way of life in which most men suffer from various kinds of performance anxiety and only a few achieve highly sought-after rewards.[10] Many men do not find their jobs satisfying and resent the time it takes away from family and other personal interests. They feel alienated and dehumanized by situations in which they are expected to take charge and "be a man" yet realistically have little control over the outcome. In an earlier time, men were recognized as the ultimate authority in family decision making, and many embraced the obligations associated with the role. Today, when few brides will promise to "love, honor and obey" their husbands, being solely responsible for any traditional men's duty (e.g., breadwinner) often seems more of a burden than a privilege. The partnership implied in egalitarian marriages is inconsistent with patriarchal notions of manhood and womanhood.

Many have argued that patriarchy hurts men, too, and that men are also oppressed.[11] Clearly, oppression is about power and women, as women have seldom had the power to oppress men. Both men and women are oppressed by various aspects of the patriarchal system. War kills both men and women, most people are exploited in the workplace, and ethnicity and sexual orientation are often used to determine who is and is not seen as most worthy of societal rewards. Alternatively, using these same criteria, both men and women can and do benefit from these systems of inequality. Nevertheless, patriarchy, by definition, calls for and leads to male dominance and female subordination. Ultimately, oppression, control, competition, and economic profit harm everyone. As a result, discussions of which gender suffers most are fruitless and divisive, since the experiences, though different, may be equally painful.

Our time would be better spent exploring how present oppressive values and behaviors could be changed in ways that would benefit all people, all nations, and the Earth itself. Such widespread transformations will require the commitment and active involvement of women as well as men. Men have been seduced into going along with the patriarchal system by a promise of rewards for "being a man." Only when large numbers of men see that these rewards are empty promises, unsatisfying and often not forthcoming, will they be willing to seek alternatives. Ongoing changes in our economy and family structure indicate that this new ideological paradigm is increasingly necessary.

## From the Industrial to the Post-Industrial Society

In his book, *The Third Wave*, Alvin Toffler suggests that the shift to a postindustrial society will alter all of the existing societal institutions in much the same way that the industrial revolution forever changed the basis of agricultural society.[12] Industrial society brought about a shift toward centralization, mass culture, bureaucratization, increased power and authority in the hands of the few, and an emphasis on order and control. Today, we are increasingly witnessing the almost antithetical trends of decentralization, cultural pluralism, egalitarian decision making and individual freedom. Machines control machines through computerized automation with much of the remaining traditional (labor intensive) assembly-line work being subcontracted out by multinational corporations to less developed countries where employee wages are only a fraction of those paid in Western countries. Global networks in communication and technology have forever changed the political, social, and economic landscape upon which we experience our lives. Clearly, these trends have changed and will continue to change gender relationships.[13]

The cultural mythology of patriarchy is grounded in notions of men having superior physical strength and size. Men are seen as the heavy laborers and warriors who both build and protect home and community; the contributions of men are defined as the most important, valuable, and necessary for the survival of the group. These beliefs have traditionally been used as the rationale for male dominance. Fictitious stereotypes, such as cavemen controlling women and other men through brute force, and images of malevolent, vengeful male gods that control people through the threat and use of violence, further reinforce outlooks of men being superior to women. God the Father demands obedience and rules over "his" people just as the king rules over his country and the husband/father rules over "his" household. The ideology of patriarchy insidiously promotes the view that women have always been expected to confine themselves to child-rearing, domestic labor, and low-status vocations while men did the things perceived to be important in society. The major world religions reflect and support these essentialist beliefs of appropriate responsibilities and statuses for men and women that have been handed down through the generations as part of the patriarchal package.

As people began to live in towns and cities, separate gendered spheres of existence were created and developed in which over time, men were seen as the rightful heirs of the public arena while women were relegated to the private domain and expected to focus their efforts on child care and domestic responsibilities.[14] Men traveled and were seen as more knowledgeable about the world, while women were tied down by work in the home, often leaving them poorly-equipped to make political decisions or handle large sums of money. Women's first priority was their family, so even when they did work outside of the home, it was typically in the subordinate, helping role.

Obviously these assumptions increasingly no longer pertain to the realities of modern societies. Even in the past, their application is often questionable— women have always worked, handled money, and performed heavy physical labor. Few jobs today are dependent on physical size and strength, and the majority of women, including those who are married with small children, work outside the home. Reliable birth control and child-care services have permitted many women to have a strong commitment to both family and career. Slowly diminishing but still quite obvious gender inequalities in pay are the result of old sexist assumptions and patterns rather than any difference in the comparable worth of the work.

The postindustrial society has also eroded the value of many traditionally male endeavors that were rewarded with much public status in the past. Warfare today is technologically sophisticated, remote, and not contained by any geographical battlefield. Terrorist bombs explode once the plane reaches a certain altitude while remotely controlled, so-called smart bombs hit targets with often deadly accuracy after being launched hundreds of miles away. Often the casualties of contemporary warfare are women, children, and the elderly. The noble warrior of the past who conquered the enemy through hand-to-hand combat is increasingly being replaced with computer screens, satellites, and weapons of mass destruction fired from isolated locations where the soldier risks little chance of injury or death. Often the biggest source of harm for the modern soldier is from friendly fire and other accidents. War is no longer glorious; in fact, it most resembles insanity and becomes symbolic of our stupidity as a seemingly civilized species that often fails to resolve conflicts in peaceful ways.

These changes have been reflected in Hollywood and the media. A few generations ago children grew up watching Westerns in which the good guys wore white hats and John Wayne single-handedly wiped out bands of evil-doing desperados. Then came World War II movies, with an emphasis on heroism and valor, and even though the costs were sometimes great, it was, of course, all worth it in the end. Good versus evil was almost always clearly demarcated with the purity of the cause always providing sufficient grounds for vanquishing the bad guys by whatever means necessary. Tens of millions of innocent people were killed during World War II on both sides, but these were acceptable losses as long as the cause was just.

Wars in the last half of the twentieth century, however, have been less popular and their objectives quite vague. Many battles fought by the United States over the past fifty years have resulted in stalemate or, even worse, failure. The media have reflected and sold some of the consequent resistance to war with characterizations of the "anti-hero"—the reluctant warrior who wanted to be anywhere other than in some futile war (e.g., M.A.S.H.). Other popular films increasingly showed the brutality and insanity of warfare (i.e., *Platoon, Apocalypse Now, The Thin Red Line, Saving Private Ryan*), making it less likely for boys to dream of growing up to be soldiers.

Instead, many young men today live in the fantasy world of cyberspace and science fiction movies. An XBox or Playstation II provides an escapist world of exotic weapons frequently set in a feudal world replete with knights, princesses, and magicians, where good and evil can be clearly distinguished. Like Luke Skywalker, faced with seemingly insurmountable odds, the player (or viewer) can still defeat Darth Vader and a whole dark star. These make-believe electronic settings are places where the noble warrior is still valued and the passive viewer can vicariously experience masculine victory, but they represent unobtainable desires for a bygone era rather than the realities of the modern world (see chapter 5 for a more detailed discussion of video games and their importance to doing masculinity).

Robert Bly and others have noted that, to many men, the loss of the warrior role feels like a loss of manhood.[15] Violence and risk-taking behavior are often motivated by the need of adolescent and young males to create an arena in which they can prove they are men. They typify the traditional roles played by sports and by the military in our society. Yet today, and in spite of television commercials that valorize belonging to certain service branches (e.g., the Marines and "A few good men"), most young men (and women) join the military to get away from home, for educational benefits, or to escape unemployment, but few see the military as a wonderful proving ground of manhood as in the past. Modern warfare is a business whose raw material is still expendable young men, and young civilians who read or listen to the daily news may not find much glory in it, let alone sacred duty or a rite of passage for real men.

Changes such as these, in turn, have had significant impacts on other societal institutions.

## The Changing American Family

Recent changes in the American family have negated many of the traditional male rewards along with the realities on which those rewards were based. For this reason it is necessary to examine how most families today actually function. Why should men voluntarily give up oppressive forms of power and male privilege and seek to be included in the feminist movement? The thesis of this book is largely irrelevant until this fundamental question is addressed. We would suggest that there are three basic reasons. First, men's traditional power and privilege has already been significantly eroded. To maintain a middle-class lifestyle today, or in many cases even to survive, often requires two incomes, with many women quite understandably demanding that they have an equal, or at least some, say in how the money that they earn is spent. This directly challenges many men's head-of-household status, with arguments over money figuring significantly in marital conflict and divorce. For many men, the stresses of paying the bills still remain but with few of the past rewards. Old solutions, such as "father knows best," simply do not work for today's problems and issues.

Second, men and women share common concerns in many areas that were often considered exclusively women's issues in the past. Equality in the workplace, safe and affordable day care, opportunities for young girls, and an end to community violence are family issues. Third, smaller families and greater affluence, in combination with living longer and healthier, have increased the expectations both men and women have from marriage and life. New values emphasize partnership, companionship, and sharing. Quite simply, patriarchy no longer offers a means for many men or women to get the things they most want out of life.

Of course, change occurs unevenly with different economic classes, ethnic groups, or regions of the country experiencing change at different speeds. There is also a gap between the reality of people's lives and the formal structure of social institutions and/or the legal system. However, the long-term trend toward gender equality is clear, and even backlash from conservative groups like the Promise Keepers cannot set back the clock. Many men are seeking ways to free themselves from old constraints and to embrace new values that promise increased personal freedom in the future.

### Traditional Sources of Male Power

Power in hierarchal settings is defined as the ability to get others to do things even when they do not want to. Anthropologist Ernestine Friedl has found that women have the greatest power and status in societies where they produced and distributed valued resources in their own names, beyond traditional domestic labor.[16] For example, women in Africa take surplus produce from their gardens to market and sell it for cash. Among the Iroquois, women raised the crops and controlled the distribution of food. In both of these societies women exercised considerable power and influence in political decision making. On the other hand, Eskimo women simply processed resources for their family that were brought home by the men. Women in Eskimo society were seen as property that could be treated, or disposed of, as a man saw fit.

In our society, power is primarily reflected and sustained by how much money one has. Men's traditional role as breadwinner—exclusive moneymaker—provided them with power while placing the homemaker wife in a subordinate, dependent role. Wives processed a small portion of their husbands' paycheck for household expenses and had to obtain their husband's approval before making any large purchase, since it was "his money." Some husbands were generous and *permitted* their wives to buy most things they wanted, while others were more difficult. Many jokes revolved around the devious ways wives used to manipulate husbands, further reinforcing the stereotype that women were untrustworthy and sneaky by nature. Women watched men for weakness and then used these to advantage in an opportunistic way. Women were also seen as gossips and preoccupied by trivial matters in life. Situational comedies (e.g., *The Honeymooners, Married with Children*) and cartoons (e.g., *The Simpsons*) often portray husbands as victims of their wives' scheming.

Social scientists have long recognized that these traits are situationally created when any group has a permanently subordinate status.[17] People everywhere seek to exercise some control over their lives and, when denied access to legitimate forms of power, they will turn to more devious methods. This becomes a self-fulfilling prophecy as stereotypes are affirmed by the behavior required for self-protection. Since women (or other oppressed groups) have acted deviously, this provides a justification for not granting them any increased power or privilege.

As previously noted, gendered spheres were created that divided public (the arena of politics and the marketplace) and private (home and family) settings. By definition, women were expected to play a supportive, behind-the-scenes role in the private sphere. The few women who entered the public arena were not taken seriously, and any success they might experience was attributed to external reasons (e.g., "She slept her way to the top" or "Her father used his influence") or was used as a proof that she was not a real woman (e.g.; "No man would have her" or "She's a dyke"). The moral was that it was impossible to be a successful woman and have a career at the same time.

All of this is changing. Women are working in increasing numbers and the income gap between men and women is slowly starting to close, especially for those who are younger. Women no longer feel they have to ask a man's permission to spend money, as more and more of the family income comes from her paycheck. As women are achieving more career success they are obtaining skills in arenas once the almost exclusive province of men. Financial decisions such as budgeting, investments, and large purchases are shared or delegated to whichever partner has the greater expertise. Quite simply, many women today, both married and single, have successful careers and their own bank accounts, and they make many large purchases. As Friedl predicts, the increasing purchasing power of women means that businesses and politicians must take them seriously, and, accordingly, women's social power and status has consistently risen over the past twenty-five years.[18] These economic changes have also forever altered gender roles within the family.

In the past, women's inability to sustain a decent standard of living, or to even provide the basics, and men's monetary power made divorce a highly unlikely outcome. Since she had more to lose and few options, there was more pressure on her to accommodate her husband's wishes and not question his authority. Today, as job opportunities have increased for women and earning power starts to equalize, the decision to continue a marriage is increasingly based on mutual choice rather than necessity.

Men are confused by changing gender expectations and the accompanying loss of power. When men initiate a date and pay for the activities, they retain control over the exchange. Today a woman may ask the man out and pay the bill or insist on paying her share of expenses. Doing so increases the women's right to have equal say in decisions. Although seldom verbalized, both men and women recognize that power and money are closely connected and that gender relationships have slowly made a real shift toward equality.

There is probably no other aspect of society that is as traditionally macho as adolescent male subculture. From football scores to scoring with women, young men are pushed to excel according to patriarchal expectations and are viciously punished by men and other boys if they fail. Many young men are taught that, to be successful, they must always be in control, the boss, "the man" when it comes to interacting with women. They carry these traits into marriage and often feel angry, frustrated, and perhaps inadequate when these expectations are not met. Quite simply, male power in the family has been eroded by conditions far beyond their control: new technologies, global markets, and changes in the social structure. As men lose financial control, much of their traditional basis for power is undermined.

### Individualism
Generations who came of age after the turbulent 1960s have been marked by a profound mistrust of politics, social movements, and formal institutions.

Young adults today are materialistic, individualistic, and very pragmatic, choosing carefully where they invest their talents and energies. They have been criticized for not voting, but they have voted with their feet, walking away from old patterns which no longer hold any meaning. The twin themes of "free to be me" and the opportunity "to be anybody I want to be" speak to the rejection of old assumptions that limit choices. Yet their choices are often limited by a lack of commitment to any larger goals beyond immediate relationships and satisfactions. Thus, this is really more about alienation than about freedom.

> Both men and women increasingly want an opportunity to develop all sides of their personalities and to follow their interests wherever they might lead. Some men seek to develop their sensitive, nurturing, and expressive side while many women are becoming more assertive and increasingly contesting being subordinated. Strong, independent men often are attracted to women with similar characteristics. Both are expected to have deep feelings and passions, an openness to new experiences and a willingness to assume responsibility for their own happiness and self development. The traditionally dependent women who expects to assume a subordinate role in a marriage is increasingly seen as a "drag" and an unwanted responsibility by many men.[19]

This new marital partnership is based, at least in theory, on gender equality. Gone are the days when girls received the apocryphal advice given to Queen Victoria by her mother on her wedding night; "Just close your eyes and think of England." Women demand sexual satisfaction in marriage. Husbands are expected to listen to them, to provide real companionship and to share interests. Life is too short to stay in an unhappy marriage and, except for perhaps when there are young children in the home, divorce is often sought on the simple grounds of incompatibility. The existence of the relatively easy escape hatch of divorce puts pressure on both men and women to make real accommodations and partake in more egalitarian behaviors.

Some men feel insecure with the growing awareness and self-confidence of woman, unsure of what is expected of them, and resentful that a man's house is no longer his castle. However, most men also recognize that it takes a lot of effort to be Prince Charming and to maintain a princess in the castle. Women's liberation created a hole in the wall of patriarchy and now men are seeing a way they can become free also. Of course, many men are very ambivalent about this new-found freedom, because it means a loss of traditional male privilege. Yet there is no way to go back, and the old ways fail to give men what they really want most, the freedom to be who they really are.

## The Two-Paycheck Family

Male privilege in the workplace is traditionally based on the assumption that it is the wife's responsibility to take care of the home and children while the husband's primary responsibility is to earn a "comfortable living" for the family and to provide material benefits and opportunities. Doors often open for men that are closed to women in hiring, promotion, and the assignment of career-advancing opportunities because it is assumed that men are "career-minded" while a woman will make family her first priority. Of course, discrimination against women based on the above assumptions is now illegal, but such bigotry continues to operate in many subtle ways.

Meanwhile, the majority of married women are now in the workforce, and many are strongly career oriented. However, changes in the labor market have increased uncertainty for both men and women and few feel the same sense of company loyalty that men commonly experienced a few decades ago. Both men and women are coming to see career as a means to an end, a way of achieving other life values and priorities. Many men are choosing to be more involved with their families and starting to make career decisions using family needs as central criteria. New social patterns continue to coexist with old gendered assumptions. Confusion results when gendered scripts are no longer clearly written.

Other trends are complicating career decisions. Women know that it is very likely that they will be working most of their adult lives and that half of all U.S. marriages end in divorce. Economic conditions often make two-paycheck families essential, and, if divorced, women must be prepared to be self-supporting. In fact, more women than men today are entering college and pursuing graduate degrees. Young women are now choosing careers with much more seriousness than in the past, are intent on obtaining the necessary training and educational credentials, and are seeking positions with the opportunity for career advancement. This means that they must be willing to make many of the family sacrifices that have traditionally fallen to men. It also means that men must assume many family responsibilities which have traditionally been considered "women's work."

These changing social patterns place young men in a precarious position, often resulting in uncertain feelings toward both family and career. In the male world, the prestige of a man is still determined by the traditional criteria of education, occupation, and above all else, income. These things determine prestige, social power and much of one's personal identity. How much a man "is worth" in the competitive male world, "where the biggest fucker wins," is based much less on private life than on the public arena of career success. Being a househusband or working part time to be with the family while the wife pursues a career is simply not an option for most men. Increasingly, men claim to be family oriented and give family needs first priority but are still drawn into traditional male work patterns by gendered societal demands.[20] This may lead to feelings of guilt and inadequacy in both family and work arenas, which often turns to anger.

Such pressures create strain in the marriage. If the wife is highly career oriented she will expect her husband to share in the sacrifices (time-consuming home and child care tasks) to equalize her opportunities for career advancement. Some couples postpone the decision to have children, often drifting until it is too late and then regretting it. Others decide to become parents in their early thirties, when the wife's biological clock is felt to be running out. The presence of a child is often experienced as a jolt in household routines and may require the new mother to reduce her commitment to work at the very time when her career is beginning to progress. Alternatively, she may have children early in the marriage, not seriously pursue her career until her mid-years, and lower her expectations to fit the needs of her family. Such experiences are the stuff out of which deep marital resentments are made.

Just as men are still judged by traditional criteria, even though times are changing, women continue to be judged by their homemaking skills and how their children turn out. A single-parent mother is still expected to bring cookies for the PTA, while these demands are seldom made on single fathers. If company drops by unexpectedly, the woman will be blamed for poor housekeeping regardless of whose turn it was to do the cleaning. Her children are expected to be neatly dressed and well behaved, her house coordinated in the latest designer colors, and she will be looked to for the many small amenities that establish a family in the community. Should her children fail in any way, she will bear most if not all of the blame, as if she were solely responsible for her children's upbringing. The criteria for a well-kept house obviously have very different meanings for women and men in terms of expected behaviors and contributions.

It would be unthinkable to judge the Declaration of Independence on the basis of Jefferson's unmet dependency needs with his mother, but people feel comfortable judging a woman's career success in terms of how good of housewife she is at home. No one would blame a husband who is successful in his career for leaving the dishes unwashed. Yet women today are expected to take home the bacon, and cook it too.[21] These external gendered expectations are very powerful, both in shaping how families adapt to pressure and in shaping the self-concept of individuals.

## Patriarchy and Self-Concept

People do not adapt well to new social patterns as long as they hold on to old ideologies. Young heterosexual men continue to report that what attracts them most to a potential partner is her looks, whereas young heterosexual women cite perceived economic stability as what attracts them to a man. Of course, there are many other factors that influence whom we do and do not find attractive, but such contradictions in values endure despite the changing realities of the modern world.

The discrepancies between what we say and what we do, and how we react to external pressures, cause marital conflict, anxiety, and self-doubt. Typically, we take out our internal conflicts on those we are closest to, our family. Guilt and regret, frustrations and resentments, are all frequently laid on significant others. Bickering may turn into major confrontations. When this occurs, nothing seems to work, and both blame one another while feeling inside that they have somehow failed. In such outcomes, happiness is a false vessel only to be found in forgotten fairy tales and myths.

Of course, all of this is really a form of blaming the victim(s) and reflects perceived helplessness. When large numbers of like situated individuals have the same problems, the cause is always structural. This is something labor organizers, social reformers and politicians have long recognized. The first step in altering an ideology is the shift from seeing problems in terms of individual shortcomings to seeing them as societal dysfunction—everyone's problem.[22] Only in recent decades have people begun to question the age-old understandings of gender. The cause of so many marital problems is the sexist assumptions of so-called normal ways of doing things, the institutionalized expectations of society itself. Most young couples recognize, and can even verbalize, how these assumptions and everyday processes have contributed to their marital difficulties. Many also see the sexist nature of these patterns, but feel powerless to change the system. Anger towards one's spouse in cases such as these often alternates with feelings of depression and hopelessness.

In addition to the discrepancy between what we say and do, there is often also a discrepancy between the values we verbalize to others and what we really think on the deepest level. Training to be a "real man" in our society is so all-pervasive that young men may not be fully aware of how much of this package they have really accepted, and how oblivious they are to much of the male privilege society bestows upon them.[23] Many men, especially those who consider themselves liberal and are familiar with feminist writings, are unprepared for their deep, gut-level reactions when they fail to live up to traditional masculine expectations.

Much of our self-concept is based on intention and accomplishment of expected outcomes. The ideology of patriarchy, at its most profound level, is an idea in our heads, a set of notions about how things ought to be, and prescribed instructions for how to bring this about. When our intended efforts are unsuccessful, we feel like failures, both in our own and others' eyes, and experience anxiety and self-doubt. Many feminist women have reacted to patriarchy by creating new perspectives, finding new criteria for self-validation, and surrounding themselves with supportive, like-minded others. These women no longer intend to "do" patriarchy, so they are unconcerned when its expectations are not fulfilled.

Many men clearly see that patriarchy no longer works, but they have not yet found alternative values and criteria for self-validation. They get just enough of a patriarchal dividend to keep them playing the game, or, as psychologists point out, intermittent reinforcement strengthens resolve to continue old behavior patterns. Most men are not quite willing to give up the chase for the brass ring even though they can see that there are far more losers than winners and that most men fail to win the prize. Like betting in Las Vegas, as long as there is a chance of winning, however slight this may be, and men win a few hands here and there, male dominance will continue to be a bull market of sorts even though most men are by definition losers in the contest. To many, the gamble seems worth it, and patriarchy is felt to be the only game in town.

What if large numbers of men redefined their intentions and simply walked away from the game of patriarchy with all its stresses and broken promises? What if men could construct a new view of reality based on gender equality, humanitarian values, and nonoppressive ways of being? What if such a world view could offer men self-validation and social acceptance in ways not yet envisioned? What would such a worldview look like, and how could it work for men as well as women? Would men then be willing to voluntarily relinquish a claim to male privilege? Can feminism offer such a vision for the future? We believe that this is not only possible, but that it is already occurring.

## Envisioning and Learning Alternatives to Oppressive Forms of Male Privilege

Both women and men suffer under patriarchy. However, there is one critical difference—women suffer because of a lack of power and oppressive forms of male privilege, while men often suffer because they refuse to give them up.

By taking on a dominant role, one ultimately assumes responsibility for expected outcomes rather than sharing this responsibility with a partner. By claiming a superior status, one is under constant pressure to prove worthiness and under scrutiny by other competitors for weakness or failure. Continuous stress, insecurity, confusion, and the inability to trust others are all prices to be paid for accepting male privilege. As has been argued throughout this chapter, archaic patriarchal ways increasingly involve more costs than rewards for those seeking male dominance.

Men often recognize this and say that they would like to be able to just chill, kick back, relax, and be themselves without having to constantly prove their manhood everywhere they go. He with the biggest toys may win, but exactly what is it that he has won? More time spent at work to afford these material objects? More ulcers? More heart attacks? Fewer true friends with whom one can share their deepest feelings? Less time spent watching one's children grow up? While patriarchal values are insidious and far-reaching, like the proverbial ball of string, pulling on just one more end might eventually unravel the entire system.

Giving up oppressive forms of male privilege may reduce some of the stresses and fears associated with playing the losing game of manhood, but this in itself does not represent the winning of something positive. An important thing that it can do, however, is remove some of the foggy haze—like the misery and pain associated with a hangover—of patriarchy that prevents men from seeking, or even seeing, alternative ways of living. As long as men believe on the deepest level that traditional, oppressively harmful gender ideals are normal, they will continue to feel abnormal and uneasy whenever they question or fail to meet sexist expectations. Only when new, nonoppressive images of gender and relationships are envisioned and acted upon will men be free to truly be themselves *and* feel good about who they are.

## Notes

1. Eisler 1987.
2. For a review of some of this research, see Bonvillian 2001; Ward 1999.
3. Ember 1983.
4. Whyte 1978.
5. Murdock and Provost 1973; Schlegel and Barry 1986; Marti 1993.
6. Sanday 1981.
7. Friedl 1975, 2001[1978].
8. Friedl 1975, 2001[1978].
9. Hughes 1995.

10. Keen 1991; Faludi 1999.
11. Kimmel and Messner 2000.
12. Toffler 1981.
13. Connell 2000.
14. Marti 1993.
15. Bly 1990.
16. Friedl 2001[1978].
17. Miller 1995; Yamato 1998.
18. Friedl 2001[1978].
19. Gerson 1993.
20. Gerson 1993; Faludi 1999.
21. Hochschild 1990.
22. See Mills 1967 for a more detailed discussion of what he referred to as the sociological imagination: the ability to take personal troubles and see them as public issues.
23. McIntosh 2000; Schacht 2001.

CHAPTER FIVE

*≈*

# Envisioning Alternatives
# to the Contemporary
# Manhood-Making Machine

As I traveled through this new landscape of masculinity, I was struck by
how many men I encountered had a feeling that something, or someone
had stripped them of their usefulness and stranded them on a new deco-
rative planet.

—John Staltenberg[1]

This chapter explores the costs of the cultural ideal of manhood and ways in
which our contemporary society has created an artificial manhood-making
machine to keep so many men addicted to playing this losing game. The
manhood game alienates men from intimate relationships with others and
from themselves, and it keeps men from gaining anything more than a superficial sense of community (e.g., male bonding settings). Healing the
wounds of patriarchy requires that men take a journey inward, to reevaluate
personal assumptions about what it means to be a man and to seek nonoppressive ways of living. Only when alternatives to the manhood-making machine can be envisioned, and then acted upon, can feminism become a lived
reality.

Integral to this discussion is the understanding that there is no one
monolithic form of manhood in our society but that, instead, being a man
is made possible through many different, sometimes even competing masculinities.[2] Directly dependent upon on one's age, race, sexual orientation,
social class, and many other factors of personal identity, there are actually
many different ways in which masculinity can be performed and manhood

accomplished. In fact, subordinated masculinities can sometimes contest aspects of the dominant masculinity, such as gay men choosing to have sex with men instead of women. Nevertheless, several important ideological themes run through hegemonic (seemingly all-encompassing ways of seeing and being) masculinity that all men pursuing manhood unconsciously or consciously adhere to.

First, and perhaps foremost, is the notion that all forms of masculinity are culturally seen as inherently superior to any forms of femininity. Such a worldview also prescribes that all "real" men should always guard against being treated as a subordinate, a woman, a loser.[3] Of course, this ultimately misogynist and homophobic ideological outlook is vitally important to maintaining male dominance. Secondly, and obviously a related theme, is that masculinity is about competitively pursuing superiority over others—being a winner while making others losers—and this is the means of ultimately proving one's manhood. Mastery, rationality, being a successful competitor, and dominance over the weak are all the traits of "real" men. One is not simply born a man but must continually prove it to others for it to be an experienced reality. Thus, demonstrating one's superiority to others becomes an important corroboration of one's manhood. Finally, regardless of the form of masculinity being pursued, manhood is always made up of four fundamental components; sex, money, power, and violence (implied or physically practiced). While often discussed separately in this chapter, these essential ingredients of manhood are obviously strongly interrelated and complementary, as those who have money also tend to have power and ready access to sex, with inferred or actual violence often being essential aspects of their masculine pursuits.

Men of conscience often feel uncomfortable when they feel forced into playing the manhood game, and some even come to dislike themselves in the process. These men may have women in their lives whom they love and respect, been raised to value fairness, and/or strive to honor Judeo-Christian humanitarian ethics (like those discussed in chapter 1). They acknowledge the pain others experience who are made losers and feel empathy for them. Yet the manhood-making machine and its expectations are so all-pervasive that men often feel powerless to resist. Whether it takes a passive form of "getting along by going along" or a more active, competitive form of playing the game to win, most men face situations where external demands for masculine conformity and performance feel nonnegotiable.

We believe that most men drawn toward feminism experience a conflict between the very real external demands for them to do masculinity (sometimes backed up with threats or actual violence) and internal feelings about what would make the world a more moral and just place for all people. They strive to live differently in ways that are not oppressive to others but often are unable to envision alternatives that would not result in their being labeled as failed men and losers. This chapter explores why the enterprises of masculinity and equality are so inherently contradictory and seeks to offer some meaningful alternatives to the harmful, superficial values and behaviors prescribed by the manhood-making machine.

## Playing the Losing Game of Manhood

What keeps so many men playing the manhood game in our contemporary society? We believe that it is the fear of losing, rather than the seemingly more valuable promise of winning, that motivates many men to keep playing this futile game. Everyone playing the manhood game knows that being a loser means being treated like a woman, some sort of lesser being, a subordinate. Such sentiments are expressed in both misogynist and homophobic terms, such as *bitch, pussy, cocksucker*, and *faggot*, and provide the important "thou shall nots" for doing masculinity. In some men's settings, especially those associated with younger men, the threat of or actual violence becomes the physical means to demonstrate who the losers are *and* provides a largely accepted method for yet other young  men to do masculinity.

While, as we will demonstrate, there are various if not always clearly specified ways for men to do masculinity, they are all offered within a very restrictive framework that strongly dictates things all "real" men should guard against and never do. *No sissy stuff, do not let anyone know they have hurt you* (even if they have), and *never let anyone, men or women, treat you as a woman* are all vitally important masculine values. In this sense, the bedrock of the manhood game—the dictated parameters for doing masculinity—is a combination of deep hatred and extreme fear of anything associated with the feminine: being a societal subordinate and loser by definition.

Almost every man, if not all men, have painful childhood memories and experiences (sometimes violent) in which they did not measure up to the standards of manhood, which serve as deep, internalized reminders of the cost of failing. Everyone has witnessed situations where "failed men" have been ridiculed, discounted, even violently attacked. Most men participate in these degradation ceremonies of other, "lesser" men so that they can feel superior about themselves, or they just passively watch and remain silent out of fear of becoming the next recipient of the attackers' wrath. It is seemingly always better to align oneself with the winners than the losers when playing manhood games.

Young boys are taught by example that failing to be a real man has grave costs. Or, as John Stoltenberg insightfully noted, for those playing the manhood game, "not to be a man is to be less than nobody."[4] Any sign of weakness— that is, being soft, emotional, queer, overly dependent on others, impotent, and so forth—will be exploited by other men and is a constant source of anxiety. Men try to ignore or forget the times when they feel weak and powerless, to bury any fears, yet all men face many situations beyond their control. Even the most successful at playing the manhood game have had experiences of being failures, moments of being subordinated to another man's masculinity, that are equally if not more memorable (albeit often repressed and not shared with others) than times of masculine triumph. Not surprisingly, for many men, trust and intimacy are seen as weakness while a posture of compulsive strength, independence, and, if necessary, violence is the armor of manhood.

Without question there is safety in running with the pack, but this security is usually only possible through hyper-conformity to patriarchal dictates—the public pursuit of money, sex, and power—and a sacrifice of the freedom to shape one's own identity. Men must constantly prove their masculinity, continually promoting their manhood successes and trophies to anyone who will bear witness to their exploits, all the while hiding any fears, self-doubts, and past failures. The public relations of the masculinity contest often is a lonely, extremely stressful endeavor, as one can never reach a fixed state of manhood but can only temporarily authenticate it. While the rewards for conformity are often vague, uncertain, and entirely fleeting, the punishment for failing to be a man, as previously noted, is swift and very real (sometimes violent) in men's experience.[5]

Both manhood's pride-of-accomplishment ethos and underlying performance anxieties often play out in the sexual arena, where women are objectified and used as the real estate—pon which masculinity is done and ultimately proven. In this model of being, emotional feelings are conceived as undermining men's sexual performance since the things associated with and often expected by women, such as love, tenderness, and intimacy, are contrary to potency and conquest. Lessons learned in the boys' locker room do not serve adult men well in sustaining meaningful relationships with women.[6]

Even a desire to satisfy a woman is often seen as a performance criterion rather than an emotional aspect of the relationship. A real man must maintain control, since women do have the power to make men feel inadequate, and pleasing her is frequently about verifying one's manhood. Both his orgasms and hers become signifiers of his virility. Simply put, many men are not emotionally present during love-making, but rather, buried deep in the head of their penis. Such an outlook prescribes that men must not only objectify women but they must also objectify themselves, and sex becomes nothing more than an instrumental practice in which any feelings of true intimacy are lost in the process. In this masculine model of sexuality, women become nothing more than signifiers to men's manhood.[7]

Sadly, highly touted male role models of this misogynist ilk are quite abundant in our society. Homely comedian Drew Carey has proudly stated that he dates only "hot" strippers, as these women are good in bed but do not desire a long-term relationship. Television/radio talk show host Howard Stern constantly has women on his program who are basically judged in terms of their "fuckability" in men's eyes. On one episode of his show, with the assistance of some of the male janitorial crew at the station, they decided which of several half-naked "chicks" who paraded in front of them were hot enough to benefit from free plastic surgery. Several of the women were judged to be so ugly that plastic surgery would be of no help and summarily dismissed from the show. Adam Carolla and Jimmy Kimmel (both quite slovenly in appearance), hosts of Comedy Central's second most popular television program, *The Man Show*, constantly utilize scantily clad women as a backdrop for their show, "affectionately" referred to as the "Juggies," and end each episode with half-naked women bouncing on trampolines. Hugh Hefner has a long history of partaking in a form of serial monogamy in which he "dates" each Playmate of the month. Recently he was publicly dating twin sisters who performed incestuous acts for his viewing pleasure. Donald Trump, finished with Ivana and Marla Maples, has proudly proclaimed that he will now date only twenty-one-year-old models.

For all these men, who are role models to many men and boys in our society, women are simply used as instrumental tools—a mere means to an end—to signify the importance of their manhood. Sadly, a significant majority of young men today would give virtually anything to live the lives these men do.[8] Of course, the heterosexist standards these men set are completely unobtainable by the vast majority of men, but by example they become idealized cultural icons, with many men aspiring to be just like them.

Money is also a vitally important source of manhood in our competitive society. Success, security, and well-being, we are told, are all commodities to be bought and sold in a capitalist marketplace. Men are taught to seek their identity in work and gain status by faithfully devoting themselves to promoting the values of corporate America and the global economy. Yet much of men's work in our contemporary society is dehumanizing, meaningless, and boring, with few opportunities for individuality, creativity, or making any sort of meaningful difference.[9] As a result, often it is not the quality of a man's job but the quantity of material possessions his paycheck allows him to buy that establishes a man's worth in society, and "shit jobs" are quite tolerable as long as they pay well. Because having the latest electronic gadget, the biggest SUV, and the hottest looking chick as an arm piece is an expensive proposition, many men live beyond their means or remain in jobs that are unsatisfying, struggling to keep up with mounting debts. Only a handful of men in our country are truly wealthy and successful (perhaps 10 percent), but most feel driven to keep up appearances, especially since the mass media perpetually sell us the notion that image is everything.

Power is the ability to control and dominate others. When the choice is perceived as to be dominate or to be subordinated, the only two possible outcomes in the manhood game, the mere exercise of power becomes an end in itself. One-upmanship, establishing one's dominance, and shameless self-promotion of one's superiority are all seen as essential masculine activities of successful, powerful men. To do otherwise runs the risk of becoming a "failed man," a man who is marginalized and "treated like a woman" and other lesser beings. Not surprisingly, other men often are seen as potential threats and cannot be trusted, since they, like all the players of the game, know there cannot be winners without losers.

While most of masculine power is exercised through consent (e.g., economic relations), it is ultimately backed up with implied threats and/or actual violence. This can range from the intimidating actions of the bully on the playground to the husband who smashes a bottle to let his wife know that he is the boss, to secret service agents who are granted lethal force to protect the president. Sometimes masculine violence is painfully evident and even celebrated (e.g., many sports), while other times it is veiled and framed as a course of last resort, but it is always a vital aspect of manhood-making machine. In a very sad but real sense, violence is the backbone of masculinity and being a real man.

The world of manhood is often a dangerous place where one must constantly be on guard against others who will exploit (sometimes violently) any moment of weakness, while always scanning the horizon for new opportunities and conquests to increase your own power. And yet, once again, most men do not have much power in our society, many lack physical prowess, and few could truly be considered manhood winners, as losers must always outnumber winners. So how is it that the masculine ideals of sex, money, power, and violence continue to be of such importance to the manhood-making machine?

# Important Venues of the Contemporary Manhood-Making Machine

Since, realistically, only a limited number of gorgeous women are to be had as trophies, and most money and power is in the hands of a few men, the vast majority of men would initially appear to be huge manhood failures. And yet late capitalist patriarchy has been rather ingenious in creating commercial venues in which men can successfully experience manhood, which in turn have generated enormous profits for the owners of the manhood-making machine. In fact, manhood is increasingly something vicariously experienced, often quite passively, through the actions of others successfully doing masculinity, and through mass-produced images and products created to reinforce feelings of masculine superiority. Although numerous cultural products can be seen as ways for both failed and successful men to experience manhood, perhaps the most important of these are pornography, television sports, gambling, video games, and alcohol.

Not surprisingly, all of these mediums, in one way or another, reflect the fundamental fodder of doing masculinity—sex, money, power, and violence—and while not every man participates in all of these activities (though many do), nearly every man has, and most continue to be, actively involved in at least one of these enterprises. Clearly demonstrating the significance of these activities to the manhood-making machine, all of these highly lucrative masculinity venues are largely (e.g., alcohol, gambling, and video games) if not entirely (e.g., pornography and television sports) dependent upon male consumers. Stated slightly differently, without male customers, the industries of pornography and sports television would go out of business overnight, while the huge moneymaking profit margins associated with alcohol, gambling, and video games would be in serious jeopardy. Finally, unlike the real world of manhood, most of these venues are relatively safe ways for men to successfully do masculinity.

## Pornography

As already noted, women who meet the cultural standard for attractiveness are a commodity the demand for which far exceeds supply. (It is ironic that a small handful of individuals, often gay men in the fashion industry, largely decide on a yearly basis what female beauty is and what men should sexually desire in our society.) Pornography is a convenient solution to the problem of a shortage of hot chicks to help men do masculinity. Mass-produced images of women in submissive, subordinating, often violently denigrating poses offer men a pictorial medium whereby they can vicariously do masculinity and experience manhood. For a few dollars, men in groups or alone can experience the pleasures of doing manhood sexuality with an unlimited number of conquests by simply turning the pages, playing the next videotape, or clicking the mouse onto the next screen. The women in pornography are a "lazy man's prostitute" of sorts, allowing any man, with little money or effort, and no emotional expenditure, to experience his manhood with an endless number of types—body sizes, shapes, colors—of women catering to every imaginable masculine taste. Or, as Audre Lorde has insightfully stated, "pornography emphasizes sensation without feeling."[10] Moreover, the beauty of pornography is that it further reinforces men's view of women being nothing more than objects to be "fucked." (This is central to Lorde's argument.[11]

Sadly, the first sexual experience for the vast majority of men is with pornography, and for many, this is the only way they can sexually do masculinity on a regular basis. This early exposure to pornography teaches young men important lessons about masculinity and men's ideologically superior relationship to women's bodies, which are conceived as nothing more than the real estate upon which manhood is realized. Without question, not only is pornography the instructional manual and propaganda of male dominance,[12] but is of the utmost importance to the manhood-making machine and the masculine identity kit that it promotes.

## Television Sports

Replete with a remote control, an important tool on many men's manhood belt, television sports offer men an array of masculine endeavors that, with the advent of cable television, is piped into men's homes 24/7, 365 days a year, on multiple channels. The one-third of the television nightly news (and newspapers) that is entirely devoted to sports is no longer sufficient, as for many men the day is not complete unless they have watched a full hour of ESPN's Sport Center before retiring to bed. While an array of television sports entertainment types are important to the manhood-making machine, such as stock car racing, professional wrestling, basketball, soccer, baseball, and boxing, perhaps none is more quintessentially American masculinity than football.[13] Whether college or professional football, every armchair quarterback can vicariously live through the violent exploits of his chosen warrior on the gridiron of masculinity. The winner's motif of "any given Sunday" is experienced by tens of millions of men every weekend, Mondays, and most Thursdays, over six months of any given year. With the advent of arena football, which is an even more violent version of professional and college football, it is probably just a matter of time before football will occupy any given Sunday year-round.

When watched in the company of other men, or while attending often expensive live football games (by far, the vast majority of sports viewing is via television), a brotherly, us-versus-them sense of camaraderie frequently arises where men cheer "their" team. Often these teams have virile names such as Rams, Vikings, Bulls, Trojans, and Gamecocks, and men cheer as if they were actually part of the contest. For example, at live games, both announcers and players promote the home fans as being the "twelfth man" on the field and an important part of winning the game.

Masculine symbolism is found everywhere in the football arena, with the few women present relegated to the sidelines as sex objects—cheerleaders or wives of the players—to demarcate the far more important masculine actions of the men on the field. Moreover, the actual players are far more than mere mortals. Realistically, they are masculine freaks whose enormous body size and physical strength make them appear almost godlike in appearance and action. Given that far more men watch football than attend church on Sunday for six months out of the year, the football arena can very much be viewed as a contemporary church of manhood where masculine prayers of being a winner, perhaps accomplished through a "Hail Mary," are answered for many men in our society.

When their chosen team wins, both players and fans bask in the victory of their masculinity. With the advent of fantasy football leagues, where fans chose certain players for positions on their own ideal teams, good choices give winning seasons to guys who never take the field themselves. Football enables the manhood-making machine to produce real men without compelling them ever to leave the comfort of their recliners. After all, actually attending a football game is an expensive undertaking, with limited seating, often in outdoor stadiums that are cold once winter sets in, so for most, television football is the way to go. Perhaps the biggest choice is whether one should be a Gamecock or a Trojan in experiencing one's masculinity. Of course, some men are so vested in the activities taking place that they are willing to bet money—put some of their masculinity down—on the desired outcome of the game.

## Gambling

For many men, just being a viewer of sporting contests is insufficient to fully appreciate being a winner in these masculine rituals. Betting is a great way for many men to have more than just an emotional investment in the outcome of a given sporting event. While nearly every state now has some form of legalized gambling (i.e., as various types of lotteries, betting on horse races, and casinos often operated by Native Americans), it is still illegal to wager

on sports in every state but Nevada. As a result, most sports gambling has traditionally either been in the form of bets placed between individuals, office
pools, or for the more adventuresome, an illegal bet placed with a local
bookie. All of this has changed with the advent of the Internet, where
through offshore accounts anyone can place a bet on every imaginable sporting event. And while the latest line for the spreads on more prominent sporting events has always been published in most newspapers, this information is
now constantly updated and always available on the Internet.

Like the manhood game itself, traditional forms of gambling, such as
cards, slot machines, and craps, entail odds that always significantly favor the
house, with "muscle" always present to ensure its take. Even though the
house still has a significant advantage in sports gambling, the bettor can
chose his champion of masculinity—his team— that will make him a winner
or loser that day. Depending on the spread for the given game, typically a win
for him means a win for his team. Moreover, winning from gambling demonstrates the bettor's superior knowledge of these masculine rituals and is indicative of his own masculine expertise. All of this gives added meaning and
significance to the given sporting event being wagered upon, and seemingly
gives the impression that he actually has some say in its outcome. Sports
gambling allows men to lay some of their own masculinity/money on the
line, and while they are still wholly dependent upon the actions of others to
determine the outcome, they are nevertheless allowed to become vested winners or losers by merely placing a bet.

Gambling in other venues is equally supportive of the underlying values
of the manhood-making machine. The friendly game of poker between the
boys rightfully invokes quintessential images of masculinity and male bonding. This good ole boys club is typically off limits to women, unless they are
periodically fetching their man a beer or whatever, ;and is an event in which
one learns important skills about winning in masculine rituals. A player can
be dealt a bad hand, but through a stoically masculine gaze, can intimidate
others into believing he is the winner, and his opponents fold. Reflective of
the rules of manhood, two kings are always worth more than two queens, and
only winners leave the table with their heads held high.

### Video Games

While pornography, television sports, and gambling on sports are spectator
activities in which masculinity is ultimately experienced passively, video
games offer men a seemingly hands-on way to do manhood in which, through
their masculine skill and knowledge, they can actually control the outcomes
of the games they play. Moreover, video games allow men to partake in mas-

culine fantasy activities, many of them quite violent, simply not available in the real world. Anybody can become Mark McGwire and hit a record number of home runs, a race car driver fearlessly running over any competition on the track, or a crime-fighting police officer who violently exterminates innumerable bad guys with the simple flick of his joystick. Such formidable masculine exploits are obviously never experienced by the vast majority of men in our society, but through his XBox, where personal skill does determine outcomes, a man is allowed to emotionally experience the triumphs of successfully doing masculinity.

Many of these games rationalize the use of violent and murderous behavior by portraying an enemy as the other and less than human—shady characters, foreign devils, nonwhite races, aliens who are often reptilian in appearance, and frequently women. Killing and destruction, getting the loot and a score that earns the chicks, are the objectives.[14] These games can be viewed as an important form of anticipatory socialization for many male adolescents, who otherwise lack means to compete, or a comfortable but seemingly mindless distraction to fill times of boredom for countless more older men.

The allure of many video games is that they not only teach many men what "real" manhood is about in our society, but they also make many of the unobtainable aspects of masculinity, especially hypermasculine often misogynist violent exploits, available to tens of millions. With a joystick a person can exercise immense power over others, amass record scores, save damsels in distress, violently eliminate the competition, use and kill women, and ultimately be a manhood winner. Video games both reflect and sustain the belief that masculinity is the best, seemingly only. game in our society. Perhaps not that surprising, they also generate enormous profits for manhood-making companies who produce and sell video games.

### Alcohol

In many ways, alcohol can be viewed as the rocket fuel that keeps the engines of masculinity burning in American society. Whether he is a whiskey drinker who periodically has Jim Beam whisper in his ear to go kick someone's ass, a beer drinker that sets out to prove he can do more beer bongs than anyone else, or just a businessman who has a few martinis over lunch, alcohol is a fundamental lubricant for many men's manhood act. While pharmacologically alcohol is a depressant that should physiologically make people mellow, even tired, when consumed in pursuit of manhood, it gives men liquid courage and enables them—by giving them a built-in cultural excuse— to partake in virtually every imaginable masculine activity regardless of how harmful it might be to others. Alcohol is for many men also an important tonic for dealing with the stresses of successfully doing masculinity and a necessary opiate to numb the pain and depression of manhood failure.

Once again demonstrating just how closely the fundamental values and venues of the manhood-making machine are interrelated, much of the advertising for alcohol, especially beer, promotes the idea that real men drink, and those who drink their brand are rewarded with pretty young women in bikinis striking pornographic poises. Unlike the babes on display, the male model on these commercials is typically quite average, sometimes even slovenly, in appearance. Frequently shown during television sport events, alcohol advertising constantly promotes the ideal that a sporting man drinks and that masculine power is to be found at the bottom of a twelve-ounce can.

Realistically, whether it be pornography, television sports, gambling, video games, or alcohol, most men appear to be nothing more than faithful disciples of the manhood-making machine and uncertain about making their own way in the world. Failing to find their masculinity in the real world, men turn to such venues to easily and "successfully" experience a sense of manhood. The substitutes require little or no effort and/or emotional expenditure—so little that male users become nothing more than passive receptacles who are entirely dependent upon the actions of other men to experience manhood. Empty promises are continually made—drink our beer and you will get the babes—and while most men know that statements such as these are lies, they keep right on playing in hopes of just once hitting the manhood jackpot. Of course, the manhood-making machine banks on men's willing conformity and does everything in its power to maintain compliance. But what does the above picture we have painted thus far say about the state of men in modern society?

## Acknowledging the Empty Promises of the Manhood-Making Machine

Not surprisingly, many men today feel confused about how to live their lives in a way that has meaning and wholeness, as the manhood-making machine has failed to give all but a few men the promised rewards. Many men feel alienated and bitter, realizing that conformity to these expectations does not guarantee happiness, let alone leave much room for real individuality.[15] They feel powerless to make any significant changes yet, as men, they often feel blamed by women for everything that is wrong. Overwhelmed by external demands and pressures, and only offered insipid venues of escape, many of today's men indeed "lead lives of quiet desperation."[16]

Clearly the manhood-making machine's unrealistic and superficial social prescriptions for doing masculinity through the pursuit of sex, money, power, and violence leave many men anxious, unsatisfied, and often socially isolated. However, coming to an intellectual understanding of this reality is insufficient to overcome the fear of being labeled a failure as a man. But what is the alternative? Under patriarchy, women have been taught to deny their anger, repress their power and competence, and limit their expectations of independence. Unfortunately, when women begin to reclaim the lost parts of themselves, the fear and uncertainty experienced by men increase.[17] Unless men have faced their own fears and taken back their strength from the manhood-making machine, they will feel threatened by the feminist movement and unable to assist in the creation of a more meaningful reality.

Men's personal being has become dismembered, wholly denied the possibility of a true individual self, and controlled by external demands for unequivocal compliance. Truly personal values and any internal moral compass are often replaced in a man with fear and anxiety about how he will be rated by other men. Paradoxically, men have become almost entirely other directed and controlled by pressures for conformity, even as independence and self-reliance are seemingly the criteria for validating one's manhood. The pressure to prove oneself and measure up in all situations removes the individual freedom to be whoever we might want to be.

Some men seek to escape these demands by entering workplaces such as the university, the service professions, or the creative arts, only to find that these setting are still dominated by manhood principles. Many seek the cheap thrills and shallow pleasures of the manhood-making machine as a way to alleviate feelings of emptiness in their lives, but by doing so, they also lose any real individual meaning for their lives. Women and material goods are the spoils of the strong, who through sex, money, and power conquer the weak to prove that they are winners—but none of this is really satisfying. Only by journeying into our selves, going back into our psyches to reclaim lost parts of our past, can we re-member ourselves and find wholeness.

The problem, of course, is that boys learn the lessons of manhood on a gut level long before they are old enough to learn moral reasoning. For centuries in Western culture, the Holy Family has been the archetype of patriarchal authority in the home. God the Father rules over the world and demands obedience and submission, threatening severe, sometimes violent, punishment for those who fail to conform. These expectations are mirrored by the father at home, the larger boys on the playground, and other male figures of authority. God the Father is remote and unpredictable, largely known through his anger while only bestowing unearned gifts when he is periodically pleased. Mary, the mother, is an empty vessel, a womb to be filled and used by the father, valued only for her innocence and subservience. Gentle Jesus is to be admired but not emulated. He is a friend to women, children, and failed men—the powerless and disenfranchised—not real men. Stepfather Joseph is worth mentioning only because of his submission to the will of all-powerful God. These images have changed over the past few decades with the introduction of feminist ideas and gender sensitive language, continuing today more in fundamentalist Christian churches than in Catholicism. Few today would consciously support this model, yet historically it has been imprinted in our culture.

Boys soon learn that what is rewarded is not the teachings of gentle Jesus or perhaps their mothers, but the power exercised by older boys and men. Decisions of right and wrong really do not hinge on morals and values but, rather, on whom we have seen rewarded and punished. Moral principles learned later in life are then filtered through these gut-level understandings learned as a child under the guise of being realistic, pragmatic, or just getting along in a world that is quite different from the one taught in kindergarten or Sunday School. Ethical relativity, expressed as rationally purposeful action, is stretched to a point where anything can be acceptable under the right circumstances—the ends are almost always more important than the means. Adult men need to reexamine their basic values, put aside oppressive, obsolete messages from childhood, and decide what principles they really stand for and are willing to act upon.

Boys are taught that to be a man means to be cool, passionless, stoic—to be a rock, an island—and to stand alone and tough out the hard times in stony silence. Only some feelings are acceptable, such as anger, pride, and courage, while "softer" feelings are for girls. Boys are not supposed to cry, giggle, or like pretty things, and they should never express feelings of being hurt or needy. Except perhaps for sex, accepting physical affection is not okay as a boy enters the teen years. To be a man requires shutting down feelings and aspects of a man's personality that might betray him with other men, rejecting closeness and intimacy, and pretending to be strong even when he feels soft inside. In a very real sense, this is one of the biggest crimes against humanity that patriarchy perpetuates and what makes oppression and inequality possible. Re-membering oneself requires reclaiming that lost and lonely childhood and mourning for the lost potential of what might have been. Only then can a man personally start to heal from the harms that he experienced in the pursuit of manhood.

It also requires coming to terms with the ambivalence men have been taught to feel about women. It is the very fact that most young boys are dependent on their mother's care and love that later leads so many of them to rebel against it.[18] Mothers, and mothering women and men, are a threat, since the experience of nurturing is often associated with personal weakness. Although men crave the warmth of emotional intimacy, they fear more the letting go of any degree of self control that might make one "entrapped" by unmet dependency needs. Men must keep their distance from women, maintain control, and put women in their place, lest they become emasculated by their own emotional neediness. Misogyny, combined with men's fears of emotional dependency on women, results in many men viewing all woman as the enemy. Pragmatic realism and rational control over the world and women, undiluted by feelings or ethical values are the criteria for traditional manhood. Of course, this is also the formula for a bully.

Children are also taught rigid, binary opposite-gender role expectations at a very early age. As previously noted, being a man means rejecting anything feminine, and gendered behaviors are accompanied by very visible rewards and punishments. Self-esteem, based on the subordination of others and the approval ratings given by those in power, is a strong motivator for conformity, while fear of losing prevents any deviation from these expectations. Boys play in larger groups than girls and are more task oriented, often obsessively focused on winning the game. They have many casual acquaintances and friends they do things with, but few they can really trust or in which they can confide. They are taught to find meaning in accomplishments that take the form of others' subordination, rather than connection. Little room is left for any feelings or meaningful relationships.

## The Journey to Re-Member Oneself

Manhood is ultimately an institutionalized social construct—a blueprint of how life should be lived promoted by religion, the mass media, sports, laws, schools, and all major societal institutions—that each man carries in his head, and is only made real through his expressed attitudes and actions. Change for a man must begin by taking an inventory of who he is now, what he believes at the deepest levels, and who he wants to become. As previously discussed, men must acknowledge what many already know in their hearts—that the manhood-making machine's promised rewards are often unobtainable, empty, and not satisfying. Further recognition must also be made that playing the manhood game ultimately robs men of the choice to decide who they are or want to be. Only when men are willing to accept the fact that the manhood-making machine is a con game, with few winners but many passive, devoted losers, will the healing begin and the possibility of living a more meaningful existence become available.

Evicting manhood assumptions from one's head is a necessary first step in becoming a (pro)feminist man, but it alone is insufficient to bring about real change. Minds do not remain empty, and often seemingly benign forms of the manhood-making machine will fill the vacuum if real alternatives are not envisioned and acted upon. Whether male or female, to create a new self, we must have a clear image of who we want to become, and then put our energy and actions into making that vision a lived reality in the present. Who do you want to be? How do you want to spend your time and energy? What feeds you, personally and emotionally?

Often we give false answers to these complex questions, answers filled with excuses, half truths, and delusions. We may say we want to be closer to nature but continually find ourselves too busy to even take a walk in the woods. Likewise, we may claim that spending quality time with our partners and children is our first priority but be so busy making a living that we have little time for our family members. Life's demands are often viewed as necessary but temporary diversions from who we really want to be. Yet, if being closer to nature, spending more time with our family, or whatever other desire were really a priority, we would find time to make it happen.

Our true priorities are actually demonstrated in how and where we invest our time and energy—actions always speak louder than words—and our life is nothing more than how we live it, not an idealized fantasy of who we might be tomorrow in an ideal world. Logically, tomorrow never exists, so our sole source of power is found in the now, the present moment. Truly honoring our priorities means we must acknowledge that we have choices and that our choices carry consequences. What are we willing to give up to become who we truly want to be? It is dishonest to say, "I would be different if only my job/partner/family-friends/society would let me." or "I am in a situation where I must be aggressive/competitive/successful/always a winner to survive." If there are things in our lives that are truly desired, then only making new choices and life changes will make them possible.

A common fantasy is that everything would be different if we could only get out of some present situation—find a new partner, get a new job, get the bills caught up, move to a new community—and then everything would be all right. Yet these life changes often do not lead to real differences in one's life unless they are also accompanied by internal changes. There is an old saying, "You can run away into the entire world, but if you take yourself with you, you really haven't gone anywhere." In any case, most men have many life responsibilities and taking a bus to Arizona or playing a guitar and trying to find yourself is simply not an option.

Envisioning an image of who you want to become is perhaps the easiest part. Most men reading this book already have sympathies for feminism and are seeking ways to develop the emotional, humanistic sides of themselves. The real challenge is to find practical ways to shift personal priorities and to put energy into one's new vision, rather than creating an idealized self that is merely an unobtainable intellectual abstraction. How can a person's vision become a conscious intention that shapes his daily living? We have to begin with taking an inventory of who we are now, of what works and does not work in our life at the present. What would your life story be if you continue on the path you are presently traveling? Where do you see yourself five, ten, twenty-five years from now? What would you like people to say about you in your obituary? Then form a vision of who you really want to be, building upon who you think yourself to be on the inside.

Most of us find ourselves stuck in places ultimately of our own creation, limited by old patterns that no longer serve us but continue as habits. Some of our past beliefs and behaviors may have been helpful or necessary in the past but are no longer needed, while others are so deeply internalized that they are accepted without question or even awareness. Old ways and beliefs often lead to circular thinking, offering few choices and no way out. The the manhood-making machine has a vested interest in the maintenance of these circular traps so that men never truly challenge the system. What does it take—what personal challenge or possibility—to pull men out of these stuck places and make real change a possibility? There is only one thing in life any one of us can truly change and that is ourselves. What commitment and action can we make that will make this possible?

How can men journey into the past and reclaim parts of their souls lost in childhood? Because of the lessons of manhood already learned, this personal quest may be much more threatening than facing any external enemy. Some men seek to do this through therapy, actively cultivating the emotional, intuitive aspects of their being. Others explore alternative forms of spirituality, such as Earth-based rituals, Buddhist meditation, or Native American traditions. Walking alone in nature, developing interest in some creative activity, or becoming involved in social causes may help some men to get in touch with their deeper selves. For yet other men, joining a men's group where they can openly share the fears and pain of childhood and reexamine the old messages about what it means to be a man is an excellent way to begin this journey.

Some men prefer to do this work rationally, intellectually, and alone. These men have too many issues with dependency, vulnerability, and control to really trust others. Men's groups are especially threatening to them, as the emotion of true intimacy with other men triggers homophobia. It is far easier to think or talk about what angers them than to allow themselves to really experience feelings of intimacy with others. Thus, the avoidance of becoming emotionally engaged in the process is a cop-out that assures defeat. Avoidance, denial, and repression of fear is the very thing that keeps men playing the manhood game.

A man setting out on this personal journey must recognize that his hopes for something different are often accompanied by fears—fear of change, and fear of unsettling the often already delicate balance of his life. How will others react once he truly begins to change? Others' reactions to his changes may raise questions about whom he wants to accompany him on this journey. This requires honest communication with significant people in his life and a reexamination of what shared values he may or may not have with others.

Others may choose different destinations and incompatible paths. Sometimes paths may merge for a distance but then separate so that each can seek his own way in the world. Often, open, honest communication can also lead to closer intimacy and growing together. Real change requires taking risks, "rocking the boat," and putting oneself emotionally on the line if men are ever to find out what is truly possible.

In sum, the need to prove one's manhood must be replaced by a form of self-validation that prescribes that a man has the freedom to choose his own life course without being dependent on other men for approval, if true personal change is ever to occur. Of course, not all men who take this inward journey will embrace feminism, but without reclaiming the lost parts of self, any commitment to feminism will be, at best, superficial. Truly listening to women and getting the message of feminism on a deep level requires an openness to the full range of feelings and experiences. It is manly to be a warrior for justice and to fight the good fight, but this often requires showing no real compassion for the oppressed or being sensitive to the feelings of those you are purportedly fighting for. Being a feminist requires giving up the need to control the actions of others and to embrace life with all its uncertainties and ambiguities. This requires getting out of our heads and into our hearts, letting go of destructive childhood lessons of what it means to be a man, welcoming true intimacy, and being fully present in the moment. The next chapter offers some specific, practical pathways men might undertake to realize a feminist worldview and way of life.

# Notes

We are indebted to John Stoltenberg for several of the arguments made in this chapter.

1. Faludi 1999, p. 468.
2. See Kimmel and Messner 2000; Connell 1995, 2000; Halberstam 1998.
3. Connell 2000; Schacht 1996.
4. Stoltenberg 1998, p. 152.
5. Faludi 1999.
6. Curry 1991.
7. Gay male sexuality often is expressed in a strikingly similar manner: see Levine 1998.
8. I (Steve) have asked male students in my classes on many occasions what they would give to be one of these men, like Hugh Hefner. Most, but not all, have said they would give up virtually anything—e.g., limbs, even testicles—to be these men.
9. Faludi 1999.
10. Lorde 1984, p. 54.
11. Schacht and Atchison 1993; Jensen 1998.
12. Dworkin 1989; Schacht and Atchison 1993.
13. Nelson 1994.
14. In the video game Grand Theft Auto III, one can make a pit stop with a prostitute for a few points, and quickly win them back by killing her when done with her.
15. Faludi 1999.
16. Thoreau 1997[1854], p. 8.
17. Gerson 1993.
18. Bly 1990.

# CHAPTER SIX

# Becoming a (Pro)Feminist

Thus far we have offered both abstract and personal reasons for our belief that men should be feminists. This chapter looks to build on these arguments and offer practical suggestions for actually becoming a male (pro)feminist. Key to this discussion is the explicit understanding that, since men are the oppressor in gender relations, they must undertake disparate journeys for realizing a feminist worldview and, as a result, their contributions to feminism will be different from those of women. Accordingly, the section that follows explores why using women's experiential models for becoming a feminist as a litmus test of who can and cannot be a feminist is ultimately a self-defeating enterprise.

From this discussion we propose what we believe should be the experiential basis of a male (pro)feminism, the explicit acknowledgment of one's oppressive attitudes and behaviors toward women. Integral to making this recognition is a clear understanding of what oppression and male privilege are, two concepts we will also explore in this chapter. We then offer what we believe are four suggestive, practical pathways for men realizing a feminist worldview. While we recognize that some readers may have already addressed some or many of the issues we propose in this chapter as necessary beginnings for becoming a feminist, we are also guessing that many readers may have little or no feminist awareness. Thus, we hope the basic, rudimentary manner in which these pathways are offered will be accessible to those just beginning a feminist journey yet still be stimulating to those who are already traveling feminist pathways.

# Moving beyond the Self-Defeating Debate over Whether Men Can Be Feminists

Those feminists activists who refuse to accept men as comrades in struggle—who harbor irrational fears that if men benefit in any way from feminist politics women lose—have misguidedly helped the public view feminism with suspicion and disdain.

—bell hooks[1]

Over the past thirty years numerous authors have proposed various definitions of feminism. While there often are ideological differences over exactly what a feminist should be, there is some general agreement on how a woman typically becomes a feminist. This consensus revolves around two interrelated themes: (1) following Simone de Beauvoir and other early feminist writers who believed that one is not born a woman but, rather, that society creates women, contemporary feminists also hold that one is not born a feminist but becomes one;[2] and (2) becoming a feminist involves a transformative process that is experientially grounded. "Experientially" means that, women through their own personal experiences, start to recognize the ways oppressive forces—often individual men in their lives—work to subordinate women as a group within society. Ultimately, this transformative, experientially based process calls for the oppressed—women—to join together to challenge and end women's oppression.[3]

Since men cannot experience women's oppression, and it is men exercising their often tyrannical authority who are largely responsible for this hegemonic reality, many women and men categorically reject the present possibility of men becoming feminists. Some reject the possibility of men becoming feminists because of personal experiences with so-called feminist men who have turned out to be just the opposite—phallocentric misogynists.[4] Other women reject the possibility that men can be feminist on the grounds that they do not experience the world as women do. As Bart and colleagues state, "We believe that one must inhabit a female body to have the experiences that make one feminist."[5] Both of these positions are summarized in the following quotes; the first is by a founding member of the current women's movement in the United States, while the second is by a male author.

I haven't the faintest notion what possible role white heterosexual men could fulfill, since they are the very embodiment of reactionary-vested-interest-power.[6]

Men's relation to feminism is an impossible one. This is not said sadly nor angrily (though sadness and anger are both known and common reactions) but politically.[7]

To categorically denounce the possibility that men could become feminists, however, is an essentialist argument that treats the categories of male and female as absolute states of being, Such a position also falls into a trap set up by patriarchy itself.[8] That is, the reality that patriarchy tries so earnestly to hardwire into each of our brains is that we live in a dichotomous, binary world: knowledge/ignorance, light/darkness, good/evil, love/hate, male/female, and so forth.[9] This either/or, us/them outlook is the bedrock of relationships of dominance and subordination. As we have previously noted, such an outlook when applied to feminism results in men, as a social category, forever being defined as the enemy and beyond redemption. The far-reaching goals of feminism are unlikely to be realized if men are seemingly framed as incapable of personal change from the onset.

Obviously one of the foremost intentions of this book is to help create a truly inclusive feminism that potentially everyone can embrace. We believe that exclusive labels are ultimately divisive and undermine the grassroots support needed for the realization of long-term feminist goals, such as an oppression-free society. Arguments over whether men can or cannot be feminists feeds the general perception that feminism is only for women and discourages sympathetic men from becoming involved. Since men often have more access to power and money, categorically opposing their participation in the struggle dooms feminism to remain a stalled social movement and an unfinished revolution.[10] Quite simply, it is unreasonable to believe that women alone will be able to construct a nonoppressive future.

Moreover, as Hawkesworth notes, the position that only women "will produce an accurate depiction of reality, either because they are women or because they are oppressed, appears highly implausible," and "adhere[s] to the great illusion that there is one position in the world or one orientation toward the world that can eradicate all confusion, conflict, and contradiction."[11] Since, ultimately, all perspectives and knowledges are partial and situated,[12] a full understanding of oppression requires that we recognize that there are multiple realities, each valid from the perspective of those having the experiences. Or as Walker asserts with equal insightfulness:

I believe that the truth about any subject only comes when all sides of the story are put together, and all their different meanings make one new one. Each writer writes the missing parts to the other writer's story. And the whole story is what I am after.[13]

Accordingly, we believe women and men have different but potentially equally valuable contributions to make toward the advancement of a feminist agenda. While it is true that men do not experience the world as women do, nor do women experience the world as men do, all individual experiences are equally real and, when woven together, tell a more comprehensive story. In fact, we believe that it is this very disparity between women's and men's experiences that, when collectively considered, provides the "whole story" and the potential to have a greater impact than either is able to achieve separately. Thus, instead of constructing litmus tests and miring ourselves in self-defeating debates over who can and cannot be a feminist, we believe it is a far more fruitful endeavor to explore what pathways men might travel to become an active participant in the creation of a feminist reality for all people.

## Making Visible Oppression and Male Privilege: The Trail Heads to Becoming a Male (Pro)Feminist

The fact that men do not socially experience the world as women does not mean that the paths they might travel to gain a feminist understanding will be less difficult. Our own experiences tell us just the opposite: Any meaningful path a man pursues in gaining a feminist consciousness is fraught with real roadblocks and doubts of his ever reaching such a destination. What it does mean, however, is that men who aspire to gain a feminist worldview have *no choice but to travel a different path* than women travel.

We believe that the trailhead of this path is ultimately predicated on a man's first recognizing that his relationship to feminism and women in general is that of oppressor. That is, if a woman's feminist outlook is born from experiences of being oppressed, then a man's feminist outlook can also be born of oppression albeit often *as the oppressor*. All men—granted, to varying degrees—have a lifetime's worth of experiences of oppressive attitudes and often behaviors that they have directed at women. Herein, and somewhat ironically, lies the most important contribution men can make to feminism. We believe that men who are willing to admit just how oppressive their attitudes and actions toward women have been, and can be, stand to make important contributions to understanding how oppression occurs and ultimately challenging its occurrence.

Some readers may find our suggestion that men's explicit relationship to feminism and women is that of oppressor to be rather extreme. We would expect some skepticism, , as most cultural conceptions of oppression, especially those found in the mass media, frame it as either the extreme act of an individual, like Timothy McVeigh, or something done by geographically remote others, like genocide in Bosnia. Thus, before proceeding, we think it would be helpful to offer a working definition of oppression. Much of this discussion is based upon Iris Marion Young's article, "Five Faces of Oppression."[14] We believe her insights will enable many male readers to better understand how their relationship to women is that of the oppressor.

Most people's conception of what oppression is very much fostered by the popular press and involves images of absolute, tyrannical, and unjust rule or actions by an individual or a small group of leaders over many subordinates. Military dictatorships, or the past practice of apartheid in South Africa, are both consistent with this outlook. These regimes are predicated on the overt use of violence to instill terror and forced obedience of subordinates. Obviously most men reading this book would not be considered oppressors as so defined.

New social movements in the 1960s and 1970s worked to expand the definition of oppression not only to include blatant examples of its occurrence, such as the obvious intentions of a tyrant, but to increasingly argue that it is also a structural phenomenon that in many ways is the insidious moral fabric of our society. This recognizes that whether we are aware of it or not (the latter most typically being the case), as dominants and subordinates we populate and make real an oppressive society. To better illuminate oppression as a structural reality, Young offers what she sees as the five ubiquitous features—five faces—of oppression, with experiences of any one of them being framed as indicative of someone being oppressed. These categories of oppression are not proposed as mutually exclusive, however, as those being oppressed often experience several simultaneously (e.g., rape explicitly involves violence and powerlessness), and most subordinated groups have experiences with all five. Young's five faces of oppression are as follows:

1. *Exploitation*: the unreciprocated transfer of power and resources from the subordinate group to the dominant group. For instance, while women do most of the productive labor in the world (estimated between 66 to 80 percent), they receive somewhere between 10 and 20 percent of all wages paid workers, and own an estimated 1 percent of all the property in the world.
2. *Marginalization*: the denying or expelling of a whole category of people from useful and full participation in society. Obvious examples of this face of oppression are traditional housewives, the elderly (most often

women) who are warehoused in retirement homes, not allowing gay and lesbian individuals marry, or the condescending manner in which the welfare state treats poor people (often women heading single parent families and their children) in our society. People in marginalized, subordinated groups are often kept in such a childlike state of dependency that anything they might contribute by fully participating in society is quickly dismissed as unnecessary, not desirable, or even in some cases, detrimental. On a more interpersonal level, as we will further discuss in moment, men often marginalize women during conversations with them by belittling or ignoring their voices.

3. *Powerlessness:* little or no autonomy of one's work and/or body. It is no accident that most service jobs (e.g., hotel maids, waitresses, secretaries), which have virtually no autonomy, almost by definition are performed by women. Nor is it surprising that women are largely absent from important decision-making positions in the political and corporate world. Moreover, seemingly flagrant cases of powerlessness, such as a woman being raped, are quite common in our society and are frequently valorized in popular cultural mediums such as pornography.

4. *Cultural Imperialism:* a practice wherein the dominant group tries to render all "other" perspectives of societal subordinates as either invisible and/or deviant. For centuries, women could get their work recognized only by presenting it under a male name. Until recently, we learned only *his*tory, the achievements and oppressive exploits of men throughout time, with little or no concern for *her*story. Women, African Americans, Latinos, and other ethnic groups are all struggling to reclaim their legitimate place in American history. Nor is it surprising that the perspectives associated with recently emerging social movements, such as feminism or civil rights, are often framed as deviant and potentially harmful to society (e.g., "feminazis"). Even in areas where there appears to be some recognition of women's perspectives, such as in literature, art, and music, women's efforts in these areas are still framed as secondary to the work being produced by men, and they become respectable only when validated by the male-controlled media. For the most part, men are seen as creating art while women make crafts.

5. *Violence:* systematic, unprovoked, legitimate use of violence by societal dominants to physically keep societal subordinates just that, subordinate. The violence occurs randomly, regardless of the actions of those experiencing the violent treatment, and is legitimate in the sense that most people regard it as unsurprising and it typically goes unpunished.

Members of subordinate groups are targeted for violence simply because they are a member of an oppressed group. To varying degrees, most people in subordinate groups live in a constant state of fear that they may be the next victim of a violent attack. Rape is a obvious form of oppressive violence against women.

As just defined, much of oppression is covert and typically so routine a practice that neither the oppressed nor the oppressor gives much thought to its outcome, as it often appears quite natural and expected.

The seemingly inevitable flip side of the hidden nature of oppression is that it also makes invisible much of the resultant privilege of dominants.[15] Privilege can be likened to playing cards with a stacked deck.[16] In many ways, white heterosexual males from upper-class backgrounds can be seen as being born with four aces (one for each privileged status they hold). While there are no guarantees in playing the game of life in competitive, capitalist societies, as even the most privileged (oppressors) are losers sometimes, certain people are afforded a significant upper hand in this real-life contest. One can lose (be oppressed) holding four aces, and one can win (become an oppressor) holding a pair of twos, but both of these are obviously highly unlikely outcomes. Being dealt a winner's hand at birth offers a lifetime's worth of protection from others' attempts of oppression, and it gives one substantial opportunities to oppress others. The key is to hold your hand so that others can never see your cards (privilege); thus leaving the impression that the game was just when in fact it was not. Perhaps the advantage of privilege is that not only is it often kept hidden from those oppressed in the process, but frequently those doing the oppressing are only unconsciously aware, at best, of both the power and unfairness of the hands they were dealt at birth.

There are important advantages, frequently entirely unearned, to being able to walk through life with limited or no experiences of oppression. This is quite easily demonstrated with male privilege. Workplace doors, especially for high-paying jobs that often are closed for women, open for men in ways that men seldom recognize. Much of it appears "natural"; for example, everyone knows that the better-paid airline pilots are almost exclusively men, while flight attendants most typically are women. Just as whites more easily advance in their careers presumably through their efforts while blacks are often stopped by an array of seemingly invisible barriers—typically covert or unrecognized forms of discrimination[17]—so men frequently move up the work ladder at the expense of women. One does not have to be an overt or even active oppressor to benefit from much of the potential competition being eliminated through discrimination and glass ceilings.

Viewed as rightful societal dominants, men are more likely to be taken seriously in business or even causal conversation, as the words of superiors are always seen as more important than those of subordinates. Men are expected to take leadership roles in our society and to be a final decision maker in family matters. Effectively beating the competition, being successful, and reaping the rewards are all things expected of men. Yet success for women often has negative connotations, such as "she slept her way to the top," "she is a dyke," "she is a frigid bitch."

Women have to justify both their failures and their successes. This is referred to as a double ontological bind,[18] or more simply a catch-22 situation, where subordinate members of society are held to such a double standard that they are oppressed regardless of what they do. Thus, women with children who work are often seen as bad mothers, while women who stay at home with their children are increasingly framed as lazy and a drain on the family finances. Similarly, the more money a woman makes and/or the higher her education, the less likely she is to be married or to have children, while low education and income levels increase the likelihood she will be married with children. On the other hand, since just the opposite relationship holds true for men—higher income and education increase likelihood of marriage and children—men are seldom asked to choose between their career or family. In most families it is largely assumed that the wife will make the necessary sacrifices and accommodations for her husband's career interests.

The actions of the rapist serve to control women through fear, violently demonstrating the vulnerability of women who are not under male protection and control. Even in America where women are among the freest in the world, a woman perceived to have no man to protect her faces real threats and dangers that a man seldom ever confronts or even considers. The stalker, the stranger met on the way to one's car late at night, the obscene telephone caller, or the most recent newspaper headline of a woman being raped and/or killed by a stranger remind all women of this truth.[19] The seemingly inherent risks of being born female in our society, combined with the accordant behavioral actions of both women and men, all work to limit women's choices and to keep women dependent, passive, and ultimately subordinated in relation to men. Most men have little awareness of the role that terror plays in many women's lives.[20] If one is fearful from the onset, it does not take much to intimidate and control them, ultimately reminding them of and reifying their subordinate status in our society.

Quite simply, by accepting and taking advantage of male privilege, a man makes possible and perpetuates women's oppression. Even men who do not actively seek male privilege but who nevertheless deny or remain silent about the harms from women's oppression receive a patriarchal dividend.[21] A few *bad* men often can be blamed for the most blatant forms of women's oppression, such as rape and battering, but until men are willing to acknowledge how they benefit from such actions necessary for maintaining male privilege and dominance.

Even those men who have never knowingly oppressed a woman will remain silent accessories after the fact. As the sayings go, "If you are not part of the solution, you are part of the problem" and "If you are not fighting the system, you are the system." Men who are willing to examine both their unearned male privilege and how their attitudes and behaviors are oppressive to women will find themselves opening a door into a feminist consciousness.

One final clarifying observation is warranted concerning oppression and male privilege. Some people often wrongly equate being miserable with being oppressed.[22] While it is true that the oppressed often have the blues and feel miserable, those doing the oppression can also experience such feelings. Conversely, through internalized oppression, wherein the subordinate party either accepts his or her secondary status as just and normal or denies it,[23] those who are oppressed can seemingly lead a blissful existence—hence the myths of the happy housewife of the fifties or the happy slave before the Civil War. Thus, as we have argued throughout this text, while systems of oppression are ultimately alienating and restrictive to everyone, the cause of any resultant misery is very different for the oppressor and the oppressed; a rapist may experience considerable anguish for his actions, but it cannot compare with the suffering of a survivor of a violent attack. Disparate pathways for becoming a feminist are obviously required for the oppressed and the oppressors.

## Pathways for Becoming a Male (Pro)Feminist

Beyond a man's basic but fundamental admission of an oppressive relationship to women, we believe that there are at least four practical pathways a man can travel in seeking a feminist consciousness:

1. Through the reading of feminists works and *actually listening to women*, he should try to learn about the depth and unjust nature of women's oppression;
2. He should consider asking himself in what ways does he personally (individually), and as a man in general (structurally), oppress women;
3. He should enter into solidarity with women and the oppressed; and
4. He should consider ways to reject traditional notions of masculinity that are oppressive to others and replace them with feminism as his referent.

These proposed ways for a man to gain a feminist consciousness are not seen as necessarily incremental steps, mutually exclusive, or exhaustive; however, in total, they are proposed as *some necessary beginnings*. Also, depending on a given man's ethnicity, race, social class, and sexual orientation, these proposed pathways will have potentially different directional meanings and applications. Those men who have the courage to take this journey will find themselves entering a world of self-knowledge and empathy that is emotionally laden and often disconcerting. He will leave behind a competitive way of life that demands that he be *always over, under, or in spite* of someone and instead learn how to truly live in harmony *with* all people.

### Learning the Depth of Women's Oppression

Men can learn about the depth of women's oppression and its unjust nature from two basic sources: a wide array of written feminist works, and feminist women and women in general. Considering the number of feminist books, anthologies, and periodicals published over the past thirty years, a man will find a nearly inexhaustible array of academic and nonacademic sources that can be utilized to address almost any given interest he might have. For men in academia, taking a women's studies course (if one is offered on his campus), or at the very least, getting a list of readings from those who teach such courses, would be an excellent start to becoming sensitive to some of the basic issues feminism explores. For men outside of academia, nearly any bookstore or library offers a wide array of contemporary feminist works.

Of equal, or greater importance for a man who hopes to gain any sort of feminist understanding is learning, perhaps for the first time in his life, how to really listen to women. Men have difficulty listening to women for several reasons. Men in our society are socialized to control and dominate discussions with women, which often means women's voices are marginalized when communicating with men.[24] Not only is this a personally sexist and oppressive behavior, but it also severely undermines any possibility of men learning anything from women. When men attempt to take control of conversations, they often do so in a paternalistic manner that insidiously promotes the idea that, like some Mafia godfather, they ultimately know best how to deal with nearly any imaginable situation. In practice, this frequently means that men interrupt women when they are speaking with them, offer unsolicited advice, and feel that they should have the last word in such conversations.

Obviously the way in which many men approach conversations, especially with women, is consistent with other important values of masculinity that prescribe always trying to be in control, never showing any weakness or uncertainty, and always trying to be a winner. Women who find themselves in conversation with men such as these often feel shut down and "put off." They may feel anger, but the most typical response is to lapse into resentful silence. Women are often left feeling unheard, as their perspective is largely rendered invisible (an obvious form of cultural imperialism) in conversations with men such as these.

Men, on the other hand, often report that they find women's conversations boring and uncomfortable. Things often feel like they move too slowly, there are fewer ways "to win" or be right, and frequently the topic discussed appears less important than the vague feelings that are being expressed. Conclusions to the conversation may seem irrational, as they are often intuitively and experientially based, sometimes in ways that men feel give little attention to facts and logic. Frustrated by their inability to actively compete in women's conversations, men often mentally withdraw and listen only marginally. Of course, this provides the fodder for many television situational comedies and jokes about women. Sadly, however, communication problems are also a major factor in the breakdown of many relationships between women and men in our society.

Obviously, if a man is sincerely interested in learning about women's experiences, he needs to learn new, nonoppressive ways to listen to and dialogue with women. Perhaps the best technique for initially learning to listen to women is to largely remain silent, saying only enough to convey continued interest. Sometimes people simply need to talk about their frustration and pain, and just being heard is enough. Attentively listening to someone's words—whether spoken or written—is always a requisite for learning more about them.

As the dialogue develops, it is important that men recognize and validate the emotional aspect of the experience the women is sharing (e.g., "I can see why you would feel so angry . . . hurt . . . betrayed"). It is far less helpful, and sometimes harmful, to make statements that minimize feelings like "It will all look better tomorrow." We believe "what" questions are always more helpful than "why" questions, as the latter often call for an intellectual justification of feelings and experiences. Why questions also often sound paternalistic, like some parent asking a child *why* her or his milk got spilled. What questions (such as "What are you feeling about this?"; "What do you really need/or want from this individual/situation?"; "What would you like to do?") encourage the speaker to explore her or his own feelings rather than trying to reframe them in such a way that they sound acceptable to the listener.

Men should avoid giving women unsolicited advice about how best to understand their own experiences. "If I were you" statements are frequently not helpful, as they fail to recognize the very different experiences and options men and women have in society. Indeed, as we have previously noted, since men do not experience gender oppression, they often have little notion of what it is like to live as a woman in our society. This is not to say that a man should not have opinions or share them with others. What it does mean is adopting a listening and dialoguing approach that is truly attentive, support-ive, and constructive instead of the traditional one-upmanship tactic of get-ting a point across no matter what, often found in men's conversations.

By truly listening to women's voices, men will come to know the truth about the oppressive realities of patriarchy and the destructive consequences of its taken-for-granted ways and assumptions. Men need to understand the personal basis of oppression and how it often harms intimate women in their lives. The personal is political, and the political is quite personal. Really lis-tening to women may result in outrage at the injustice of their oppressive ex-periences. Anger can be a healthy emotion if it is channeled into purposeful action to contest the injurious outcomes of oppression. One especially fruit-ful avenue men might pursue to this end is to take the new knowledge they have learned from listening to women and start to address additional ways in which they personally oppress women.

## Question the Individual and Structural Ways in Which Men Oppress Women

> In what ways do I exploit women, put them down, ignore them? How do I benefit from the system? Are there ways that I could act which will bet-ter recognize the contributions of women and equalize opportunities?
>
> —Harriet Gill[25]

While there are untold ways in which men oppress women, perhaps one of the most basic, rudimentary methods is at the interpersonal level through sexual-ity. Numerous feminists have examined the way in which heterosexuality as an ideological practice is used to dominate and control women.[26] Whether it be in the more blatant forms of rape, incest, sexual harassment, prostitution, and the presentations of these found in pornography or in consensual sex, het-erosexuality is frequently a tool used by men to dominate and control women in all settings.[27] Dominant and subordinate roles are built into our cultural ex-pectations of sexuality and our definitions of what it means to be masculine or feminine, and they play a major part in sexual attraction. Consensual sex is often based on men and women willingly playing these roles.

Perhaps the bedrock of this ideological practice is the social process of ob-jectification. Andrea Dworkin states, "Male supremacy depends on the ability of men to view women as sexual objects."[28] From a very early age, men in our society are taught to think of themselves as subjects and women (and other perceived lesser beings) as objects and, therefore, not quite human. Expressed through heterosexuality, objectification, then, provides all men with an instrumental practice whereby they can differentiate themselves from "others" so that they can ultimately feel relationally superior to some*thing*: all women. Some men struggle to unlearn these messages from adolescence with varying degrees of success, but this is difficult in a society where men are surrounded by media images, jokes and conversation, and practical situations that reinforce this objectification.

Recognizing this most fundamental insight begs the question for men who hope to construct and live a feminist reality. Quite simply, men (both gay and straight) who are trying to break from patriarchy should explore and try to learn new ways of viewing women and men that do not involve sexual objectification. Since one can only rape, sexually harass, or exploit an object, viewing and treating women as real people (subjects) diminishes, if not completely eliminates men's predisposition to oppress women. Moreover, if men were to start to view all people as subjects, then the whole patriarchal construct of oppression, in the numerous ways it manifests itself, would truly become contested and more easily eliminated.

Men who truly desire to view women as subjects, instead of sexual objects and subordinates, would be well served to personally address some of the following questions. All of them touch on issues of power and vulnerability found in societally prescribed scripts of sexual attraction that ultimately promote male domination and female subordination. As most men's first sexual experience in our society is masturbation using pornography, one might also benefit from considering where one's ideals of attraction originated and what values these sources promote.[29] Although we are guessing that many male readers will be uncomfortable with some of their answers, we are hopeful that this recognition will also lead them to search for new ways to view women as subjects.

- What sorts of women really turn you on?
- When viewing women, do you fixate on certain parts of their anatomy, such as breasts or legs, and use these as the criteria for evaluating their sexual attractiveness?
- Are you primarily attracted to women who are physically slender, smaller, and weaker than you? Who make less money? Whom you perceive as less intelligent than you? Whom, in general terms, you see as easily subordinated?

- Do you like the status conferred upon you from other men when seen in the company of a societally attractive women?
- Conversely, what sorts of women turn you off?
- Do you find unattractive women who are physically heavier, larger, and stronger than you? Who make more money? Whom you perceive as more intelligent than you? Whom, in general terms, you see as an equal or perhaps even superior?
- Are you uncomfortable if a women takes the initiator role in sexual interactions?
- Do you find it sexually exciting to play the protector role with women?
- When actually having sexual relations are you more focused on the act—sexual pleasure—than the relationship and shared experience of closeness?

(Pro)feminist men need to honestly consider the sources of what they find sexually attractive and the oppressive implications of such outlooks for others and themselves. Building on the ideas of feminist authors like Audre Lorde, new images and ideals of the erotic need to be envisioned and acted upon.[30] There is nothing inherently evil or good per se about sexuality. Our own personal experiences tell us that experiences of sexuality when shared between equals can be some of the most profound and personally moving. On the other hand, when sexuality is used for oppressive purposes, such as rape, the act becomes one of the most destructive experiences known to people. (Pro)feminist men obviously need to seek and explore nonoppressive forms of sexuality.

The home is another context in which many women are oppressed on an interpersonal level that (pro)feminist men can easily question and personally change. Although today most women are employed outside the home, they are still largely responsible for most of the housework and child care. This "second shift" means that the average woman works fifteen hours longer each week than a man (over a year's period this equals an extra month's worth of twenty-four-hour days) and that there is a considerable gap between leisure time available to men and women.[31] Moreover, since women are also largely responsible for the emotional upbringing of children, by parental example, many children are socialized to expect and accept exploitive gender roles from the onset of their birth.

Marriage has been described as a 60–40 proposition traditionally organized around the wife's meeting family needs—both her children's and husband's—for care, comfort, and support. Her primary function is to serve the emotional needs of others in the family, which by definition renders her a servant of sorts. Just as masters seldom take seriously the needs and perspectives of servants, many husbands discount the views of their wives and take for granted their dominant status in the family. Such an outlook is further bolstered by the fact that men often make a greater financial contribution to the family, along with an array of societal expectations that define him as head of the household. This often unspoken inequality prevents the creation of healthy relationships. We believe the following questions are helpful in illuminating who has family power and how they exercise it, and they may suggest needed changes in some readers' personal lives who desire more equitable ways of being in the world.

- Is there limit (implied or stated) on how much money one can spend independently without consulting the other? Is the limit the same for both parties? Does your spouse have the same amount of discretionary funds for spending on pleasure and luxuries?
- How much personal sacrifice would you be willing to make for your spouse's career advancement? Would you move to a different location? Refuse a promotion? Conversely, what sort of expectations do you have of your spouse concerning these questions?
- Who has the final say on major financial decisions, such as buying a home or a car?
- If your relationship were to end, how much financial security (i.e., benefits, property, and income) would your spouse have? How much would you have?
- Is family income spent equally on your spouses' interests, hobbies, and personal needs?

Who has power in a family is often indicative of other forms of oppression occurring in far too many contemporary homes. Expecting women to be the primary ones responsible for most household chores and child care is an obvious form of exploitation found in many homes, especially in those where the mother is employed full time. (Pro)feminist men should learn how to move from "helping around the house" to *equally* sharing in completing these vitally important tasks. To this end, and recognizing that men often overestimate the amount of time they spend on household tasks,[32] the following are some basic questions that a man might ask himself:

- Who primarily does the dishes or scrubs the toilet?
- Who primarily does the grocery shopping and the laundry?

- Who is primarily responsible for changing the diapers on an infant or the feeding and bathing of the children?
- Who is responsible for putting the children to bed or getting them up in the morning?
- Who primarily attends to the children when they are in need of comfort, support, or a ride to an activity they are involved in?

Conversely, who does and does not have time (and money) for leisure oriented activities often is a strong indicator of who does and does not have privilege in our society. Given gendered expectations about housework and child care, as previously noted, these same inequities concerning the availability of free time are also found in many contemporary homes. The following questions address this arena of potential inequalities.

- Do you and your spouse spend equal amounts of time socializing with friends and pursuing activities outside of the family?
- Are holidays and vacations equally restful, or is it a time of added chores and responsibilities for your spouse?
- When entertaining visitors in your home, do you share in preparing for and cleaning up after the activities, or does your spouse do most of the work?
- And in more general terms, who (you or your spouse) has the most free time to pursue leisure activities and how does he or she spend it?

While this is far from an exhaustive list of questions that a feminist man might ask himself concerning family relationships, we would guess that many such men might not like the answers if they were to respond truthfully.

(Pro)feminist men need to learn ways to actively appreciate and value household labor and child care. We believe this is most easily accomplished by men adopting a peer approach in their close personal relationships. This means viewing one's spouse, girlfriend, or boyfriend as a true partner, someone with whom all responsibilities and decisions are equally shared. Not surprisingly, Pepper Schwartz has not only found "peer marriages" to be a growing trend in our society, but individuals in such relationships often report the highest levels of marital satisfaction.[33]

(Pro)feminist men should also consider ways in which they are a participant and/or silent witness to women's oppression in the workplace. We believe that addressing the following questions would be helpful to many men hoping to better understand the office politics that often promote and sustain women's exploitive experiences of oppression while at work.

- Is sexual harassment encouraged or tolerated where you work?
- Do men in gender-exclusive groups make sexist, objectifying comments about the women present? Do you participate in these conversations? Or do you contest such comments?
- Are women excluded from informal conversations or get-together's?
- Have you personally benefited from a good-ole-boy network that excludes women?
- Do women advance at the same rate as men?
- Are women's voices seen as valid and taken as seriously as men's?
- How do you treat women in subordinate or superior positions at work?
- Have you offered to assist or mentor your women coworkers?

While we are guessing that most male readers do not purposely partake in sexist practices at work, we also think it is of the utmost importance for (pro)feminist men to acknowledge the ways they have remained silent, thus both inevitably supporting and often benefiting from women's workplace exploitation. This requires that one actively start to recognize the way that gendered expectations shape both oppressive attitudes and behaviors. In the next chapter we will explore ways in which men can fruitfully move from a position of silent witness to that of an active challenger of women's oppression.

### Entering into Solidarity with Women and the Oppressed

Paulo Friere said it best:

> Discovering himself to be an oppressor may cause considerable anguish, but it does not necessarily lead to solidarity with the oppressed. Rationalizing his guilt through paternalistic treatment of the oppressed, all while holding them fast in the position of dependence, will not do. Solidarity requires that one enter into the situation of those with whom one is in solidarity; it is a radical posture . . . true solidarity with the oppressed means fighting at their side to transform the objective reality.[34]

At the most basic level "entering into solidarity with the oppressed" means putting people first; justice, inclusion, and equality should always come before self-interest and personal gain. It requires not only being vigilantly aware of the impact of one's own actions on others, but also explicitly recognizing the harm done by the system (e.g., other oppressors) to women, children, and other oppressed groups, often made possible by men's silence. It means refusing to play the patriarchal game of winners and losers, and instead entering into true solidarity with the oppressed wherein an egalitarian reality is ultimately made possible.

Traditionally, being sensitive to women's needs has meant doing inane things that emphasize dependency and helplessness, like opening doors, buying drinks, lighting cigarettes, and other gentlemanly gestures that men are expected to show toward women. These typically are condescending offers, as they often come with exploitive expectations (e.g., drinks for sex), and they often camouflage the oppressive intentions of the seemingly benevolent giver. In the quest for impersonal sex, this has also meant men feigning interest in women's activities, welfare, and/or saying they love someone when in fact they do not.

Women have also been taught to pretend interest in male activities and to appear more needy and dependent than they actually are, with the promise that through such actions they can find "true love." Thus women are more likely to be seeking an ongoing relationship while men are looking for "no-strings sex." Of course, actions such as these are largely manipulative, as getting what you want often requires observing certain expectations, but there is less sincerity or integrity in the man's words or actions.

Obviously an important aspect of entering into solidarity with women means contesting oppressive forms of male power and privilege. As previously discussed, men in our society are given an array of unearned advantages and privileges not afforded women. Peggy McIntosh makes the important distinction between positive advantages and negative advantages.[35] Negative types of advantage are ones whose explicit intent is to further reinforce the hierarchical realities of our society. These are privileges that not only subordinate and oppress people but also further reinforce and magnify the status of the dominant individual who is exercising them over the dominated individual.

Negative advantages include those of the executive who uses his trophy wife and attractive receptionist to bolster his business status, with their subordination signifying his obvious superiority and power. If a man's power/status comes from being able to purchase an attractive woman, her status comes from being someone who was purchased. Her level of responsibility or competence in job performance is ignored and she is discussed primarily in terms of her body parts. Other examples of people who serve the explicit role of enhancing the status of dominants are the maid, the doorman, the chauffeur, the cheerleader at a sporting event, and even the greeter at Wal-Mart stores. The resultant increased status of the user of the given service is always made possible, and ultimately purchased—an obvious form of exploitation—at the subordinate party's expense.

In a violently extreme example, the rapist is given many cultural clues (e.g., pornography) that he is entitled to have free access to women's bodies, and when he exercises this perceived privilege, his feelings of superiority and sexual pleasure (often one and the same for many men) are made possible by a woman's forcible subordination.

On the other hand, positive advantages are qualities necessary for survival and personal growth, such as earning a living wage and having adequate housing, nutrition, and health care, all things everyone should be entitled to. However, since many of these positive advantages are available only to certain people (especially white, middle- and upper-class men), they presently remain an unearned and unfair privilege. Single women as heads of the household are the largest group below the poverty line today, and their number is rising. Often abandoned by the husband/father, women and children on welfare struggle to simply get by. Recent changes in welfare legislation will result in many of these women using up their lifetime benefits while still being trapped in the cycle of poverty. Thus, (pro)feminist men should look for ways to resist negative advantages often conferred upon them while at the same time working to extend positive advantages to all people and to make them the norms of a just society.

Perhaps a starting point for entering into solidarity with women and the oppressed is to never make assumptions about what they think, feel, desire, or need. Far too often dominants assume that subordinates' silence means they are in agreement or have no opinion on a given matter. When combined with male privilege, this often means that men paternalistically make choices for women without even being aware that they might want something different. In short, and related to learning to actually listen to women, men need to learn how to truly ask women what they want and to be respectful of any response they receive. A position of solidarity with the oppressed demands that the actual voices of the oppressed be welcomed, heard, respected, and validated as worthy of concern by all involved parties.[36]

Entering into solidarity means sometimes using, almost ironically, male privilege to open workplace doors for women and other oppressed people. One of the things that frequently keep women and minorities from advancing in their careers is the lack of mentors who can teach them the insider skills often required for being promoted. (Pro)feminist men can often fruitfully use their male privilege to redirect resources and information toward those who have traditionally been excluded in most work settings. This can be as simple as mentioning someone's name in a meeting or could, more actively, involve taking personal time to teach an individual the ropes of the organization, to provide her with the insider information, and to act as a sponsor and/or advocate for her. Of course, these are the same things male mentors have always done for other men. A (pro)feminist man will equally, if not more so, look to also do this for women and minority colleagues.

In sum, (pro)feminist men who truly desire to enter into solidarity with women and the oppressed need to acknowledge how unearned male privilege gives them status at the expense of others. Entering into solidarity means giving up this privilege, or using it only to contest the oppressive treatment of societal subordinates. Solidarity ultimately demands that the voices of the oppressed be heard, validated, and acted upon in a way that promotes a transformation of the objective realities of society.

### Replacing Masculinity with Feminism as Referent

A feminist writer has observed that "men who resist masculine dominance cannot become women, they become failed men and betrayers of masculinity."[37] While it is true that men who reject traditional notions of masculinity are betrayers of masculinity and cannot become women, we believe such men are anything but failures. If one agrees with Stoltenberg's assertion that "the belief that one is male, the belief that there is a male sex, the belief that one belongs to it is a politically constructed idea,"[38] then rejecting such a position is also a political statement. In other words, while men who betray masculinity are seen as failures in the eyes of patriarchy and death, they would also be successful survivors in a reality of feminism and life. Or, as more elegantly stated by Carlin,

> Exposing the monster's false power, thus breaking the spell, happens when a man dares to enter the realm of women's reality. A man breaks rank with other men when they make women's reality their referent. All the power of the social order gathers itself to prevent his going there. . . . Where he is going, he risks being regarded with suspicion, of not being readily accepted, because of what he has left. . . . He understands that to save himself means not grasping patriarchy closer, but letting it die—even the part of it that resides within himself.[39]

A man who aspires to have a feminist worldview should not view such a commitment as a part-time undertaking, when it is convenient or to his advantage. Rather, to become truly committed to a feminist reality means he should try to act accordingly in *every* possible setting in which he finds himself. Moreover, as Sonia Johnson notes, we believe such a feminist orientation is found in the present, not the future.

> When we envision the future without first changing our present feelings, without undoing our indoctrination, we project all our unexamined assumptions into the future, recreating the old reality, making it inevitable. Anything we

try to do without grounding ourselves in new and powerful present feelings and perceptions will be compromised from the onset, hopelessly contaminated, simple tinkering at best, perilously complicit at worst. . . . This means that our feelings about ourselves *in the present moment* are the sole source of change, and that they are therefore our only source of power.[40]

To actually live such a reality means not only giving up oppressive forms of male privilege and replacing it with feminism, but it ultimately demands that men learn new ways to perceive themselves and to relate to all people in the present.

(Pro)feminist men need to learn how to be compassionate in their pursuit of living an oppression-free life. As compassion is often framed as a feminine quality, it is a difficult concept for many men to embrace. Frequently men view compassion as an outlook predicated on vulnerability, which is seen as making one weak, a "mush," a "fag," a "pussy," and inviting attack from other men. Moreover, compassionately viewing one's own shortcomings is nearly an impossible task for untold numbers of men in our society. This is truly unfortunate, as it makes it extremely difficult for men such as these to hear ways in which they might improve their life without getting defensive and feeling that some unfair judgment is being made of them.

Compassion is a special type of skill and strength, neither cynical nor naive, but sensitive to feelings—others' and one's own—and always open to new truths. Hearing the distress and pain of others and wanting to alleviate the suffering of others is ultimately not feminine but, rather, what it means to be human. However, like many characteristics defined as stereotypically feminine, such as nurturing and freely expressing one's emotions, (pro)feminist men have much to gain by exploring and embracing these values and behaviors. Actually doing so will not only make men far more aware of how harmful oppression is, and the intimate role each of us plays in its occurrence, but with women and feminism as their referent, (pro)feminist men can play an important role in contesting patriarchal boundaries.

Since men who truly embrace feminism very much run the risk of being ridiculed by other men and even women, they need to become centered in themselves, inner directed, and less dependent on the reactions of others, especially other men, for approval and self-validation. We believe that this is a far more healthy and less oppressive way to be a true individual than following the latest manhood-making trend. For men struggling to succeed in the competitive world of sex, money, power, and status, this will involve making many difficult choices, as numerous social forces are in place to keep him from ever leaving his oppressive ways of being. Yet, as previously discussed, male dominance runs more on fear than hope. If we are motivated more by our hopes than our fears, then change will not appear as overwhelming.

Whether male or female, truly coming to know ourselves at a deeper level involves honestly acknowledging our innermost desires and fears. What are the lost dreams of our youth? What values do we really stand for? What things truly bring meaning and satisfaction to our lives? We must also honestly consider how consistent our behavior is with our values and acknowledge ways in which we have been co-opted by the promised goodies of male dominance. We need to ask ourselves what sort of talents and strengths we have if we truly want to make a difference in the world. We must assess whether our dreams and goals are obtainable without using oppressive patriarchal means to reach them. We need to envision and make real a world where all personal needs can be pursued compassionately, always balancing the desires of others with our own. We need to learn how to focus on the possibilities instead of the limitations of life.

## Moving beyond Patriarchal Boundaries

Rolling, and pushing out the boundaries, beginning to explore our deeper mind where we know so much more than we know we know, so much that we never get to consider because we're always staying on the surface explaining the same ideas over and over.

—Sonia Johnson[41]

Some who read this chapter may still be unconvinced that men can become feminists. Such a position is not only based on the same dichotomous thought that underlies patriarchy—male/female—it also sets up boundaries that men need not go beyond, excuses men from gaining any sort of feminist understanding, and overall, spares them from having to change anything in their personal lives. We believe that the time has come to reject this oppressively limiting yet ultimately artificial boundary and move beyond it. The suggestive paths we have tentatively outlined in this essay are not well worn or known to many men, but they are something beckoning,

something real and urgent. Another way, another path, another door. A door patriarchy says isn't there; *insists* isn't there, which is evidence of its existence. That which doesn't exist doesn't have to be denied.[42]

Although the pathways men will have to travel to exit patriarchy into a new feminist reality have many obstructions and dead-end forks, we have attempted to delineate some preliminary trailheads and road signs that may be found on this journey.

Women and men, people of color, gay and straight, and people residing in Third World countries, all have to travel disparate paths in realizing a feminist reality, but our differences are also "that raw and powerful connection from which personal power is forged" and new realities are constructed.[43] Thus, on our different journeys toward a feminist reality that is inclusive and egalitarian, we must forge new connections between autonomous people, regardless of their gender, race, sexual orientation, or other socially constructed categorizations. We believe then, and only then, can we truly start to live, instead of slowly dying in a patriarchal reality.

## Notes

Portions of this chapter were adapted from Schacht and Ewing 1997a.

1. hooks 2000, p. 115.
2. Beauvoir 1953.
3. Morgan 1978; Stanley and Wise 1979; Johnson 1987; Collins 1991; Steinem 1992.
4. Stanley and Wise 1979; Bradshaw 1982; Leonard 1982; Stanley 1982; Showalter 1987.
5. Bart, Freeman, and Kimball 1991, p. 191. We should also note that over the past few years we had, wrongly, come to the conclusion that most women feel that men cannot be feminist. While the list of people who feel men cannot be feminist is far from complete, in actually reviewing the literature to write this essay we have found just the opposite: most feminist women now appear to feel that men could be truly feminist. Interestingly, many of the accounts that we have read that take a stance against the possibility of men being feminist are often written by men; see Jardine and Smith 1987.
6. Morgan 1970, p. xxxv.
7. Heath 1987, p. 1.
8. Johnson 1987, pp. 282, 304.
9. Hekman 1987; Haraway 1988; Hawkesworth 1989, pp. 539–40; Delphy 1993.
10. Taylor 1989.
11. Hawkesworth 1989, pp. 544–45.
12. Haraway 1988.
13. Walker 1983, p. 49.
14. Young 1988.
15. McIntosh 2000; Schacht 2001.
16. Another example that works well here is likening life to a foot race. Those who are women, who are people of color, and/or who come from poor backgrounds

start life's race at, or very close to, the beginning line. Conversely, those who are men, white, and/or who come from affluent backgrounds start life near, or in some cases with one foot almost over, the finish line.

17. Yamato 1998.
18. Frye 1998.
19. While many women fear attack from strangers—the stereotypical man lurking in the bushes—her most likely assailant is a man she knows, most typically a husband or boyfriend; see Russell 1982.
20. Hanmer and Maynard 1987.
21. Connell 1995.
22. Frye 1998.
23. Yamato 1998.
24. Thorne, Kramarae, and Henley 1983.
25. Gill 1992, p. 152.
26. Brownmiller 1975; MacKinnon 1989; Dworkin 1987, 1989; Wilkinson and Kitzinger 1993.
27. Schacht and Atchison 1993.
28. Dworkin 1989, p. 113.
29. While we strongly believe that masturbation can be a healthy expression of one's sexuality, when done to pornographic images of women's subordination, a rapist mentality often results where the pornography user comes to equate sexual pleasure with women's oppression.
30. See "Uses of the Erotic" in Lorde 1984.
31. Hochschild 1990.
32. See Kathleen Trigiani's home page for a more detailed discussion of how men over-estimate the amount of housework they do: http://web2.airmail.net/ktrig246/out_of_cave/gv_notes.html#133
33. Schwartz 1994.
34. Friere 2000 [1970].
35. McIntosh 2000.
36. Lyons 2001.
37. Ramazanoglu 1992, p. 347.
38. Stoltenberg 1990, p. 185.
39. Carlin 1992, p. 124.
40. Johnson 1987, pp. 305–6—emphasis in the original.
41. Johnson 1987, p. 133.
42. Johnson 1987, p. 49—emphasis in the original.
43. Lorde 1984, p. 122.

# CHAPTER SEVEN

# Being a (Pro)Feminist

In a sense, *becoming* a (pro)feminist is the necessary but insufficient condition to *being* a (pro)feminist. Perhaps like all newly embraced personal identities, it is easier to say one *is* a feminist than to actually *be* a feminist, and realistically, no one will be able to truly live as a feminist as long as inequality and oppression exist. Most people who continue to be attracted to feminism seem to reach a point, however, where they move from verbally supporting notions of gender equality to actually trying to consistently live them on a regular basis. We believe it is at the point where one moves from awareness to informed action, called praxis, that an individual truly starts being a feminist.

Praxis in feminism varies significantly by individual, with some never reaching this state, and it often signifies a new and different set of considerations. While there are many social forces that keep most men and women from ever considering *becoming* a feminist, there are perhaps even more powerful societal mechanisms in place that directly contest anyone from ever consistently *being* a feminist. Even the most devoted feminists are prone to sexist relapses, being a feminist one moment and not the next. To actually live as a feminist, as we have previously noted, involves a full-time commitment to be vigilantly aware of the many obstructions that will keep her or him from ever living such a state of being.

This chapter explores several factors that often make being a (pro)feminist a difficult endeavor and offers some suggestive strategies for dealing with them. Accordingly, whereas previous chapters offered many reasons for (pro)feminism, this chapter has a more how-to emphasis. Like the paths outlined in chapter 6, the obstacles and suggested ways for dealing with them discussed here are not conceived as mutually exclusive or exhaustive, but, from our experience, they do seem to be some of the necessary considerations for being a (pro)feminist. Ultimately, *being* a (pro)feminist means learning consistent ways of viewing and interacting with *all* people in an egalitarian manner.

The section that follows examines some of the impediments to a man's successfully being a (pro)feminist in the presence of other men. Suggestions are then offered on how a (pro)feminist man might effectively respond to other men's misogynist and homophobic comments and actions—how best to move from fear and silence to find strength and a voice in these situations. The second half of this chapter offers some suggestions for constructively being a (pro)feminist in the presence of women, both in terms of entering women's spaces and general ways of relating to women as equals. Much of our advice here focuses on possible ways for dealing with women's understandable mistrust of men and learning new, supportive (versus competitive) ways of socially interacting with others. The chapter ends by discussing how being a (pro)feminist man can enable one to serve as an important bridge between the oppressed and the oppressors, forging fruitful alliances between the two.

## Being (Pro)Feminist in the Presence of Men

### Some of the Impediments

You are standing at the bar waiting to order your first round of drinks with a group of your male buddies. An attractive woman walks by on her way to the bathroom. One of your friends quickly gives her a fairly inconspicuous once-up-and-down glance out of the corner of his eye, as if scanning her entire body, while she passes by. As soon as she disappears behind the door, he blurts out for all to hear, "Man, I'd like to fuck her so hard she'd bleed for a week." Another man immediately responds, "Yeah, me too!" giving the speaker of this obviously misogynist statement a friendly slap on the back. Everyone, except perhaps you, is nodding his head in agreement, with now quite obvious grins on their faces. The bartender, who has overheard the entire exchange, laughs and says, "Take it you boys are out to have some fun tonight." Another friend quickly changes the first round of drinks from beers to shots of tequila.

When the woman returns from the restroom, everyone, including the bartender and perhaps even you, are now "discretely" trying to "check her out" as she passes by this time. The woman, noticing the not so subtle and unwanted attention she is now receiving, quickly averts her eyes, as if now staring at the ground, and quickens her pace. Then the shots finally arrive. The initiator of the bonding session makes a toast, "Bitches, you gotta love 'em." Everyone laughs, throws back their shots, grimaces for a moment, with this look of pain quickly replaced with warmly shared smiles and nods of affirmation.

We are guessing that many male readers of this text are quite familiar with this vignette.[1] The particulars may be somewhat different in your experience, but the general intention of the scenario is played out quite frequently in all male groups. But what is the intention? Isn't it just some innocuous, friendly banter privately shared among friends? And even assuming you might find the entire description personally troubling, as we are guessing many readers do, why is it that so many men go along with the sentiments of the moment or are speechless when they find themselves in situations such as these?

The fear of how one's male friends will react is frequently what keeps so many men silent, even when they fully recognize the rapist mentality of statements such as the above. Rationalizations in situations like this are abundant: "It's just a joke." "My friends are all good guys and would never rape a woman." "They're just letting off steam." "It doesn't hurt anybody." Most men who find "raunchy" comments like these personally troubling will nevertheless either play along or remain silent out of fear that they will become the new target for the hostile put-downs (e.g., "You a faggot? Don't you like women?"; "Shut up, bitch.") and as a means to bond with their male friends.

Situations such as this are further compounded by the power relationships within the group. It is much more difficult to object if the initial statement is made by a boss or a core group member (versus a peripheral group member). Conversely, one's own group status strongly influences the likelihood, and the effectiveness, of speaking out. Many men's groups are highly competitive, and typically members of these groups are acutely aware of who does and does not have power and valued resources, whom it is best to back down from, and who is considered marginal and expendable. A group leader who is highly respected for doing masculinity well can afford to take more risks and can more easily take a moral stand on any social issue. The same stance by a man with lower status and power will often be taken as evidence of weakness and a sign that he does not deserve to be in the group. In a group of close friends who are of equal status it may be easier to contest sexist comments. Even here, however, violating group norms and questioning accepted behavior can raise suspicions about whether one really belongs. The perceived costs for speaking out frequently appear much greater than any potential benefits.

This scenario may also play out a little differently, depending on the backgrounds of the participants (e.g., age or other social status) and the setting in which they occur, but the underlying misogynist message, and dilemma for a (pro)feminist man, remains the same. Sexist cartoons and jokes freely circulate in many work settings, men will put down "dumb women" in casual lunch conversation, and smirk while ogling the secretary. From the swimsuit model calender posted in the workroom to the request for "your girl" to do some task, many men partake in an array of subtle behaviors that can create a hostile and intimidating work environment for women. (Pro)feminist men sometimes find themselves in work situations in which they feel personally offended but remain silent because job security and advancement depend upon the favorable opinions of those whom they find objectionable. Perhaps not so ironically, this fear of those with contextual power is why women often remain silent about sexual harassment they experience in the workplace. At what point is it worth it to take a stand against sexist behavior? Somewhat understandably, for many men it is enough to just remain a silent nonparticipant because, after all, You can't change everybody, can you?

As briefly discussed in chapter 5, we believe the underlying social control mechanism here that ultimately keeps so many men passively silent—perhaps the very bedrock of masculinity—is a combination of misogyny and homophobia that prescribes both the hatred and the fear of anything associated with the feminine. Since we believe that truly being a (pro)feminist means actively confronting one's own misogynist and homophobic feelings, the next subsection explores these strongly interrelated impediments to finding a (pro)feminist voice.

### Misogyny and Homophobia: The Tools of Masculine Conformity

We still live in an essentially misogynist society. Since it is impossible for either women or men to escape this hegemonic reality of male dominance, those pursuing a feminist future need not only to speak out against misogyny, but to acknowledge and confront those aspects that are alive and all too well in each of us. Contesting misogyny for women often means dealing with internalized oppression and self-loathing.[2] For men, like becoming a feminist, resisting misogyny obviously means reexamining one's own assumptions and the basis of one's personal identity.

Hegemonic masculinity not only demands that men hate women but, of equal importance, that they constantly guard against being viewed as effeminate in any way.[3] This often means eternally trying to prove one is a man. All men know that to be seen as feminine often means being treated like a women—a second-class citizen, to be easily and appropriately subordinated. Or as John Stoltenberg states, "Not to be a man is to be less than nobody,"[4] ultimately not human but womanlike. Thus, men are taught not only to despise virtually everything associated with women, but they also very much fear the feminine, as if it were some contagious disease, easily acquired but difficult to cure. Much of men's anxieties about the feminine, specifically its potential application to them, often manifests itself in a strong fear known as homophobia.

The power of homophobia is clearly evidenced in an endless array of derogatory slurs and put-downs that a man can use against other men ranging from the seemingly innocuous statement of disapproval, "that's gay," to the taunt of "fartknocker," to the far more condemning utterances of "queer," "faggot," "cocksucker," or "shut up, or I'll bend you over and fuck you like a bitch." The speaker of "cut downs" such as these frames the recipient as less than human, womanlike, and appropriately subordinated. The targeted party must seemingly always reassert his masculinity and prove to all present that he is not what the attacker claims. To do otherwise means a risk of validating the accuser's words. Straight men are always expected to ward off any accusations associated with being gay, and a successful disavowal often involves directing equally homophobic statements back at one's attacker.

Either way, the hatred and the fear of the feminine, really two sides to the same coin, form a powerful restricting mechanism that coerces many men into acting in ostensibly masculine ways when they might not be in fact so disposed. The hegemony of misogyny, and its twin brother, homophobia, pack a one-two punch of sorts, so powerful that many men feel the constant need to prove their masculinity by denigrating anything associated with the feminine. This both frames and validates the importance of their own masculine attitudes and behaviors. Failure to do so in many men's groups means that one risks being seen as effeminate and becoming the real estate—like women and the feminine—upon which men do masculinity.[5]

Homophobia has long been used as a highly effective tool to assure conformity to traditional gender expectations and as one of patriarchy's primary weapons to keep people from identifying with the feminist movement. "Everybody knows" that all radical feminists are man-hating dykes and all (pro)feminist men are faggots! While it may be okay for a man to sometimes verbally support feminist causes, actually being a (pro)feminist man often earns one the label of "queer," especially by other men. In short, the fear and resulting panic associated with homophobia obviously keeps many sympathetic men from ever expressing (pro)feminist ideals, especially in all male groups, effectively silencing their voices.

Not surprisingly, then, until one personally deals with his (or her) own misogyny and homophobia, serious identification with feminist principles is not possible. As long as woman-hating and gay-baiting slurs personally hurt and intimidate, as opposed to generating revulsion for the hatred they represent, it is highly unlikely that a given man (or woman) will contest their usage. To the contrary, since silence often is seen as confirmation of their "appropriate" application to the targeted party, he will typically use similar terms in his own defense.

And yet some (pro)feminist men have and do contest misogynist comments when confronted with them. What factors differentiate these individuals from the much larger silent majority? From our experience, for men who speak out, the principle of contesting statements such as the above often becomes far more important than fear or a cost-benefit analysis of the situation. Self-confidence and security with one's own gender and sexual identity are also of the utmost importance, as counterattacks almost inevitably involve some attack on the speaker's manhood. Respectively, the next two subsections explore ways of personally confronting misogyny and homophobia and how to find confidence and integrity in a (pro)feminist outlook.

### Confronting Misogyny and Homophobia

Many (pro)feminist men earnestly start to explore their own personal feelings of misogyny in the process of becoming feminist. In learning about the depth of women's oppression, addressing ways that he may personally oppress women, and entering into solidarity with women, a sincerely dedicated (pro)feminist man will move from feelings of hatred (many of which he may have been previously unaware of) to a position of compassionate appreciation of both women and the feminine. This is obviously an important first step in his realizing a feminist outlook, but it does not necessarily entail confronting misogyny's relationship—often most readily expressed in homophobic attitudes and behaviors—to himself as a man. Just as (pro)feminist men come to a different, far more affirming appreciation of the feminine when they enter into solidarity with women, perhaps the most effective way to deal with internalized feelings of homophobia is to publicly enter into some form of solidarity with gay and lesbian individuals (the same can be said when dealing with issues of racism, classism, and other forms of oppression).

The truth is that, like all other isms, homophobia is a deeply rooted and quite oppressive societal outlook that we all—including gay and lesbian individuals—suffer from, whether we are aware of it or not.[6] Thus, many liberal straight men will often vehemently deny that they are homophobic yet refuse to ever participate in a gay parade or any other gay-sponsored event. These men may have a gay or lesbian acquaintance that they sometimes socialize with, perhaps even consider a dear friend. As long as these interactions are kept on the dominant individual's turf, however, such friendships also can be a form of tokenism whereby the "friend" is kept subordinate in the relationship.[7]

To fully understand how homophobia and other isms operate, straight men need to publicly enter into situations in which they are no longer dominant in the setting. It is in circumstances such as these that they can come to experientially appreciate what it feels like to be a contextual minority. For example, one may feel unsafe, unwanted, and vulnerable— all common feelings that societal subordinates experience in daily interactions. It is also in situations such as these that entering into solidarity with the oppressed is most likely to occur.[8]

Another risk is that contact with the "other" can reinforce oppressive stereotypes, a straight man using the experience to validate the "fact" that he is not one of "those weirdos." One must always enter settings such as these with a truly open mind, ultimately searching for ways to build alliances across difference.[9] Cooperative endeavors where everyone is viewed as equal and work together towards a shared goal are perhaps the most effective at contesting oppression, both within and external to the individual.

Ranging from many gay or lesbian bars to an annual gay pride parade and celebration to PFLAG (Parents, Families and Friends of Lesbians and Gays), today there are a growing number of formally established gay and lesbian venues that accept and welcome straight people. Participation in such settings can be a wonderful way to come to terms with personal feelings of homophobia. For those who have little exposure to gay communities, a trip to a straight-friendly gay bar can be a remarkable learning experience. If possible, going to a gay bar is made easier and perhaps best accomplished when accompanied by a gay/lesbian or a gay-friendly friend, as such a person can provide sponsorship and make one less anxious in entering the setting.[10]

When going to a gay bar, the most important thing to observe is not "them," but rather your gut-level, emotional responses to being in the setting. While far from an exhaustive set of questions one might ask oneself, we think the following are useful issues to address during or after being in a gay bar or any other contexts that might elicit a homophobic response.

- What is it about the setting and the people in it that is making you feel anxious and fearful?
- Does it trouble you to see men kissing and hugging each other in a sexual manner? Do you have problems showing physical affection toward other men in nonaggressive ways?

- Are you afraid that someone will "hit on you," treating you like a woman, and/or think you are "one of them"?
- Do you feel like a social minority, perhaps for the first time in your life, since being a straight male is no longer the most privileged status in this setting?
- If it is a bar where drag shows are staged and/or transgendered individuals are present, does it make you feel anxious that you are unable to discern who the "real women" are, especially if you find them sexually attractive?

Honestly answering these questions can not only lead to profound personal insights about homophobia, but it can also experientially fragment dichotomous outlooks of male and female.

The purpose of these contacts is not to alter a man's sexual orientation and make him gay, but rather to confront the fear and panic many men feel from any male intimacy, or even being witness to it, that is potentially seen as "queer." Coming to terms with homophobia, and becoming secure with whatever sexual identity he might have, allows him to enter into alliance with others who have sexualities different from his own. Through respectful interaction, old stereotypes, which both reflect and sustain patriarchy's divide-and-conquer orientation, give way to new possibilities. People become free to explore who they are and truly want to be, and to experiment with alternative ways of living. They start to understand that everyone should be free to love whomever they want, regardless of their "sex," and that that choice is ultimately available to each of us. We have noted over the years that not only do (pro)feminist men typically have many gay and lesbian friends, but they are also often involved in publicly supporting various queer activities, and that these alliances are often the result of their adopting a feminist outlook.

Men who consciously confront and deal with personal issues of misogyny and homophobia will also find homophobic taunts and slurs to have less effect on them. Instead of becoming defensive and trying to fend off being labeled, such men are able to question the attacker's hateful intentions in using such terms and phrases. Sometimes a simple series of "why" questions (e.g., "Why do you use misogynist/homophobic terms to describe people and/or things that you disapprove of and/or dislike?") can be quite effective. Other men will often become confused or angry when they encounter an unexpected reaction and are uncertain about how they should subsequently respond. At this point they might actually listen to the target's point of view, or out of frustration, they may walk away and leave him alone, but in either case a potential confrontation is often avoided. The actual consistency with which a (pro)feminist man challenges other men's misogynist and homophobic attitudes and behaviors not only attests to the degree he has personally confronted these issues, but it is also a measure of the integrity of his own feminist outlook.

## Finding Confidence and Integrity in a (Pro)Feminist Outlook

Often the confidence with which one speaks reflects both the strength of an individual's personal values and the connectedness he feels with other likeminded individuals. A strong (pro)feminist man typically has an extensive network of men and women who accept and support his feminist beliefs. Not only is there strength in numbers, but as social beings, we all need sources of self-validation for our beliefs. For many men, pursuing a feminist state of being often involves significantly expanding one's reference group or entirely changing it. Some men have found considerable approval, support, and important mentors and role models in joining a (pro)feminist group, while others find confirmation in a wide array of personal friendships and settings. Some (pro)feminist men may find it necessary to temporarily or permanently break with old friendship groups, and perhaps even seek out new types of employment.

Perhaps more typically, a (pro)feminist man will purposely create a large network of friends and supporters from a wide array of people and groups that will slowly become of equal or greater importance than, and in some cases entirely replace, old reference groups. Consistent with the inclusive model of feminism we have promoted throughout this book, we believe that the diversity of one's friendship groups, especially with traditionally oppressed people, directly speaks to both the breadth and potential efficacy of one's feminist outlook. If his voice is genuinely grounded in a variety of very different experiential standpoints, a (pro)feminist man will clearly understand his relationship to gender oppression as that of oppressor, and to change this, he must enter into solidarity with women. Dependent upon his race, class, and sexual orientation, he will also be able to explore and speak about other forms of oppression he might participate in or experience. While those who speak from a position of ignorance often have many insecurities—homophobia is an excellent example of this—truly sincere and knowledgeable individuals can confidently enter into fruitful discourse with a limitless number of people.

The power and integrity of any feminist stance by a man or a woman is ultimately measured in the consistency of his or her expressed attitudes and actions. This is strikingly apparent in being a (pro)feminist in the presence of other men. Any contradictory behavior, even the utterance of a single sexist statement, will immediately be seized upon as evidence of your true colors ("See, he is actually one of the boys after all") and often provides the grounds for dismissing any feminist ideals one might express. Because of this, striving to be a (pro)feminist man often results in feeling that one is constantly under the microscope and the judgmental eyes of others and that one must constantly be on guard to never say and/or do something that other men (and women) might interpret (usually correctly, although misunderstandings can arise) as sexist or oppressive.

While this can sometimes feel like a significant burden, it often has rather ironic, quite positive consequences. To begin with, some of the most vigilant scrutinizers of a (pro)feminist man are other sexist men. Given the slightest opportunity, they will frequently do anything in their power to discount or prove wrong a man's feminist ideals, and perhaps one of the easiest ways for them to accomplish this is if a (pro)feminist man partakes in any sexist behaviors himself. The astute (pro)feminist man, however, can use these men as a consciousness raiser of sorts. Since these men are the obvious experts on doing sexist behavior, if they see a (pro)feminist man's words or behavior as such, there is a high probability that their assessment is correct.

When these men correctly make note of any sexist actions by a (pro)feminist man, he can either "act like a real man," and try to simply dismiss their words, or, more constructively, he can admit the error of his ways, let others know why he thinks his previous sexist actions were wrong, and then try to make amends for them. When the latter occurs, an opening for a learning experience for all becomes possible. The (pro)feminist man realizes yet one more way in which he can be sexist and then works to not repeat the action, while his antagonistic critics are given a real-life example of how a man can acknowledge and change his sexist ways. Of course, these "lessons" do not work well if the given (pro)feminist man frequently acts in sexist ways, but for those who are consistently not sexist, and who regularly contest other men's sexism, these situations can be wonderful occasions to illuminate for everyone present what oppression is, how it operates, and why it is so harmful.

Much of the power of a (pro)feminist voice obviously comes from the courage to speak, something that takes far more bravery and strength than timidly going along with the crowd and doing oppressive forms of masculinity. However, speaking up is not the same as being heard. For a (pro)feminist to communicate effectively, he must learn new noncompetitive and nonaggressive ways to dialogue with other men. This means learning patience, how to be *passionate* but keep a calm tone of voice (shouting matches seldom lead to anything except perhaps a fight), and accepting the fact that it is not necessary, nor perhaps desirable, to have the last word in every conversation.

Obviously it also means allowing others every opportunity to express his own viewpoints, sincerely listening to what he says, and validating his concerns when appropriate. As issues of race, class, sexual orientation, and other forms of oppression will often be illuminated in these conversations, the (pro)feminist must learn to also be *compassionate* and understanding when interacting with other men. Moreover, discussions such as these often provide wonderful opportunities to highlight the ways in which all forms of oppressions are interrelated and interconnected. The purpose of dialoging about feminist issues is not to ultimately win arguments, as such an outlook is a dichotomous patriarchal trap, but rather to share the feminist compassion with others and the passion for explaining why an oppressive-free future is in the best interests of both women and men.

When all of these conditions are met, old limitations can give way to new possibilities, and other men will actually start to hear the validity of a (pro)feminist man's voice. In fact, if his sense of personal security is firmly rooted in feminist groups and thinking, his voice will often come across powerfully strong and may earn him the respect of other men. Drawing on this inner strength of being, he will feel freer to show all aspects of who he is— strong and competent yet caring and compassionate. Strong, interconnected voices of men who do power *with* others (versus the traditional "power over" models of male dominance) stand to make an important contribution in contesting and ending gender inequalities.

## Being (Pro)Feminist in the Presence of Women

### Entering Women's Spaces

Once upon a time a fox trotted up to a henhouse and softly knocked on the door. The hens nervously peered through the cracks in the shed, fascinated with the potential intruder's gentle and novel approach, but none moved toward the door.

"Let me in," pleaded the fox, "I want to be your friend and help protect you from the farmer's exploitation."

"But the last time a fox entered our hen house," replied one of the more outspoken chickens, "there was a terrible racket and afterwards we discovered one of our sisters was missing and several were hurt."

"I heard about that," the fox said in an ever-so-compassionate tone, "but I am a vegetarian fox and very different from others of my kind."

Unconvinced, the hens clucked amongst themselves, but they did not open the door. The fox strutted proudly around the structure, finally posturing himself so that the moonlight glistened magnificently off his coat.

He seductively continued, "With my help you will be stronger, wiser, and safer."

Taken in by his appealing words and appearance, one of the younger hens cracked open the door to get a better look at him. The fox returned her potentially welcoming gesture with a wide friendly smile.

"Oh my, is that a feather on your chin?" gasped the now embarrassed hen, slamming the door shut in his face.

"Ah . . . of course not," replied the fox, snapping his mouth shut.

The hens breathed a collective sigh of relief as the fox threw all his weight against the door again and again. All through the remainder of the night they listened to him howling outside in frustration and indignation.[11]

(Pro)feminist men often feel unwelcome when trying to join or contribute to feminist women's groups. Women have long been taught to defer to men, to stay in the background, and to permit men to control and dominate conversations, activities, and decisions. They have also been taught to value the approval of men over women. Since feminist women seek to totally reject these sexist notions, they will often become angry if they find themselves falling back into old patterns or feel uncertainty in the presence of men. Maintaining women-only space, or, when this is not possible, being abrasive toward men are both ways to defensively guard against such sexist societal expectations for interaction between the genders. Of course, women have many valid reasons for distrusting men, as many a seemingly well-intentioned man will have feathers on his chin, but some of their negativity directed at men may also come from a woman's own feelings of vulnerability. As with truly (pro)feminist men, feeling secure with one's own competence and identity are both important requisites for women hoping to work cooperatively with those who are different.

Feminist women are often hesitant about admitting (pro)feminist men into their circles, cautiously waiting to see if subtle patterns of dominance and control emerge. Styles of conversation, speaking, and listening are all carefully scrutinized. Many women will become silent and move away from men who have a competitive, aggressive style of conversation. A hostile way of joking, even about those seen as the opposition, suggests a way of objectifying and putting down those not in agreement with the speaker. Since men often dominate conversations with women by claiming superior knowledge and offering "expert" advice; this too increases suspicion.

The following or similar questions will be implicitly asked whenever a man looks to join a feminist women's group. The verbal and behavioral answers a man gives to the below questions often determine initial reactions in a feminist women's group, and the potential for any (pro)feminist man to be rejected or fully accepted. First impressions are often hard to change, and they set up a pattern for future interaction that may either marginalize a (pro)feminist man as an outsider or open doors for his acceptance.

- Does he provide unsolicited advice or information in a way that suggests he views himself as the expert, with superior knowledge of the subject matter?
- Is he willing to initially accept a marginal group status, pay his dues, and patiently wait for inclusion? Or does he demand immediate acceptance as a core member and/or group leader?
- Does he patiently take turns speaking, thoughtfully and attentively listening to others' words? Or does try make his voice more heard and important than others present?
- Does he speak to women "I" to "I" with vulnerability and humility? Or is it all about him and his agenda?
- Is he sensitive to the feelings of quieter women who seldom speak? Or does he assume silence means agreement and/or compliance?
- Using large expansive body movements, does he move in the setting as if he owns the place and is used to being in charge? Or does he act like a respectful guest?
- Does he argue when he should listen?
- Does he always have to be right?
- Does he devalue women's experiential knowledge and favor abstract theory?
- In general, does he seem sincerely committed to giving up male privilege and interacting with group members as equals? Or, like the fox, does he still have feathers on his chin?

In light of these implied questions when entering women's spaces, we believe there are some simple attitudes and behaviors a (pro)feminist man can undertake to increase both the likelihood of his acceptance into feminist groups and of any subsequent contribution he might make. Considering and acting upon these basic issues will increase a (pro)feminist man's credibility and ability to fruitfully work with women to construct a feminist future. Part of entering women's spaces is recognizing that women have the same needs that, to varying degrees, have always been afforded most men in patriarchal societies. The foremost of these is the inalienable "right to physical privacy . . . essential to personal freedom and self-determination."[12] Beyond respecting women's right to physical privacy, this also means that men should learn how to respect and honor women's need for a "room of their own." That is, not only should individual woman be able to control their own personal space but men should also recognize women's need for "a room" with other women.

Since a truly cooperative relationship between men and women assumes men giving up male power and privilege, men should always wait for an explicit invitation before entering women's space. Once there, men should tread softly and act like a guest in someone else's house. This may be quite difficult for many men who are used to being homeowners and arranging the furniture how they please. Feminists will look more carefully at what a man does than what he says—how he treats women at work, at home, and in his personal relationships. Women notice when men volunteer for what is traditionally thought of as women's work—for example, making coffee, bringing cookies, or stuffing envelopes. Women also notice when men expect to do all the "important" work, such as formulating group goals and policies or representing the group to outsiders without first "paying their dues."

Ultimately, men should ask themselves what they can *add*. By that we mean, What insights from a man's feminist perspective can he offer to support and strengthen the activities taking place in the given setting? If there appears to be nothing that he can contribute, or if his presence will be disruptive, then he should graciously decline the invitation. We will revisit and further explore issues of men and women entering into alliance in chapter 9.

**Truly Relating to Women as Equals**
Beyond learning new ways of interacting with feminist women in public settings, (pro)feminist men need to learn new ways of relating to women in *all* settings. The way a man treats women in his personal life will also be one of the determining factors of acceptance or rejection by feminist women. To truly relate to women as equals often means learning fundamentally new personal styles of viewing and communicating with women, and then practicing them to the point that they almost seem second nature. We believe that it is at the point when one moves from forcibly trying to not be sexist (becoming a feminist), to truly, almost effortlessly, relating to women as equals that one is actually being a (pro)feminist.

As discussed in chapter 6, part of becoming a (pro)feminist is learning to view women as subjects instead of objects. As simple as this may sound, for most men (including many gay men) this is a quite difficult task to accomplish and very much a long-term goal. Removing any pornographic images of women from your view is obviously a good starting point. Men can also teach themselves to look women in their eyes instead of focusing, even discretely, on various body parts. This significantly cuts down on the possibility of objectifying women and makes it far more likely that the female speaker will be viewed and heard as a subject. If consciously practiced over time, a man will increasingly experience interactions in which he does not objectify a female speaker. This can be taken as a strong sign of truly relating to women as equals.

Truly viewing women as subjects will also have a profound impact on the way a (pro)feminist man will communicate privately and publicly with women. He will thoughtfully listen as much as he speaks and not look to control discussions or have the last word. He will often speak passionately but never aggressively or try to drown out another's voice by speaking louder. He will sometimes speak with humility, acknowledge his vulnerability, own his emotions, and always be receptive to and appreciative of women's emotional feelings in a conversation. Again, when a man starts to consistently interact with women in this manner, it can be taken as another sign that he is truly relating to women as equals.

Another meaningful way of relating to women as equals is found in a man's labor expectations of men and women. Whether at home or at work, a truly (pro)feminist man does not have gendered—his and her—expectations about whatever work needs to be done. In the home he will equally share all domestic responsibilities, the ensuring of his children's emotional well-being, and all important economic decisions. At work he will view his female coworkers as colleagues and serve as a mentor to women whenever possible and appropriate. When consistently practiced, these are all important commitments toward equality between women and men.

A final and quite telling sign of truly relating to women as equals is found in both the quantity and quality of alliances a (pro)feminist has made with strong feminist women. Such men will publicly and privately have strong connections with feminist women. In these relationships they will create a shared space that is inclusive of the feminist outlooks of both parties but always respectful of difference. It will be in these alliances that a (pro)feminist man comes to most experientially appreciate the power and beauty of egalitarian ways of being across gender. Men such as these will be an important bridge in a realizing a feminist future.

## Men as a Bridge to a Feminist Future

(Pro)feminist men who sincerely try to live their lives by feminist principles—truly being (pro)feminist in attitude and behavior—will find themselves cast into a salient new role within the larger feminist movement: a bridge. A truly feminist-oriented man can perform four important functions when he assumes a role as a bridge: (1) he can educate other men and build a strong foundation for feminist social change amongst them; (2) he can gain access to settings where women are excluded and, utilizing a feminist lens, explore and expose these settings to a larger feminist audience; (3) he can serve as a bridge to the established power structures, translating feminist agendas to the "good old boys"; and overall, (4) he can provide an important linkage between feminist women and men.

Fear of co-optation and far too many experiences with self-serving men who steal key insights from feminism but give nothing in return has rightly led many feminist women to conclude that men can add little, if anything to a feminist reality.[13] Clearly, however, the kinds of far-reaching social change envisioned by feminist goals cannot be accomplished without the active support and participation of men. Men who truly have a feminist consciousness can serve as a bridge of understanding between genders separated by sexist traditions that have now been practiced for thousands of years. This is the promise truly feminist men hold: an important addition to the larger reality that is presently being constructed. The role of a bridge is both explicitly and implicitly found in the next two chapters that discuss (pro)feminist parenting and forging radical alliances with women's groups.

## Notes

1. I (Steve) have used this exact scenario in my classes for nearly ten years now, and the men in my classes have always grudgingly admitted to having almost this exact conversation, or one quite similar, with their male friends, often on a regular basis.
2. Yamato 1998; Newton 2000.
3. Connell 1995; Schacht 1996.
4. Stoltenberg 1998, p. 152.
5. Schacht 1996.
6. See Laud Humphreys' 1975 discussion of the breastplate of righteousness, an outlook wherein those who partake in the given activity are most likely to condemn it.
7. Ann duCille (1994) has insightfully named this the "driving Miss Daisy syndrome."
8. Friere 2002 [1970].
9. Bystydzienski and Schacht 2001.
10. Schacht, 2004.
11. This story and some of the materials that follow in this section originally appeared in Schacht and Ewing 1997b.
12. Dworkin 1987, p. 102.
13. Stanley and Wise 1979; Bradshaw 1982; Leonard 1982; Bart, Freeman, and Kimball 1991.

CHAPTER EIGHT

◆

# (Pro)Feminist Parenting: Learning How to Mother and Be a Positive Feminist Role Model

This chapter, like others in this book, is loosely grounded in our personal experience, in that one of us was raised by a feminist mother, while the other was a feminist mother raising a son. In this sense, we offer a unique—both sides of the equation—perspective on some of the trials, the tribulations, and ultimately what we believe to be the promise of (pro)feminist parenting. While there are obviously many different considerations for feminists raising sons and daughters, and no guarantees that any child will turn out as a parent hopes, we also believe that there are many important benefits feminist parenting styles have to offer.

This chapter begins by revisiting some ideas initially put forth in chapter 2 about how the contemporary role of fatherhood is at a crossroads, and why (pro)feminist parenting is needed. Next, we explore the archetype of feminist parenting and the feminist mother-and-daughter relationship, and then we note the contradictions and possibilities for feminists raising sons. Building on the pioneering efforts of feminist mothers, we then propose a (pro)feminist model for parenting wherein men would learn how to mother and make themselves emotionally available to their children and partners. Ultimately, we believe that children are taught more from their parents' actions than their words, so we next discuss ways in which men might become positive feminist role models for their children. The chapter ends by arguing that children and their parents have much to gain from feminist parenting.

## Fatherhood at a Crossroads

Most, if not all, attempts at feminist parenting over the past thirty years have been made by individual mothers struggling to find alternative models for childrearing. While successes have been realized, especially with daughters, we believe much more progress could be made if men were to become actively involved in the feminist parenting of their children, both daughters and sons. While assuredly this is already happening in some homes in the United States, (pro)feminist parenting is nonetheless a largely invisible model for raising children, especially in a society that still clings to the ideals of traditional fatherhood. Yet we also believe that recent societal changes have made feminism an increasingly attractive approach to effective parenting for both women and men. Thus, before sketching out an image of what we envision a (pro)feminist parent might look like, we think it would be helpful to explore why the present state of fatherhood is at a crossroads.

Two generations ago we had fairly clearly prescribed cultural standards of what a "good" father was supposed to be. Very much based in the values and visibly promoted practices of the white middle class, the ideal father was a breadwinner and family protector, a wise and final voice in making important family decisions, and a pal to the children on the weekends. He backed up a stay-at-home mom when the rules needed to be enforced and helped with the chores, especially those traditionally male (i.e., mowing the lawn, making household repairs, and taking out the garbage), but it was implicitly understood that "work" would be his top priority. As schedules allowed, fathers were expected to participate in leisure activities with their children (e.g., going fishing or attending a baseball game) and the family (e.g., church, holiday gatherings, and vacations). Being a good provider, which made these outings possible, frequently required time-consuming careers, and family time was often sacrificed for financial success. Harry Chapin's song, "Cat's in the Cradle," expresses the unfulfilled promise of spending time together with one's father; both children and fathers would come to wish that somehow it all could have been different. While not every father lived up to these expectations, or was able to, they were accepted as the norms and ideals of doing fatherhood correctly.[1]

The feminist movement has convincingly pointed out the exploitive, sexist basis of contemporary family arrangements that require women to work a double shift while men largely still work one.[2] Often using models of androgyny, feminist women in the 1970s demanded that fathers start to become more physically affectionate, show emotions, and become fully involved in nurturing children of both genders. While all laudable goals, the real problem was that most fathers had little experience in affectionate nurturing—something typically framed as an unnecessary, even undesirable quality for men—and few could look to their own fathers for role models.

Understandably, many fathers resented that they were being told to do something for which they had little knowledge, women's work at that, and mothers employed outside of the home resented the fact that they were increasingly expected to "take home the bacon and cook it too." The Archie Bunkers responded in disbelief to the notion that being the breadwinner was no longer sufficient to afford them "lord of the castle" status, while others resisted their wives' entry into the workforce, even when it was financially necessary.[3] Both working fathers and working mothers were left feeling indignant that their spouses did not fully appreciate the importance of their respective contributions. In many ways, the cultural scripts for being a father and mother were forever lost when significant numbers of women entered the workforce. Combined with new feminist demands for men to more equitably share in domestic responsibilities and to be more emotionally available, men often felt confusion, anxiety, and anger.[4]

Although some notable right-wing groups of our society are still strong proponents of seemingly traditional notions of fatherhood,[5] growing numbers of both women and men are beginning to question this antiquated social model. As previously noted, most middle-class families need two paychecks to maintain their standard of living, while those in the lower working classes often need two paychecks to merely survive. Nearly 50 percent of all marriages today end in divorce, often leaving women to raise their children in single-parent families with little financial support from the father. As much as the conservative right wants to extol the breadwinner-father and the stay-at-home-mother roles of the not too distant past, the reality is that the *Father Knows Best/Donna Reed* family is on the verge of extinction and has always been more of a romantic ideal than a reality lived by most.[6]

Many young men have accepted this cultural fact and, as previously noted in chapter 2, see marriage to a working woman who meaningfully contributes to the family income as far more attractive than being sole provider and having a stay-at-home wife.[7] Help with keeping up with the Joneses, maintaining a comfortable standard of living, or, in many causes, just paying the bills is a welcome relief from bearing all of the significant responsibilities of being the exclusive breadwinner. However, while the norm is now for women to share the provider role, many of the expectations associated with fatherhood have been slow to change. Accordingly, women are still expected to be the primary individuals responsible for most of the child rearing and household labor, while many men continue to believe that they should have a final say in important family decisions. The frequent punishment for women who contest this family arrangement is divorce. Typical of periods of rapid social change, there is a significant cultural lag between the fact that most wives are now members of the workforce (public) and men's willingness to make appropriate adaptations to this reality in the home (private).

Obviously, there is much resentment, frustration, and conflict today concerning parental roles for raising children. While men are now slightly more likely to help around the house, women continue to bear the brunt of household and child-care responsibilities.[8] And yet there is a sad irony in men's continued resistance to equally sharing parenting and home responsibilities. Research is increasingly demonstrating that those involved in peer marriages who consciously try to share all family responsibilities often report the highest levels of marital satisfaction.[9] Moreover, research has also consistently shown that children whose fathers are actively involved in their lives benefit in many ways, and, should divorce occur, such men are more likely to remain involved in their children's lives.[10] For men who are truly concerned about the welfare of their children, and who see marital or relationship happiness as an important ingredient for raising children, we believe that (pro)feminist parenting has much to offer. Based on the efforts of feminist mothers and their daughters, the next section begins to sketch out some of the basic ideals of feminist parenting.

## The Feminist Parenting Archetype: Mothers and Daughters

The mothering efforts of feminists over the past thirty years have largely been directed toward empowering daughters, in hopes of giving them the skills and knowledge necessary to successfully survive and compete in a man's world while trying to shelter them from the harmful messages of female inferiority so forcibly fed to them by patriarchy. Resources such as children's books and music, creative nonsexist toys and games, confidence-building activities and strong women role models have all been used to successfully empower girls and young women.[11] Feminists have understandably valorized the mother-daughter relationship as special (and an important source of third-wave feminism), worthy of untold time and energy, as with each new generation of women the possibility of gender equality seems ever closer.

Feminist child rearing for girls often involves a permissive parenting approach that emphasizes a full range of behavioral choices, including many of those traditionally offered to boys, and a general emphasis on striving "to be all you can be." An environment is cultivated where it is all right to get dirty, to play with trucks, to climb trees, to serve tea to your dolls and teddy bear, and to cry. Support is given for being strong and brave but much room is also made available to be playful, sometimes even silly. The feminist mother looks to create a strong emotional bond with her daughter through which, like a mentor and a close friend, she can nurture her daughter's development, support the many aspirations she may have, and help her overcome some of the sexist impediments the mother may have faced as a child. Instead of traditional models of parental "power over" children, feminist parenting focuses on the mother trying to do "power with" her daughter in hopes of empowering her.

A feminist mother also looks to be a positive role model to her daughter. Regardless of whether she is single or involved in a relationship with a man or woman, by example, she tries to teach her daughter the importance of being both treated by and treating others in an equitable manner. Feminist mothers recognize that how they handle their affairs, both personal and professional, will provide important lessons for their daughters. How she spends her time and money are also important considerations here, as actions always speak louder than words. Many adult daughters (and some sons) today very much appreciate, and often share, both the sacrifices and triumphs of their feminist mothers

In sum, the ideals of the feminist mother/daughter relationships are based on openness whereby the mother tries to nurture an environment that enables her daughter to bloom into adulthood while trying to minimize the very real physical and mental damage that our male-dominated society so often inflicts upon young women. Feminists have been quite vocal about the special basis of the mother-daughter relationship, have spent much time and energy in its creation and maintenance, and have made available many resources to nurture it. In many ways, the efforts of the second wave of feminist mothers made possible and assisted in the emergence of third-wave feminism, a movement now most associated with their daughters (metaphorically and, in some cases, literally). Much of a feminist mother's success comes from her providing a positive feminist role model for her daughter and is visibly found in the present generation of young feminist women.

At its deepest, most powerfully radical level, feminism is simply an ideology that prescribes equality and life-affirming ways of relating to all people in the world. In this sense, feminism is nether female nor male, but more a way of being in the world in relation to others. If, however, one is going to fruitfully pursue living a nonoppressive existence, there are obviously certain values and behaviors that are far more conducive to this end than others. As suggested throughout this book, we believe being compassionate yet patient, caring yet strong, loving yet independent, and sometimes self-sacrificing yet never losing a sense of self are all vitally important characteristics for living equality.

In many ways, we believe these same features describe the past and present parenting efforts of feminist mothers with their daughters and, in a few cases, sons. These pioneers in parenting rejected traditional notions of mothering that entailed selflessly playing a behind-the-scenes role, always their children's and husband's needs before their own. These strong, independent women cared for their children with the same passion as any mother, and realized that they could and should provide positive role models for their daughters. By being both strong and nurturing, feminist mothers literally opened up new—we believe, far more healthy—approaches to parenting. We believe that (pro)feminist men stand to gain much from adopting similar parenting styles.

## The Contradictions and Possibilities of Feminists Raising Sons

There are no books that adequately serve as maps providing males of all ages with a feminist education by explaining what patriarchy is, how it works, and why they should be committed to a feminist movement that opposes sexism and sexist oppression.

—bell hooks[12]

As bell hooks observes, feminist advice on raising sons is conspicuously absent and rife with all sorts of inherent contradictions.[13] While feminist mothers seek to empower girls, should they, conversely, try to disempower sons, the privileged gender? Girls can be given gifts of athletic equipment, construction sets, and scientific toys, but what should you give boys? Few parents would choose dolls, toy stoves, and an apron "just like mommy's." Giving boys the same toys as girls often ends up reinforcing preexisting sexist attitudes. A girl who can play soccer often gains status, while a boy who bakes cookies stands to lose it. To some feminists the mere notion of a feminist raising a son may sound like a difficult undertaking at best[14] and an oxymoron at worst.[15]

Men's studies literature is also largely silent on this issue. (Pro)feminist men have written extensively about boyhood experiences, predominantly focusing on two issues: (1) how patriarchal groups and institutions shape young boys into different adult masculinities and (2) the tremendous pain and suffering experienced by some boys who fail to conform to patriarchal expectations.[16] While all of this literature is extremely helpful in better understanding what masculinity is, how manhood is accomplished, and the costs of doing masculinity for some men, little practical advice is offered on alternative strategies for raising feminist sons or for (pro)feminist parenting. Given that so much of growing from a boy to a man is predicated on successfully undertaking various models of masculinity—doing privilege—it is perhaps not that surprising that little has been written on feminism and sons. Yet as we enter the fourth decade of the most recent women's movement, we note that many feminist women and perhaps even a few (pro)feminist men have successfully raised sons during this period.[17] In light of our own experiences, we now explore what we see as some of the general limitations to, and possibilities of, feminist women and men raising sons. Key to this discussion is our belief that feminist parenting is more about the process of sharing feminist *values* than potentially coercing our children into ready-made feminist *identities*. Ultimately we believe that an important part of being a feminist is making others aware of how our own attitudes and behaviors can be oppressive to others and ourselves, that we often have choices about how we are treated by others, that we always have choices about how we treat others, and that equality is the only way to undo oppressive realities. We believe these are all important values in general for successfully raising children.

Unless parents totally isolate a child, it is impossible for the child to escape the gendered imagery upon which our society is based. Everywhere one looks in public settings women and men are "appropriately" gendered and presented as being in only one of two dichotomous categories. Activities in everyday settings are also gendered—men most typically hold important positions of authority while women fill lesser mothering and/or subservient roles—that both reflect and reinforce male dominance and female subordination. Not surprisingly, most children, even the very young, are all too aware of differences in gender expectations, and both girls and boys will be quick to tell another child what is appropriate behavior for each gender.

Feminist parents must counteract these messages as much as possible by explaining alternative ways of viewing gender and by ultimately demonstrating in their own behaviors the untruths and the oppressive limits of sexist assumptions. A mother who is strong and competent and makes valued contributions in the outside world and/or a father who is gentle and nurtures his children both teach by example nonsexist ways of being in the world. Such parents not only contest the present gender-role expectations, but they also clearly illustrate that it takes a multitude of behaviors to successfully raise a child, none of which are ultimately the domain of either a mother or a father. Such parenting styles offer both boys and girls an environment in which the possible ways of acting out gender roles far outnumber the limitations found in the traditional male-dominated home.

Contrary to the perhaps uninformed public perception that feminism emasculates young boys,[18] a feminist no more wants to raise a "sissy" son than they do a daughter.[19] No parent wants his or her child to be a target for ridicule by bullies or to appear weak and dependent. Thus, an important aspect of feminist parenting is to look for ways to add instead of take away from typical boyhood activities. Feminists want their sons, like their daughters, to be active, adventuresome, independent, and fun loving. In pursuing these objectives, however, feminists also try to share with their sons that it is not necessary to be aggressive or exploitive and that it is important to be able to express feelings to others. In many ways, feminist parents teach their sons that it takes much more strength and courage to be compassionate, caring, and sensitive to others than it does to be merely a traditional young man.

Sons raised by feminist parents can have a significant advantage in navigating the often turbulent years of adolescence. As previously noted, a large part of being a feminist parent is teaching children how to openly express feelings, to be sensitive to the feelings of others, to view other people as equals and not mere means to an end, and nonviolent methods of conflict resolution. If these values have been learned prior to puberty, it significantly increases the likelihood that parents and sons will continue to communicate during these years. Early family patterns learned before adolescence, along with the fact that the personality becomes fairly fixed in early childhood, give the feminist parent unique opportunities to continue to play an important role as their sons enter their teenage years.

In all probability, a boy raised by a feminist(s) will still partake in some risk-taking behavior with his friends that he will not discuss with his parent(s), but he will also feel more free to talk about significant moral dilemmas that he will face when trying to adapt to peer expectations. Feminist parents can offer alternative perspectives, nurture approaches to sound decision making, and support the judgment of their sons in making informed decisions. For this to occur, however, parents need to be defined as part of the "we" rather than an oppressive "them." Parents who have exercised "power with" their children—versus "power over," whereby parents are often defined as the outside enemy—will be in a much better position help their sons (and daughters) negotiate the often confusing teenage years. Perhaps not surprisingly, the parenting efforts of many feminist mothers have an explicit "power with" orientation that is emotionally open to but independent of their children. We believe (pro)feminist men would stand to gain much from adopting a similar parenting style wherein they would learn to mother and become more emotionally available to their children.

## Learning to Mother as a (Pro)Feminist

Few men in our society truly know how to mother. Men have long been taught to play the role of the patriarch, the family ruler who, like a distant but caring god, wisely exercises power over his children (and wife)—his flock—to protect them from harm and to punish them for doing wrong. Conversely, as an ideal, mothering is a nurturing approach that, through comfort and care, children are emotionally and physically nourished so that they can fully develop as individuals. Mothering often involves playfully doing "power with" children, to empower them so that they can more confidently explore the world around them. This requires really listening to children and empathically seeing and feeling things from their perspective. It also requires recognizing that things that sometimes appear inconsequential can be of central importance to children's emotional well-being and self-concept. In contrast, the quick-and-easy answers that the traditional father is expected to give his children through commands and punishments frequently trivialize feelings and convey a message of emotional unavailability.

Being emotionally distant is a common complaint that many young adults have about their fathers today.[20] Dad might have been a great provider, a fun pal on the weekends, willing to share a smile during a moment of triumph (and anger during times of disappointment), but many fathers in the past and today have real problems hearing and effectively responding to the fears and tears of their children. Frequently, as for many of their stoic fathers before them, any emotions that make them feel vulnerable are to be guarded against, repressed when necessary, and certainly not shared with others, as doing so is seen as making them potentially defenseless and easily attacked.[21] Boys, especially, are given the message that they should guard against any emotional feelings that will make them appear weak: "Real men don't cry!" Nor do real men verbally express feelings of love.[22] By example, and sometimes by dictate (e.g., "Quit your crying or I'll give you a reason to cry"), many past and present fathers make it quite clear that there are real limits to their emotional availability to children (often their spouses, too) and that, for the most part, such a stance is seen as quite desirable for "real" men. Of course, these messages do not keep the fears and tears from happening. They do, however, often demonstrate that its is unsafe to express these feelings with one's father.

Obviously (pro)feminist men need to not only more equitably share in household tasks and in making important family decisions, but they must also break this cycle of being emotionally inaccessible to their children. We be-lieve this would most effectively be accomplished by men learning how to mother. As we have previously noted, the actual behavior of mothering, like feminism itself, is neither inherently female or male, but rather a way of be-ing in relation with others. At its perhaps most rudimentary level, and much like feminism itself, mothering is a loving, creative life-force that looks to nourish, nurture, comfort, and protect others from harm. Such an outlook is attuned to a child's laughter, anger, *and* his other fears and tears. Mothering is based on a deep commitment to the growth and well-being of children, a nonjudgmental stance of compassion and acceptance that assumes the child will always be loved no matter what happens. It creates a safe environment for the child to explore and experiment, to discover who he or she is and wants to be, and to have that discovery validated. While mothering is per-haps most easily focused on one's children, we also believe such an outlook has important implications for how we might view and treat others in gen-eral. Whether female or male, those who approach life in a loving, caring manner, who are truly concerned about the welfare and growth of others, and who look to live an egalitarian reality will all be important agents in the so-cial change that will make a feminist future possible.

Putting this into actual practice, we believe the archetype of feminist par-enting, the feminist mother-and-daughter relationship, is a suggestive model for (pro)feminists who are interested in learning how to mother. Again, in raising their daughters, feminist mothers look to be a parental figure who is compassionate yet patient, caring yet strong, loving yet independent, and sometimes self-sacrificing yet never without a sense of self. (Pro)feminist men who seek to make themselves more emotionally available to their chil-dren will find these vital feminist mothering values and ways of being quite conducive to this end. Of course, the actual praxis of feminist parenting will entail different behavioral approaches for women and men to accomplish them. Nevertheless, these important values for mothering should guide the parenting efforts of both feminist women and men.[23]

Ultimately, for men to learn how to mother, they must be willing to give up control and the self-serving comfort of always thinking they know best. They must develop ways to be more open and vulnerable, sharing some of their own uncertainties and fears and tears with their children. Doing this re-quires a sense of personal security and self-awareness that many men today simply do not have. It also requires time and patience for them to hear and see who their children really are and want to be, rather than seeing them through a preconceived and limiting lens with which many fathers view their sons and daughters. Self-disclosure requires a foundation of trust. If children perceive that their father has a set of fixed expectations about who they can be, they won't feel truly free to share with him their deepest fears and desires.

Fathers need to teach their children the difference between being strong and being hard. Teenage boys and many men frequently confuse hardness with strength. Hardness is fear driven and callous, typically demonstrated by a rigid, compulsive stance of toughness that precludes the ability to show any feelings of vulnerability. On the other hand, strength involves being flexible and adaptable to new circumstances without losing one's center. The truth is that caring and sensitivity do not make one weak if his or her life is consistently guided by self-honesty and internal convictions. No one values a weak, indecisive individual, male or female, but people do very much respect those who are truly strong. Fathers must learn to mother in ways that teach their sons and daughters how to be strong but caring and sensitive toward others.

Perhaps someday the role of mother will become truly celebrated instead of being one that, beyond fictitious lip service (e.g., Mother's Day), is conceptualized as a significant burden that second-class citizens called "women" are seen as most appropriately filling. (Pro)feminist men who learn to mother, their own children and all people, will be important change agents and role models in the construction of an egalitarian future. By example, and in alliance with feminist women, (pro)feminist fathers will help usher in new, less oppressive ways to be in the world.

## Teaching Feminism by Example

Children learn as much from what they see as from what they are told, or more. Actions always speak louder than words. Through observation, children learn who has the power and is dominant in the family even when it is never overtly expressed. Families in which the father is the important one, busy with career and the external world, while mother's needs and opinions have lower priority, are unlikely to produce feminist children. On the other hand, homes in which decision making and responsibility are truly shared, in which both parents are actively involved in childcare and household responsibilities, and in which the mother is a strong and independent woman in her own right are obviously more conducive to raising children with feminist values. Adult role models illustrate "normal" ways for families to operate, and children are motivated to repeat these patterns in their own marriages. Any problems (e.g., alcoholism, family violence, infidelity, authoritarianism) existing in the family of origin are likely to be reproduced. The values and assumptions that underlie such patterns are deeply entrenched and, although not always fully recognized, will often manifest later in life.

Many children today are being raised in female-headed households, and society has often expressed much concern about the effects of such child-rearing arrangements, especially on boys. Critics suggest that the lack of male role models in a boy's life leads to effeminate boys and/or aggressive behavior toward women. Of course, there is no one answer to this issue, as many other factors are involved. Single mothers can be aggressive and dominating or exploitive in their relationships with men. They can also be passive and dependent, blaming all of their misfortunes on men who have victimized them. Yet many sons and daughters come to respect their single mothers who are both nurturing and hardworking as they struggle against patriarchal institutions to support their families. Egalitarian attitudes are learned by watching mothers who are neither dominant nor subordinate but who, in a quietly competent manner, do the things that must be done.

Children carefully observe differences in how they and their brothers and/or sisters are treated in the home. Are there different rules (such as curfews), different chores and responsibilities, different privileges and importance given to needs, or are brothers and sisters treated equally? Are both boys and girls expected to learn how to cook, clean the house, and do the laundry, as something every adult needs to know how to do, or are these tasks "women's work"? Do adults actively listen to daughters? Are daughters included in household repair work, playing catch, or the fishing trip? Parents cannot teach nonoppressive values while encouraging gender-specific behavior. Consistently observing parents act in egalitarian ways will not make children into feminists, but it will increase the likelihood that the children will also enter into truly peer-based marriages and relationships.

Both boys and girls learn important lessons about life by watching how their fathers spend their time and money. When the father spends long hours at work, children often feel that he cares more about work than them. This sentiment is further accentuated if the father's pursuit of money and material possessions is understood as validating his masculinity. (Pro)feminist fathers need to learn new ways of balancing work with family so that their children do not feel as though they are lost in the shuffle of his work.

Power, and the abuse of power, are constant themes in childhood. From the bully on the playground to a multitude of adult authority figures that oversee their activities, children quickly learn that their wishes and perceptions are easily overridden by those with power, regardless of who is "right." If children feel unheard and that their wishes are always dismissed, sadly, the most important lesson they learn is to aspire to power for themselves. Statements like "because I said so" teach children, and especially boys, to seek out those with less power so that they can oppress them. (Pro)feminist fathers need to model alternative ways of exercising legitimate authority when protecting their children from the risks and negative experiences posed by society, while still giving them a real sense of their personal power and independence. This involves actually sitting down and taking the time to truly listen to children, and then teaching them that there are always choices to make and repercussions to their actions.

Fathers who have an aggressive, competitive style of speaking and relating, often putting down those with whom they disagree and treating them as inferiors, teach their children oppressive ways of always having to be right. Children notice how their fathers handle situations of anger and sadness, what sort of jokes they laugh at, and what makes them feel uncomfortable and defensive. Fathers are the archetype for "how men are" for their children. (Pro)feminist men need to provide a consistent role model for their children of practicing nonsexist ways of relating to women and dealing with everyday situations.

Ultimately, children look to their fathers and mothers for guidance and values in learning about the world, not so much for what they say but more for how they live life. Feminist parents need to role-model real-life values of equality and to consistently demonstrate their commitment to those values in the way they live their daily lives. They must enter into open, intimate relationships with their children based on full integrity and authenticity. The bottom line for a feminist parent is always about living equality in the present rather than teaching children about some abstract feminist future. This is certainly a lofty goal, but on it rests the true hope of a feminist future.

## Feminist Flowers that Bloom

From our own personal experiences, the ultimate promise of feminist parenting is perhaps more found in the long term as one's child matures and becomes more secure in defining his or her own individual identity. Although the overwhelming pressures of the womanhood- and manhood-making machines make feminist parenting a difficult undertaking, especially with children in their teens, with adulthood come many more opportunities for individuality not found in youth subcultures. We would like to end this chapter on a personal note of hope.

### Steve

Whenever I am faced with a dilemma or troubling situation, almost inevitably it is my mother's values and behaviors that most inform my subsequent actions.

With much admiration, I recall her seemingly eternal patience as she compassionately attempted to share her feminist wisdom with me. Much of what she taught me was by example and not authoritative dictates. While I realize that, filtered through a lens now over twenty years old (my mother passed in 1980), some of my words may glamorize our actual relationship, especially as I entered my teenage years, the fact remains that she has nevertheless had an incredibly strong impact on me in the long run. When I think of positive role models for living my own life and relating to others, she is always one of the most prominent. I believe I am finally becoming the feminist flower my mother planted as a seed in my head—a thought and way of being—so many years ago.

**Doris**
My son recently completed a master's degree in social work and is now employed as a counselor for at-risk teens. Quint is typically masculine in appearance and presentation of self, and as a result, often serves as a role model with whom many of the teens can identify, yet he continues to hold many of the values of his feminist mother. Young people of all genders feel free to share deep personal issues with him and often seek him out for advice. He is an adult man in a position of responsibility and leadership but is still able to listen with compassion, truly helping others make their own choices and find constructive solutions to personal problems. Best of all, he is "cool"! He consistently practices nonviolent ways of conflict resolution, treating both genders with respect and true caring. If asked, Quint would say he is a feminist, but this is not central to his personal identity. Nevertheless, he is doing important feminist work, and he is a caring, compassionate individual. There were times during his adolescence when I felt unsure of how he would turn out, so I feel very pleased to see that the feminist values that I planted are now blooming.

A feminist perspective in children who have been raised by feminist parents seldom fully develops until their mid-twenties. This awareness is typically gradual, often brought about through experiences of oppression—for daughters, experiences with being oppressed, and for sons, observing the discrimination and oppression of women they care about deeply. Herein is the true hope we can have for children raised by feminist parents. There are places in the desert when rain comes only once every few years but, when this occurs, seeds that have long lain dormant in the earth suddenly sprout and the desert blooms in magnificent splendor. So let it be with the generation of daughters and sons who have now been raised by feminist mothers and (pro)feminist fathers who have learned how to successfully mother their children

# Notes

1. Rubin 1992.
2. Hochschild 1990.
3. Rubin 1992.
4. Faludi 2000.
5. This family model is relatively new, largely the result of industrialization and jobs that took men out of the home. Subsistence farming and most cottage industries involved women working side-by-side.
6. Coontz 1993.
7. Gerson 1993.
8. Hochschild 1990.
9. Hochschild 1990; Schwartz 1994.
10. Schwartz 1994.
11. For example, see the Boston Women's Health Book Collective 1992.
12. hooks 1992, p. 111.
13. Two notable exceptions are Lorde's 1984 chapter entitled "Man Child," wherein she discusses the problems and possibilities of raising her son as a feminist, and a *Journal of the Association for Research on Mothering* 2000 special issue on feminists raising sons. It is also noteworthy that Christina Hoff Sommers, poster child of the conservative Right, has written a book entitled *The War against Boys: How Misguided Feminism Is Harming Our Young Men.*
14. Lorde 1984.
15. Johnson 1989, 178–79.
16. Connell 1995, 2000; Kimmel and Messner 2000.
17. Again, see *Journal of the Association for Research on Mothering* 2000 special issue on feminists raising sons.
18. Sommers 2000.
19. Ironically, in our experience, the "sissy" son often is the result of an overbearing, quite father who defines him as a manhood failure. See Faludi 1999 for similar examples and arguments.
20. Faludi 1999.
21. Faludi 1999.
22. For example, on an episode of the television program, *That 70s Show*, family patriarch Red Foreman instructs his son that real men don't say "I love you" unless they are drunk, dying, or there is no way out.
23. For a wonderful example of nonsexist, feminist parenting, please see Marge Piercy's 1976 science fiction novel, *Woman on the Edge of Time*, where she contrasts the oppressive realities of today's society with a feminist utopia in the year 2137. The story is told through the eyes of a poor Latina woman named Connie Ramos who, through her mind and the assistance of an individual in the future named Luciente, enters a world wherein dichotomous gender identities of male and female have ceased to exist. This hopeful feminist community of tomorrow is a place where all oppressive behaviors have almost entirely ceased to exist, diversity is truly celebrated,

and all children are raised with three co-mothers, regardless of the parents' biological sex, which is often difficult to discern, and the true assistance of the entire community. The number of births allowed each year is strictly limited to any losses—just replacement level—and the mothering of a child is seen as a true privilege, honor, and one of the most important responsibilities in the community.

◊

# Feminist Women and (Pro)Feminist Men: Moving from Uneasy to Radical Alliance

In our view, a feminist future will not be possible until women and men enter into truly radical alliances as shared partners in pursuit of this egalitarian reality. This chapter considers some of the very real impediments in contemporary society that make such coalitions highly unlikely and fraught with all sorts of difficulties. To move beyond these limitations, we first explore some of the often disparate expectations and experiences that men and women have when undertaking feminist activism, and how these differences might be redefined as strengths for alliance building. We next provide some current examples of feminist coalitions at the margins. Building on the insights that these groups provide, we then offer some suggestions for making possible truly radical alliances between men and women at the center. We end the chapter on a hopeful note of envisioning a fourth wave of feminism wherein women and men would fruitfully enter into true partnership in the pursuit of an oppression-free future.

## Present Impediments to Alliance Building

Many (pro)feminist men's groups have formed in Australia, Canada, England, and the United States over the past twenty-five years.[1] These groups have been organized around feminist principles, and most have general mission statements that call for the elimination of all forms of violence, oppression, and inequality. Recognizing that men are usually the perpetrators and seeming benefactors of violence and oppression, they work primarily with other men in an effort to change their attitudes and behavior.

Such groups have developed a wide array of educational materials that offer suggestions about ways healthy relationships might be formed and alternatives to using violence to resolve conflicts. Many organize seminars and group discussions on a diversity of topics ranging from nonsexist parenting to combating sexual harassment, the prevalence of rape and pornography, and challenging racist and homophobic societal realities. Some work with children and teenage males in hopes of providing positive role models. Others facilitate consciousness-raising groups for men who use violence against women (battering and rape) and for those men sexually and/or physically abused as children.

Given such visions and actions, it seems that strong alliances would occur between men's (pro)feminist groups and women's feminist organizations, but such positive relationships often fail to develop.[2] This represents a lost opportunity for both groups that weakens and sometimes directly undermines efforts to achieve shared goals.[3] While there are many impediments to alliance building between feminist women and (pro)feminist men, we believe the biggest limitations to such an end are the result of two general and very restrictive social outlooks.

First, the notion of essential gender differences is learned from infancy and is reinforced (both forcibly and through consent) until death, with both males and females being taught to view the opposite gender as "other," and as someone who can never be fully understood or trusted.[4] Social acceptance in adolescence, especially for boys, requires a rejection of all parts of oneself that are suggestive of the other, and the developing of a dichotomized "we/they" perception of reality. Simultaneously, young women are taught, and frequently learn through personal experience, that most men are potential predators to be feared and to always be on guard against unwelcome intrusions. No other sense of difference and mistrust seems to be as deeply entrenched and seemingly so fundamental as that of gender.[5]

Second, this sexist predisposition is further compounded by contemporary identity politics. As discussed in chapter 1, almost every emerging social movement over the past thirty years has been based on some fixed, typically single and rigid—albeit socially constructed—identity; such as nationality, age, race, gender, or sexuality.[6] The second wave of the women's movement that began in the late 1960s is a quintessential example of this approach. Fundamental to every emerging ideology is some definition of an oppressor group, a common enemy, and an operational—to be excluded from the ranks—other. For the women's movement this has obviously and understandably been men. While identifying the oppressor is a realistic and important first step in the formation of any social movement to challenge oppression, in the long run it often means the exclusion of sympathetic individuals—members of the very groups targeted as in need of change—that might be quite helpful in realizing larger movement goals.

The third wave of feminism (beginning after the failure to ratify the Equal Rights Amendment in 1982) is far more diverse in ideology and membership than the predominantly white middle-class women's movement of the 1970s. Poor women and women of color, however, have often resisted the feminist label because they perceive its acceptance as joining with white middle-class women against their own men.[7] Gender discrimination is just one of the forms of oppression that these women experience, and often other efforts for collective action are seen as requiring equal priority (e.g., the womanist ideology of Alice Walker).[8] Third World women frequently view economic and political imperialism and neocolonialism as the most important cause of their problems, including gender exploitation.[9] Women's groups in Third World countries often talk of a complementary basis to gender roles and work together with men to bring about political and social change.

Nevertheless, in the United States (and in many other similar countries, such as Canada, Great Britain, and Australia) the term *feminist* is still strongly associated with white middle-class women. This view places feminism squarely in the tradition of identity politics—a single-issue collective social movement, with men defined as the oppressive other.[10] This perception, perpetuated by the media and politicians, clearly influences those who join the women's movement and the stance taken by feminist organizations. Thus, while much of contemporary feminist ideology rejects notions of gender duality and radical separatism, in practice, feminist women have had problems building and sustaining working alliances with men. Today it is more common to blame patriarchy, an institutionalized system of male dominance, for injustice and oppression rather than portray individual men as the enemy. Yet long-held perceptions, expectations, and experiences create mistrust and continue to influence gender interactions in ways that might be unrecognized by the participants. Men often continue to be excluded or marginalized in feminist undertakings because of the personal realities of the women involved.

## Issues of (Pro)Feminist Men in Relation to Feminism

Male (pro)feminism consists of a loosely structured network, primarily made up of local men's groups working on activist projects and a handful of men in academic settings, who often receive little public recognition or support. The feminist movement has largely ignored or, at best, marginalized the efforts of these men, and many men in these groups feel unseen and undervalued. They are seeking alliance with feminist women, and many are hurt and confused by women's refusal to accept them as "the good guys." (Pro)feminist men, as we have defined them here and elsewhere, recognize the harm that patriarchy inflicts on both women and men. They want feminist women to make a distinction between culturally defined masculinity and being male as a biological category and to recognize that they, too, have been harmed (not to be confused with oppressed) in playing the masculine societal gender role. (Pro)feminist men attempt to adopt a feminist stance in hopes of finding nonsexist, nonoppressive ways of being and look to feminist women and feminism in general to guide them in this pursuit. However, since feminist women remain a largely silent and absent partner, (pro)feminist men are unfortunately often left in isolation to debate what sort of accountability and responsibility (pro)feminist men's groups should have toward women.

While women embracing a feminist worldview may find empowerment, a (pro)feminist male identity can lead to feelings of guilt, self-hatred, loss of confidence, and increased feelings of vulnerability. Moreover, many people tend to condemn men who refuse traditional forms of masculinity, labeling them "gender traitors," "wimps," "faggots," and in general view them as "failed men."[11] There are few role models for being a strong (pro)feminist man while simultaneously meeting social expectations for successful manhood. (Pro)feminist values and behaviors conflict with a lifetime of trying to repress perceived feminine aspects. Thus, while many of these men are willing to reject overtly violent and oppressive forms of masculinity, they still seek alternative ways of being a man. Given that masculine behavior is defined by feminism as the cause of women's subordination, they understandably have little interest in redefining what it means to be a "real man." Women insist that men have to give up male privilege, and reforming masculinity intuitively feels counterproductive to such this end.

Many (pro)feminist men see the exclusionary practices of most women's groups as not only discriminating against men but also against other women. Alliance formation that transcends single-identity politics is always more difficult when additional aspects of personal being are considered. Feminism itself is segmented over issues of race, class, sexual orientation, age, and nationality.[12] Although there is an overall stated commitment to inclusiveness and ending all forms of oppression, feminists often are resistant to taking nongendered forms of oppression seriously and see them as potentially diverting already scarce resources away from what is really important. Just as coalition building for men requires them to give up male privilege, many

feminist women need to give up white, class, and/or sexual orientation privilege to make possible larger alliances of women. Many feminist women,
however, are unwilling to relinquish the little privilege they might be afforded in a society where this determines both one's status and life chances.
There obviously is no guarantee that being a feminist means that an individual is strongly opposed to all forms of oppression and many forces keep
one from ever taking such a stance.[13]

(Pro)feminist men critically observe the internal dynamics of feminist organizations and the ways in which power is sometimes used to subordinate
and oppress other women. Dogmatic pressures for a common point of view
and the maintenance of whatever little status the given women's group might
have can become stifling, and those expressing alternative views sometimes
are dealt with harshly.[14] Consensus models of decision making may be used
in small groups, but large feminist organizations often operate in an ironically
hierarchical, patriarchal manner, leaving members feeling exploited and
powerless. Regardless of how worthy the stated cause of the feminist women's
group, many appear to be more of a replication of oppression than a challenge to existing patterns of dominance.

(Pro)feminist men may look at these inconsistencies and conclude that
feminism as a movement is more "against men" than "against oppression."
Unfortunately, many feminist groups often seem more about protecting privilege and advancing the interests of a small group of white middle-class
women. There seems to be a double standard—men must give up male privilege, must use process models of decision making, must carefully examine issues of power, dominance, and control in their personal lives, whereas
women are not held to the same rules of accountability. (Pro)feminist men
are constantly suspect and under scrutiny for any slight infringement of the
rules that could be taken as an indicator of underlying sexist attitudes. They
are placed on permanent probation by women who may or may not conform
to these rules themselves. Power and control tactics are often incompatible
with feminist ideology, leading groups to do things that are very different
than from what they say.

## Issues of Feminism in Relation to (Pro)Feminist Men

Because of a long history of oppression and subordination, women are understandably very protective of their space. Opening membership to men in
women's feminist organizations poses real danger. The presence of even a
small number of men in women's spaces often changes group dynamics.
Some women may hesitate to state their opinion freely; they may focus on

male approval or try to make their ideas more "reasonable" to a male audience. Suspicion about male motives may lead to defensiveness and focusing on only tangential issues. Personal experience tells us that if male membership reaches perhaps even a third, the very nature of the organization changes (some feminist women argue that allowing just one man into the group does this ).

If a man speaks with authority or is at all assertive, he often will be seen as a threat. Women often fear domination from men in any guise, as seemingly equitable relations between otherwise societal unequals can often be a subtle form of domination, even if a given (pro)feminist man is well intended and committed to feminism. The outside world, especially the media, will often cast a man into a leadership role, preferring to deal with feminism on a "man-to-man" basis whereby men's voices ultimately interpret and decide what feminism is and is not. Thus, a man might be the president of the board of a local women's shelter, make an academic career out of putting forth the "women's studies issue," or create a lucrative professional position for himself crusading to end violence against women. Men, and even other women, are more likely to rally around a male speaker and leader while discounting the exact same ideas if spoken by a woman. This infuriates feminist women, who have had many experiences with being discounted.

Even entering into cooperative agreements with a group of (pro)feminist men can be problematic, as women know from experience that such alliances often lead to co-optation, resulting in the weakening of organizational goals for minor successes. Many feminist women's groups already feel that they have insufficient resources to adequately address the pressing issues that confront women. Why should valuable time and energy, already in short supply, be spent on men's issues?

When these real concerns of men's involvement in feminist women's groups are combined with identity politics, exclusiveness seems an inevitable outcome. Such a stance is required for the successful identity formation of any given group. However, like any other disenfranchised collective, feminist women's groups see empowerment of their membership—taking back their power from men and male-dominated institutions—as a major goal. Realistically, this can only occur in safe, exclusive women's spaces where process may be more important than task, consciousness raising and education more important than social action. The initial step of defining a social problem and constructing an opposing identity to confront it is probably best undertaken by those who are most adversely and directly affected by the given issue. When this is true, alliances with (pro)feminist men and men's groups are largely irrelevant.

Like a flower garden, if feminism is to grow strong, flourish, and to truly become a mosaic of colors, shapes, and sizes of blossoms, eventually men will have to be included. Nevertheless, in initially deciding which men should be granted entrance, women will have to be very careful. Weeds grow in even the best-kept garden. Some weeds are obvious, while others look like flowers in the early stages of growth. Quite clearly, phenomena such as the Promise Keepers, The Million Man March, Robert Bly, and the Men's Rights Movement are about re-establishing male dominance and cannot claim to be (pro)feminist in any sense. Other pseudo-allies, such as those in men's studies or Sam Keen, may be harder to detect, as they use feminist insights and rhetoric to support their arguments. A similar problem exists in classifying the many local consciousness-raising groups for men. Both men and women with feminist sympathies may be taken in by their criticism of traditional patriarchal institutions and their attempts to make men more humanistic and sensitive.

For feminist women, the bottom line is, "Who benefits from the group's or individual's ideology and activities?" Is the purpose to broaden the scope of masculinity so that men who have been marginalized can now realize a bigger patriarchal dividend? Is the activity mere tinkering to reform the more obviously disagreeable aspects of patriarchy while ignoring the very real and unearned privileges men are afforded as men? Is it directed toward alleviating the pressures associated with the heavy responsibilities and guilt that are assumed with male privilege? Do these groups primarily focus on the ways in which men suffer and are purportedly oppressed by patriarchy while ignoring or minimizing women's experiences? Many men only want to change the rules a little so that they have a better chance of winning ( e.g., see our previous critique of men's studies).[15] All this is self-serving, as men will never be free from the pain of patriarchy until they are willing to give up male privilege. Such men are obviously unwelcome, harmful weeds in a feminist garden draining away important resources that can be better spent elsewhere.

Relatedly, another source of weeds is the male power broker who offers feminist women assistance in achieving their goals, but in return he advances his own career by becoming a spokesman for feminism. Although some are sincere, others are not and may use the women's movement as a less competitive arena for their own personal ambition. Social causes always attract moral entrepreneurs who crusade to improve their own status with little regard to the underlying values of the movement. Again, the question ultimately is "Whose interests are really being served and who benefits?"

In the short run, an exclusionary approach has been necessary, as to do otherwise would have been far too dangerous. After all, women have had enough problems protecting the garden from the weeds brought in by women. Meager assets and energy have been best spent exclusively on women's issues. The potential costs of male membership, or even partnerships with (pro)feminist male groups. has understandably appeared to far outweigh any possible benefits from such alliances. The fact remains, however, that exclusionary politics is a form of segregation, which is a tool of inequality and ultimately antithetical to realizing nonoppressive ways of being. Perhaps some men, with the help of a little plant food, could become flowers—especially considering that all cultivated flowers began as weeds. Without such risks, feminist ideals will never flourish and gain widespread acceptance nor will they be able to bring about large-scale social changes.

## Alliances between Women and Men: At the Feminist Margins

Alliances between women and men currently seem to work best at the margins;[16] when both have some form of deep antioppression/feminist commitment and/or even when there is merely a superficial commitment to feminism. Either way, feminism in these groups at the margins is really a secondary issue, as what they are trying to accomplish is only indirectly related. In the first situation, there often is a fluidity of gender roles, a form of "gender bending," where both men and women are committed to antioppression/ feminist goals and a process model of interaction. In the second, both men and women largely share traditional gender expectations and, although seemingly feminist in orientation, the leadership tends to be task oriented and the organizational structure quite hierarchical. Problems typically occur in both instances when individuals with different values and expectations try to join the group.

A friend once commented, "If we had five genders instead of just two, we wouldn't have all of these problems."[17] Gay men and lesbians can often create a group with multiple genders, successfully working on projects together to confront the oppression they experience in their lives.[18] Since both groups are marginalized in the larger society and share an outsider status, they often find a common ground that respects multiple gendered differences. Of course, there are gay men who are quite misogynist and lesbian separatists who want nothing to do with men. However, when gay and lesbian individuals make a personal choice to work together, the resulting alliance often is quite strong. Since both groups tend to be sensitive to the oppressive effects of patriarchy, gender- inclusive and consensus-based organizational models are more likely to result. And although not always explicitly feminist in orientation, often referring to themselves as "queer," many alliances such as these do implicitly address feminist concerns.

Another instance where "gender bending" leads to strong alliances between men and women is in the Earth-based spirituality movement. Such groups are deeply committed to feminist principles, and the men who join are most typically seeking ways to develop intuitive and feeling aspects of themselves (i.e., they are motivated by a desire to reject aspects of traditional masculinity). Such groups include both gay and straight men and women, but women are usually the group leaders and the men involved often viewed and treated as "honorary women." Although these groups are at the margins of both feminism and society, they still do have a potentially important impact because members frequently take their experiences and insights back into other (pro)feminist/feminist groups in which they are involved.

Liberal humanism, at another margin, permits alliances between men and women working toward feminist goals, but without either women or men deeply embracing feminist principles. It is no surprise that these alliances are most likely to occur between those who are white and middle class. Often these coalitions are practical and short-term, involving, for instance, the passing of a particular piece of legislation, supporting a political candidate, sponsoring a public event, or raising money for some cause. Such activities often get widespread community support from political leaders, the media, and sometimes even the church. Men's concern and involvement are increasingly seen in efforts to address concerns traditionally classified as women's issues, such as community activities for children and teens, health and education, and youth violence.

At least in principle, liberals are opposed to all forms of injustice and work together using traditional models of organizing to reform existing social and political structures. These types of coalitions, however, are inherently unstable, as they are usually organized around a single issue rather than any sort of expressed commitment of the participants to a broad-based feminist agenda. Sexist gender expectations almost always go unchallenged and organizational work is done in traditional hierarchical ways. Women are expected to be, and usually are, grateful to the men for helping with "their cause." Men frequently hold the key leadership roles. Only when these movements attempt to form permanent alliances with a broader feminist agenda do real problems arise.

Socialist men are yet another margin where alliances between men and women can be found. These men share many concerns with feminists, and their ideological outlooks usually affirm feminist principles, but they have multiple priorities and often a complex political agenda. Practical compromises and shifting priorities often result in women's goals and issues being given only

secondary importance. According to socialist theory, the exploitation and oppression of women is a by-product of capitalism and the economic arrangements in a society. While feminists often are opposed to capitalism, they see
sexism as much older and more deeply entrenched than any economic system.
Some socialist men are truly (pro)feminist, but others are only verbalizing politically correct views. As such, alliances between men and women under a socialist banner tend to consider feminist issues as secondary concerns at best.

A final site at the feminist margins with which we are familiar are the alliances between feminists and (pro)feminist academic men, especially in the
humanities and the social sciences. Male academics are a resource sometimes
tapped by feminist women to move issues through the university structure
and decision-making process. Unfortunately, although many of these men
pay strong lip service to feminist issues, they frequently have not incorpo-
rated feminist commitments into their personal identities and daily lives. As
a consequence, they sometimes can be difficult to work with and may also be
a source of goal co-optation. The university setting itself, for both men and
women, tends to be more focused on forwarding one's career—tenure and
promotion—than advancing any sort of meaningful feminist agenda. Most
classroom teachers today dutifully mention the achievements of women, often showing their contributions to male goals and structures. This is far different from advancing a feminist agenda that exposes the patriarchal assumptions and institutions in our society. Thus, while important theoretical
statements about gender inequality emerge from the university settings, any
alliance building that does occur between women and men often tends to be
more about career building and only of marginal importance to the larger
feminist movement.

## Forging Radical Feminist Alliances between Men and Women: New Beginnings at the Center

Most contemporary societies are based on a hegemonic world view that emphasizes power, dominance, and oppression. People everywhere are hurt by
values and ways of being that treat women, the Earth itself, and even men as
things to be manipulated and controlled for personal gain. Eliminating oppression is obviously a massive undertaking that will require the efforts of all
people of goodwill who truly champion justice and equality. Like all aspects
of existence on our planet, all forms of oppression are interconnected, so tinkering with the present system over single issues will not bring about significant change. Women cannot do this alone, nor can they bring about desired
changes by focusing only on women.

There are men who truly are (pro)feminist and deeply committed to living a feminist, nonoppressive reality. These men provide a valuable service to feminism by working with other men to change masculine culture and to reduce violence and other forms of oppression directed at women. Such men are a bridge between feminist women and masculine audiences. It is a sad and unfortunate truth that men seldom listen to women about issues of masculinity and male oppression. Feminist women often are dismissed by most men as nothing more than lesbian separatists and/or man-haters with an axe to grind at men's expense. These same men, however, often will listen to a (pro)feminist man utter the same or even more radical words condemning patriarchy and offering suggestions for more egalitarian ways in its place. Ultimately, the prevention and ending of oppressive masculine attitudes and actions is men's work. (Pro)feminist men addressing such issues very much deserve support and recognition from feminist women.

For the foreseeable future, feminist alliances across gender will probably best be realized using a threefold approach—women's space, men's space, and shared space. For a variety of reasons, as outlined throughout this chapter, feminist women and (pro)feminist men will continue to need same-gender groups, spiritual retreats, and conferences where they can comfortably focus on their own needs and issues with other experientially like individuals. Potential allies should recognize and respect that all groups deserve a room of their own. Shared spaces should also be created where feminist women and (pro)feminist men can come together to cooperatively work on projects. Herein lie the promise and beginning of a truly radical alliance between men and women in the pursuit of a nonoppressive feminist future.

For such alliances to be forged, however, we believe that both (pro)feminist men and feminist women will have to consider the following suggested criteria for getting along.

*Men* will have to: (1) acknowledge and give up their male privilege; (2) be willing to apply feminist principles to their personal lives; (3) affirm that the elimination of oppression against women and people in general is a central priority; (4) advocate for social and institutional change to promote equality and justice for women and all people; (5) learn nonhierarchical forms of communication and decision making; and (6) demonstrate respect for women and women's spaces.

*Women* will have to: (1) recognize oppression is socially structured and not an innate biological characteristic; (2) agree that men are also harmed (not to be confused with oppressed) by patriarchy; (3) sincerely recognize and value the contributions of (pro)feminist men by viewing them as comrades in a larger struggle; (4) demonstrate respect for (pro)feminist men and (pro)feminist men's space; (5) support all efforts to end nongendered forms of oppression; and, where appropriate, (6) acknowledge and give up any non-gendered forms of privilege they may have.[19]

Reflecting on our own working relationship, we have found that by agreeing on the above criteria for feminist interaction—first implicitly and now explicitly—we have been able to envision new ideas and ways of being from our quite different social identities and accompanying backgrounds. Moreover, it has been through the *process* of working together that our awareness about and appreciation for our discordant experiential perspectives have deepened, as has our friendship and overall commitment to realizing a feminist future. This has been accomplished by not minimizing the very different gender experiences we each have as a woman and a man but, instead, respecting them and then using them to strengthen our understanding of gender inequality and oppression in both personal and general terms. In sum, we believe such an approach has enabled us to forge a radical alliance across our differences of gender and age.

Forming strong radical alliances between diverse groups would require a consensus on goals, practices, and principles. Such a consensus is not found in either the women's movement or in the (pro)feminist men's movement, so it is not surprising that even greater difficulties occur when (pro)feminist men and feminist women attempt to work together. Yet such coalitions are forming on the local level around a variety of community issues and projects. It is not necessary that all groups have a high level of feminist consciousness before the work can begin. Often it is the work that brings about a deeper feminist consciousness. Too often, demands for ideological purity become divisive and waste meager resources on infighting and pointless controversy. Since none of us absolutely knows *the truth*, beyond our own limited experiences, there must be room for all people of goodwill to work cooperatively regardless of their ideological perspective.

Both men and women have a tendency to place all the blame for whatever social problem confronts them on the "system," to minimize their own responsibility for personal change. For many this a cop-out ("I will change if the system changes first") or a statement of powerlessness and frustration ("You can't fight/beat the system"). Such thinking is circular, as it perpetuates current attitudes and patterns of social behavior and resulting inequalities. Systems and/or societal structures are not concrete entities in the traditional sense of being some physical object such as a rock, a car, or a body. Instead, they can be viewed as ideological maps in each of our heads whose reality can only be measured in terms of our individual actions and their quite real consequences for ourselves and others. Labels like "the system"

carry with them emotional baggage that is counterproductive to efforts of social change. When people believe they have choices and are free to act on
these choices, it alters the reality of their lives. Thus, while it is true that an
individual cannot change societal structures alone, it is equally true that a
group of people can change structure when they collectively see and do
things in a different way. For empowering radical feminist alliances to be
forged between women and men, new ways of envisioning the world will
have to be created *and* acted upon.

## Forging Radical Alliances in a Feminist Frontier

At one time many people felt the planet was flat and one would fall off its
ominous edges and disappear if one ventured too far from the known. Exploration of this mysterious horizon proved this previously very real and limiting boundary to be fictional. In its place was found a circular, interconnected
reality upon which the survival of all peoples is dependent, called Mother
Earth. Perhaps feminist women will come to view men as a last largely un-
explored frontier of sorts—the fourth and hopefully final wave of feminism.
Real change will obviously require the efforts of both women and men. Only
then will previously dichotomously and rigidly conceived gender and other
social boundaries give way to life-affirming and egalitarian ways of being.
Men and women will have to become comrades in scouting out and creating
this new territory of being—a nonoppressive future.

When men have tried to do it alone (patriarchy), they have brought the
planet to the brink of destruction. It is just as naive to think women can do
it alone. The efforts of everyone working cooperatively toward a shared vision will be required to bring about significant change. There are presently
(pro)feminist men who truly do get it and are interested in joining women in
exploring ways to bring about an egalitarian future. Without such men, feminist women will be forever resigned to investing precious time and energy
into simply treating the symptoms and consequences of existing gender inequalities, without ever truly challenging their cause—a misogynist, patriarchal society that resides in each of us. (Pro)feminist men often have access
to very different audiences and resources than those tapped by feminist
women.[20] Women lose a real opportunity for change if they fail to support
the efforts of such men. Misunderstandings will occur, but in an atmosphere
of honest communication and mutual respect, they can be resolved. We must
all recognize that a feminist vision will be realized only through the efforts of
both women and men working together as partners to bring about change.
Now is the time to build that alliance.

# Notes

An earlier version of this chapter appeared in Bystyzienski and Schacht 2001.

1. For a sampling of (pro)feminist groups, see the Appendix of Schacht and Ewing 1998.
2. Leornard 1982; Stanley 1982; Canaan and Griffin 1990; Ramazanoglu 1992.
3. Friedman and Sarah 1982; Hagan 1992; hooks 1992; Starhawk 1992.
4. Lorber 1994; Connell 1995; Schacht 1996.
5. Ewing and Schacht 1998.
6. Aronowitz 1992; Gitlin 1993; Gamson 1995; Rupp and Taylor 1999.
7. Baca Zinn et al. 1986; Spelman 1988.
8. Walker 1983.
9. Bystydzienski and Sekhon 1999.
10. Rupp and Taylor 1999.
11. Stoltenberg 1990, 1993.
12. Baca Zinn et al. 1986, Spelman 1988.
13. Hagan 1998; Schacht and Ewing 1997; Schacht 2000.
14. When women have power they can be just as vicious as men in exercising it and sometimes more so, as power often is new to them.
15. Schacht and Ewing 1997a.
16. In using the term "margin," we are not asserting that the given group discussed is marginalized (which may or may not be true). More specifically, we are defining the given group as being on the edges, fringes, and/or periphery of the feminist movement.
17. We thank Shekhinah Mountainwater for this insight. Personal correspondence.
18. Schacht 1998.
19. Hagan 1998; McIntosh 2000.
20. Schacht and Ewing 1997b; Schacht 1997.

CHAPTER TEN

# Undoing the Original
# Phallic Sin: Envisioning a
# Fourth Wave of Feminism

The gendered basis of American society has changed dramatically during the past fifty years. Financial necessity has made the two-check family a norm of today, and women are now entering every occupation in burgeoning numbers. Many of these women are ambitious and career oriented, becoming more rational and assertive, knowing that advancement requires thinking and acting "like a man." Women now serve in the armed forces, even in combat situations, and we all know that in modern warfare there often is no explicit "front line." At the same time, increasing numbers of men are becoming disillusioned with the notion that work should be their primary source of affirmation.[1] Some of these men are becoming more nurturing and starting to assume a more vital role in family life. As much as conservatives may lament their loss, traditional gender roles are not options for the vast majority of people today.

Much of this book has focused on individual ways of helping men understand and adapt to these larger societal changes. We have noted on numerous occasions that growing numbers of men today are becoming dissatisfied with old scripts for being a man and are actively seeking alternative ways of interacting and relating with women and all people. However, male domination and gendered ways of viewing the world are increasingly being played out in a global arena. R. W. Connell has noted that the globalization of masculinity has led to the creation of a contemporary world gender order.[2] It is to this worldwide focus of understanding gender that we turn our attention in this final chapter.

Over the past five hundred years, European forms of male dominance have come to shape reality on a worldwide scale, leading us to make fictitious assumptions about what is natural, just, or even possible. Alternative, often more egalitarian forms of gendering, such as the practices of the indigenous people encountered by the explorers of the New World, have been rendered invisible or deviant through practices of cultural imperialism associated with these conquests. Today, whether found in the hegemonic forms of Western masculinity, or in the subordinated, often competing forms of masculinity (e.g., al Qaeda and the Taliban), male dominance and female subordination are a worldwide phenomenon. Thus, as we will argue in this chapter, many, if not all the world's problems are best understood as highly gendered in basis, with realistic solutions ultimately requiring a fundamental paradigm shift away from male dominance to be replaced with an inclusive, nonoppressive worldview.

This chapter explores the gendered basis of all inequalities and how ideologies of male domination and female subordination are played out on the individual, national, and world levels. We begin this chapter reflecting on the recent events of 9/11 and exploring how they can be viewed as masculine politics as usual being played out on a world scale. We next examine the gendered basis of all oppression and argue that this original sin must be undone on the individual, local, and international levels for equality to ever be realized. We point out how this gendered outlook of the world has also resulted in significant environmental damage being done to Mother Earth herself. We end the chapter arguing that a fourth wave of feminism must emerge if we are to reverse the cataclysmic direction in which we are now headed. This new social movement must be attuned to both the hegemonic basis of masculinity being played out throughout the world and create a new ideological outlook that would enable both the oppressed and the oppressor to join forces to undo all the unnecessary, self-destructive harms that accompany the oppression of both people and the planet.

## Masculine Politics as Usual: 9/11 as a Seemingly Inevitable Outcome

R. W. Connell has put forth a compelling argument that masculinity is a global phenomenon whereby, through conquest, colonial empire building, and postcolonial policies, Western ideals of masculinity have come to dominate in the world gender order.[3] The history and creation of the present standard of hegemonic masculinity is the outcome of many conflicts and wars, some of them on a global scale, such as World War I, World War II, and the

Cold War. Men in developing countries and all subordinated masculinities are at a decided and obvious disadvantage when competing against and/or contesting the oppressive practices of contemporary Western masculinity. This often leads these men to feel as if they are being treated "like a woman," and often the only way that they can act like a man is to strike back with deadly force.

Whether on the nightly news, CNN on the half-hour, or in newspapers and magazines, the media feed Americans a steady diet of images of ethnic conflict throughout the world. Often the violence captured for our viewing pleasure and entertainment is that of the most desperately poor protesting the oppressive realities with which they are forced to live. We see young teens with semiautomatic weapons, grandfathers with grenade launchers, and even babies dressed as suicide bombers. Most Americans dismiss these images as the product of violent, backward cultures who lack the benefit of Western ideology and institutions. Sadly, many Americans have become so desensitized to these scenes of poverty and suffering that they forget that these oppressed people have the same hopes and dreams as theirs.

In all contemporary cultures today, being a man means having respect and being seen as of value to the community, being able to protect and provide for his family, and having a sense of competence and control over his life. What happens to the spirit and self-worth of men who are defined as expendable pawns in the global game of masculine politics? To men who lack the means to sustain their families at a minimum survival level? To men who feel despised by their own governments? In many of the poorest countries reactionary political movements and religious fundamentalism offer hope that through violent resistance things can be made better. For many of these men the only way they can prove their manhood is with a gun. Often responding to the systematic exploitation and violence of the world's wealthiest nations, especially the United States, terrorism and random violence are the acts of the desperate who can see no other way.

Americans need to recognize the direct role they play in the exploitation of poor countries and accept responsibility for undoing the many harms that result. The United States is a mere 4.5 percent of the world's population yet consumes over 25 percent of our planet's resources while the majority of the people in the poorest countries live in abject poverty. Multinational corporations exploit the natural resources and labor in these countries, often causing permanent environmental damage in the process, all to maintain our high standard of living and greedy ways. In many poor countries, agriculture has shifted from producing food for its populace to growing crops for export to raise monies to pay off debt to the World Bank.

Corrupt governmental officials and entrenched elite made wealthy by their contacts with Western business, siphon off vital resources and try to use police and army violence to stifle any resistance to their exploitive practices. Is it any wonder that warfare is such a common ongoing reality in many poor countries?

In short, our high standard of living is sustained on the backs of the world's poor. Is it really all that surprising that so many people in these poor countries hate Americans and wealthy Western countries in general? In all honesty, it is actually fairly understandable that worldwide terrorist networks exist that both preach and practice violence against Americans and its allies. In the worldwide matrices of hegemonic masculinity, those denied access to "normal" ways of being a man will inevitably resist their subordinated status, often using the very tools of violence that have been used for so long to continue their oppression.

The suicide plane attacks on the World Trade Center and Pentagon can easily be framed as a subordinated masculinity striking back against the most hegemonic of all masculinity-based powers, the United States, and is rife with symbolic gender imagery. In this framework it seems almost too appropriate that the targets to be assaulted were the two tallest phallic symbols in our country, the World Trade Center, that represented the means by which much of the world is economically "fucked," with the Pentagon being the "balls" that back up the United States' exploitive policies toward the rest of the world. As most people in the United States watched these attacks on live television unfold, their disbelief was quickly replaced with terror. Fighter planes were scrambled with orders to shoot down any unaccounted-for commercial jets. Thethe commander in chief of hegemonic masculinity, George Bush, was whisked away to a fortified hole in the ground for "security purposes." Perhaps the most telling and, in a sense, shocking aspect of these attacks was not that they occurred, or that nineteen men with box cutters could so easily wreak such havoc on the most powerful nation in the world, but rather that it struck terror into the minds of men who were the self-ordained leaders of the world gender order.

Unlike the Cold War and World Wars I and II, this terror was based on a new sense of vulnerability, that such a small number of men who were losers in the game of hegemonic masculinity could wreak such devastation on and cause such chaos in the strongest nation in the world. Many people in the United States, both women *and* men, felt powerless, a feeling typically reserved solely for the oppressed. Reactions were largely symbolic, such as flag waving, prayer meetings, and making seemingly cathartic donations to charities created for victims of the attacks. Stores sold out of gas masks, gun sales increased, and people canceled their travel plans, passively retreating to their homes all in an attempt to allay feelings of fear and vulnerability. Billions of dollars have been allocated for "homeland security," even though it is quite clear that they are largely ineffective measures for dealing with suicide attacks. Our basic assumptions about the seeming hegemony of United States masculinity and the security that it is supposed to afford us had been temporarily called into question.

Worldwide, women have long lived in fear of rape and other forms of men's violence. From the man lurking in the bushes to the man on the street who sexually harasses to the battering husband in the home, the threat of male violence is a ubiquitous feature of every contemporary society. Even a woman with considerable status, one who has followed all the rules and taken all the precautions, is not immune from some man, in either a public or private setting, wreaking havoc on her life. Likewise, those living under the rule of authoritarian governments around the world, and the poor and minorities everywhere, constantly fear the random attacks of the police and the military, frequently one and the same, never knowing where the next oppressive assault will occur and often feeling that there is nowhere they can safely hide.

What was seemingly so shocking about 9/11 was not only did the attacks elicit fear in women but men in the United States also felt a strong sense of terror. Yet, unlike women and other subordinated people for whom experiences of violence are often highly probable, most men in America are not accustomed to living with terrorist based fear. Thus, while all men were experiencing similar feelings of terror from the attacks, the basis of this fear may have been very different for men of privileged status than it was for subordinated peoples. Women's fears are based on the reality that they are the frequent targets of men's violence. On the other hand, men's fears in response to 9/11 are the result of seeing their personal privilege, and the security that accompanies it, thrown into question.

Dominant masculinities have a long history of tolerating and sometimes even outright supporting the violence often associated with subordinated masculinities.[4] Wars are constantly being waged throughout the world between subordinated masculinities, and, beyond perfunctory condemnation, the United States seldom does anything to intercede in these ongoing conflicts. At home, since the early 1800s our country has a long and rich history of violent subordinated masculinities in the form of gangs. In fact, in musicals such as *West Side Story*, movies such as *The Warriors*, or numerous Mafia/Godfather–based television series like today's immensely popular *Sopranos*, we very much like to romanticize and celebrate the violent struggles of subordinated masculinities. Given the divide-and-conquer orientation of hegemonic masculinity, as long as those hurt and killed in the conflicts of subordinated masculinities are these men themselves, often accomplished by keeping their activities localized to a certain implicitly agreed-upon territory, their violence is seen as tolerable, often desirable, and in some cases, even entertaining.

Periodically, however, an innocent bystander is hurt or killed by gang violence, or warfare in other countries spills into areas where we have economic interests. Or worse yet, a member of a subordinated masculinity purposefully attacks the dominant masculinity. Timothy McVeigh, the Columbine school shootings, and the 9/11 attacks are all examples of subordinated masculinities successfully striking back with deadly force against the dominant masculinity.[5] It is cases such as these that cause moral outrage and strike fear in the hearts of men who are cultural or world dominants. The resultant fear here is very different from that experienced by subordinated people where threats of violence and actual violence are used as constant reminders and as a means to keep them in their lesser position. To the contrary, forced to recognize that the master's tools can also be so effectively used against the master himself, his fear resonates from an insecure place of losing status and being treated as a subordinate—like a woman—all the worse for being at the hands of a very few determined losers. In the present matrices of hegemonic masculinity, this terror is almost always quickly replaced with a swagger of righteous anger (even though the fear and insecurity remain beneath it) and the use of violence whereby the subordinated masculinity that dared to question the master's superiority is forcibly put back into its lesser position or eliminated outright .

Since 9/11, like a playground bully on a world scale, the United States has responded swiftly using all its violent—most cutting-edge—military technology in an attempt to exterminate the subordinated masculinity of Islamic fundamentalism in Afghanistan. The United States first bombed Afghanistan into submission while leaving the more dangerous ground fighting to local warlords opposed to the Taliban. Once this campaign of hegemonic masculinity was successful, America sent in its ground troops to further secure the conquered territory through mopping up actions and to interrogate captured prisoners. Correctly recognizing that there are many other upstart masculinities in the world, President Bush has promised that the "new" war on terrorism will continue into the indefinite future along with a war on what he once called the Axis of Evil. Of course, all of this can be restated to say that the United States, through significant expenditures of its enormous wealth on defense spending, will, as in the past, do anything to maintain its dominant masculine position in world politics, and anyone who might challenge this position can expect to be dealt with in the harshest means available.

Money spent on the military is fictitiously called "defense spending" when in reality it is really an "attack budget."[6] The monies spent on health, welfare, and education are our true defense budget. Defense is what is required to protect families and children from harm. As long as we confuse defense spending with the hegemonic masculine politics of domination through violence and aggression, and see the protection of economically exploitive political policies as the defense of vital national interests, warfare and world instability will continue. Violence and other forms of oppression can be used to force people into submission, but this will never produce peace. True peace will only be made possible when there is a recognition of and respect for the needs of all people on the planet.

The 9/11 attacks on the World Trade Center and Pentagon are obviously quite consistent with viewing masculinity as a hegemonic force that drives history. Weapons of mass destruction in the hands of an ever-increasing number of nations have made it possible for a few men to threaten all people. Militarism, brinkmanship diplomacy, ever more efficient killing weapons, and nationalism all seem to be an extension of nothing more than a boys-on-the-playground mentality, an international pissing contest or circle jerk to see who is the biggest and strongest. Wars are fought for economic positioning, lofty "principles," and for revenge but seldom are concerned with the general welfare of all people. We believe the time has come to quit fighting for the "fatherland" and turn our attention to nurturing the "motherland" and undoing all the harms that have been done to her.

## Undoing the Harms of the Original Phallic Sin

And the rib, which the Lord God had taken from man, made he a woman, and brought her unto the man. And Adam said, "This is now bone of my bones, and flesh of my flesh: she shall be called woman, because she was taken out of man."

—Genesis 2:22–23

Five thousand years of ever hegemonic forms of patriarchy have resulted in a world gender order where male dominance and female subordination are the moral fabric of every contemporary society.[7] This assumption of gender inequality is fundamental to the traditional religious understanding of the world in which men are superior and intended to have domination over all of nature while women are merely created to be their helpmates and appropriately subordinate. Although many forms of categorical inequality exist today, gender can be viewed as the first socially created inequality and the model upon which all others are based. In social class terms, Thorstein Veblen argued that the social categories of male and female made possible the first industrious (women) and predatory (men) classes and provided the blueprint for all subsequent divisions of have and have not, oppressor and oppressed.[8] In this sense, the categories of male and female are the source of the first known forms of inequality, oppression, injustice, and rightfully viewed as the original sin. This basic insight of inequality became the fundamental basis of the radical feminist outlook most developed and publicized in the late 1960s and early 1970s.[9]

This is not, however, to say other forms of oppression are less powerful or meaningful than gender oppression. After all, mutant strains of a given disease can become even more powerful and destructive over time, and people's experiences with oppression are often multifaceted, varying significantly over an individual's lifetime or even daily experience, frequently rendering them an oppressor in one circumstance and the oppressed in yet another. But what this seemingly radical outlook does suggest is that there is a gendered basis to all inequality. Thus, it is not surprising that this same binary male/female ideological outlook of oppression is conveniently embedded in all relations of domination and subordination; for example, rich/poor, gay/straight, white/black, Western nation/developing country. Nor is it surprising that the prescribed states associated with these statuses have an inherent gender basis; e.g., active/passive, leader/follower, independent/dependent, good/evil, logical/irrational.

The harms from dichotomous beliefs of gender inequality are far-reaching and ever present—they are hegemonic. Writers, such as Mary Daly, have illuminated the ways in which ideologies of male dominance, perhaps most easily seen in patriarchal religions, have locked women into oppressive social structures and stunted their growth. She laughs at the absurd notion that Adam gave birth to Eve, that Eve's desire for knowledge of good and evil is the original sin from which patriarchal religion tries to save us, and that all suffering from the world comes from women. Daly defines the "original sin" as follows:

> State of complicity in patriarchal oppression that is inherited by women through the socialization process; socially transmitted dis-ease involving psychological paralysis, low self-esteem, hatred of self, emotional dependence, horizontal violence, and a never ending conviction of one's guilt.[10]

Much of this definition is obviously equally applicable to other subordinated groups in any given society. Gloria Yamato calls this condition internalized oppression, and defines it as situations where "members of the target group are emotionally, physically, and spiritually battered to the point that they begin to actually believe that their oppression is deserved, is their lot in life, is natural and right, and that it doesn't even exist."[11]

Jean Baker Miller has analyzed the effects of dominance and subordination and concluded that the stereotypical characteristics attributed to women are shared by all subordinate groups.[12] Whoever fills subordinate roles is perceived as less competent, passive and dependent, lacking self-confidence, and more concerned with gossip, which is often the source of valuable information needed for personal safety. Moreover, subordinates who demonstrate competence and strength, especially in arenas traditionally reserved for dominants, risk increased vulnerability and are taught, sometimes violently reminded, not to push things too far. She points out that these are pragmatic, learned behaviors that are often necessary for survival when one is a member of subordinate group.

What is perhaps the most harmful aspect of inequality is that those who are subordinates are often oppressed regardless of what they do (what we have previously referred to as a double ontological bind or a catch-22 situation). The very futility that oppression represents often leads to feelings of worthlessness, helplessness, isolation, and powerlessness, all conditions that are directly associated with depression. The time has come to end all forms of oppression and the unnecessary harm it causes. As we have argued throughout this text, for this to occur, both the oppressed and the oppressor must recognize the deplorable pain and suffering caused by inequality and how needless and destructive it is for all. Feminism and other progressive social movements of the oppressed have long recognized the harms of inequality. The time has come, too, for the oppressor, on the individual, societal, and international levels, to also acknowledge the unnecessary suffering and pain caused by their actions. Only then will the formation of truly radical alliances, powerful enough to effectively challenge and dismantle oppression, be made possible.

Undoing the harms of the original sin, the assumption of male dominance, not only requires a radical transformation of how women and other subordinated people are to be treated, but it also demands that we drastically change how we view and care for our planet. Our survival as a species may very well depend upon our making this happen. Patriarchy has long viewed our "mother," the Earth, as an object that "men" are supposed to rape, exploit, and plunder for their own profit. As made clear in the Bible, all of

Mother Earth's mineral and living resources are seen as the rightful domain of men to use however they see fit. The gendered imagery here is unmistakable. The abusive, neglectful manner in which we have done much harm to the planet is nearly identical to the way in which many women and other subordinated people are treated throughout the world today.

Many scientists believe that we have a small window of opportunity to contain and undo the ecological damage we are doing to our home, Mother Earth. Worldwide overpopulation is permanently damaging the ability of the environment to feed people and to sustain the many other forms of life with which we share the planet (when Steve was born in 1960 there were 3 billion people, whereas in 2001 there were 6 billion). Antiquated moral values severely restrict the availability of birth control to most people worldwide and much of the world's population lives in abject poverty. Over the past five hundred years, oppressive greed has resulted in the extermination of untold species of animals, with numerous species being on the brink of extinction today. Domestic animals are often raised in wretched factory-like conditions that deplete grain stocks to feed the gluttonous appetites of those in wealthy nations while significant numbers of people worldwide go hungry every day. While the proverbial horse has long since been let out of the barn, we are just now beginning to seriously question the consequences of genetic engineering and the constant altering of the environment through technology.

Wealthy nations continue to get richer through the exploitation of poor country's labor and mineral resources who, in turn, are rendered ever poorer and dependent from these oppressive practices. Political instability, war, terrorism, and violence in general are inevitable outcomes of present oppressive worldwide policies, needlessly killing many and leaving untold others homeless, injured, and desperate. These will continue to be normative outcomes as long as we fail to acknowledge the unnecessary harm and suffering caused by such "business as usual" ideologies. We must do better or, through warfare and/or environmental degradation, we run the very real risk of exterminating ourselves as a species.

We are told that the health of our economy is entirely dependent on consumer spending. Advertising is designed to convince us that our selfish wants are actually needs. After 9/11, we are told that buying a new car, preferably a gas-guzzling SUV, or taking a vacation is the patriotic thing to do and that doing otherwise will lead to more jobs being lost and a deepening of the recession we are in. Patrons of this marketplace, which is most everyone in the United States, have accumulated trillions of dollars in credit card and personal debt, effectively making them indentured servants of the capitalist system. Even more devastating is the pollution, the depletion of nonrenewable resources, and the waste that directly result from political policies that define societal health in terms of the monetary value of the goods produced and sold (e.g., GNP) in a given quarter or year. Sadly, the profit margins of Fortune 500 companies in the United States are almost always seen as more important than the availability of social services or a healthy environment, both basic standards needed to support the quality of life for everyone.

The United States has been extremely resistant to doing anything that might jeopardize its dominant position in the world economy. While world leaders struggle to create an environmental treaty that would limit the release of harmful gases into the atmosphere (e.g., the Kyoto Agreement), the United States is conspicuously absent from the negotiating table. In fact, we resist any international agreements that would our restrict our ability to do business as usual, meaning exploiting the world's resources and many of its people for our own profit and personal gain. Instead of using all of our considerable wealth to be a beacon of progressive politics, we invest these monies into what we call defense spending to protect the investments throughout the world that are necessary to maintain our overprivileged and wasteful standard of living.

By the year 2000, 165 nations had ratified the United Nations Convention on the Elimination of All Forms of Discrimination against Women. The only four countries who have refused to sign this agreement are North Korea, Iran, Afghanistan, and the United States (ironically, the United States has much more in common with the Axis of Evil than it is willing to admit). The United States Senate has repeatedly refused to approve this accord. In the hegemony of the world gender order, this is not surprising, as having an oppressive view of women is certainly consistent with viewing the rest of the world as subordinate to us, as our helpmates (e.g., other wealthy nations aligned with us), and/or as our rightful servants (e.g., countries whose labor and resources we exploit). Like the malevolent God described in the Old Testament of the Bible, we punish those who do not see the wisdom of our beliefs (e.g., Cuba), exterminate those who refuse to accept our desire for their resources (e.g., Iraq), and devalue those who question our sovereign right to pursue our national interests at the expense of others (e.g., the United Nations).We reward only those who more appropriately worship no false gods and pay homage only to us and our ways (e.g., our allies, such as Japan and England).

Since we do wield such considerable power worldwide, it is infuriating to recognize that those doing business with us must, in many ways, adopt our oppressive outlook on women and Mother Earth, and that our gendered values realistically set the standard for all other countries.[13] This is especially troubling because we *could* do so much better here. Is it any wonder that the stereotype of the "ugly American" exists worldwide, with many people throughout the world outright hating us? For this to change, just as (pro)feminist men or whites must give up unearned privilege,[14] as a nation we need to find ways to effectively share the considerable wealth we have with others and start recognizing the harm that results from our overprivileged, greedy, and wasteful lifestyles. To finally undo the original sin, and all the needless oppression associated with it, we must envision ways to effectively challenge male dominance on the individual, group, national, and worldwide levels. For this to occur, we need to explore and illuminate ways in which the oppressed and the oppressor, of all sorts, can become partners in the pursuit of a more egalitarian future.

## Envisioning the Next Wave of Feminism

Over the past two hundred years of feminism, there have been visionary voices calling for a major paradigm shift in how we view gender and the oppression that accompanies it, but these broad-based outlooks of gender equality were set aside for more short-term, practical objectives. The first wave of feminism was first sidetracked by the abolitionist movement and the Civil War. Then, after expanding significant energies in the campaign for the right for women to vote, and convinced all was seemingly well and fair after its passage, women rested. After 1920, notwithstanding a few notable exceptions (e.g., Margaret Sanger and Jane Adams), feminism as a social movement was largely dormant until the 1960s.[15] With increasing numbers of women entering the workforce, women in the late 1960s and 1970s again joined together to challenge the sexist basis of the family, work, the law, and politics. Rediscovering the works of their grandmother's suffragette generation and the accomplishments of "Rosie the Riveter" in their mother's time, they again started to question the basis of the societal arrangements that led to women's oppression. Women were now better educated and more financially and socially independent, and many increasingly demanded equal rights and opportunities in all public areas. Some moderate changes, and the failure of the E.R.A. in 1982, left many feeling that all had been done that could be accomplished at that time.

While the second wave of feminism was largely a movement about "women's rights," and primarily attracted white middle-class women, the third wave of feminism during the 1980s and 1990s attempted to establish a broader base that was sensitive to other equally powerful forms of inequality, such as class, race, sexual orientation, and nationality. Goals were redefined and inclusion, at least for women as a group, and the end of all forms of oppression became the idealized values of the movement. The suffering of women in developing countries was increasingly recognized. There was growing awareness that the same political and socioeconomic values and assumptions that are the bedrock of sexism are also the root of all other forms of inequality. Unfortunately, much of this new, often quite abstract feminist thought was restricted to academia and isolated feminist groups.

As noted at the beginning of this text, feminism, as a social movement, is presently seen as being in a period of abeyance.[16] Many women continue to press for small changes in the system as they are affected by it, but refuse to self-identify with the label *feminist*. The third wave of feminism simply "ran out of steam" and stalled because of the lack of mass support. Ironically, there are many girls and young women today who are making very feminist choices in their lives and who support many of the goals of the women's rights movement, but they refuse to call themselves feminists. Through the misogynist tactics of the conservative right (e.g., coining terms like *feminazis*) and the mass media, the word *feminism* has acquired much negative baggage in our society.

Obviously, things need to change if feminism is ever to become a vital social movement again and realize its far-reaching goals. The past efforts of feminist and other progressive groups suggest to us how those goals might be achieved. There is a significant and quite radical potential when women and men, the oppressed and the oppressor, enter into alliance to challenge oppression. If one looks at all of the progressive social movements of the past three hundred years, it has been exactly those times that the oppressed and the oppressor entered into alliance that oppression was successfully challenged. In fact, quite arguably, the only times progressive change has occurred has been when dominants and subordinates have joined forces together to bring about positive social change.[17]

The abolitionist movement in the United States that successfully brought an end to slavery was made up of coalitions of blacks and whites, men and women, oppressor and oppressed. While their successes were limited in the long run—more symbolic than meaningful in the lives of most blacks—drawing on a broad base of people, the abolitionist movement nevertheless brought to an end perhaps the most contemptible form of oppression, that one human could own another. The Nineteenth Amendment that gave women the legal right to vote in 1920 was made possible by coalitions of women and men,[18] oppressed and oppressor, and ultimately passed exclusively by men who could vote. The limited successes of the Civil Rights movement that most visibly emerged in the 1950s and culminated with symbolic legislation being passed in the late 1960s and early 1970s was again made possible by progressive blacks and whites joining forces. The recent passage of same-sex unions in Vermont was made possible by progressive straight people entering into alliance with gay and lesbian individuals. Consistent with each of these examples, there is a growing body of social research that strongly suggests that alliances created across difference, especially those between the oppressed and the oppressor, will also be the politics of the future.[19]

We are beginning to see a new social activism reminiscent of the 1960s, primarily directed at the oppressive practices of organizations such as the World Trade Organization, the World Bank, and the International Monetary Fund. Protests against them have attracted strange bedfellows, creating alliances between previous enemies who now agree on one thing: Exploitive business practices and the systems that support them are destroying the planet. Strife and discontent, even in wealthy nations, seem to be the norm of the present human condition, and no present ideologies seem efficacious enough to reverse the direction such outlooks are heading us. There seems to be some general agreement on what is wrong and who is to blame—greedy corporations and corrupt politicians (two more worldwide norms of the contemporary masculine politics)—but not on how the problems can be fixed. Depression and anomie are widespread in all wealthy nations with many people in these countries turning to drugs, alcohol, and other opiates to numb and escape the pain of feelings of personal failure and alienation that oppression causes. People are ready and anxiously waiting for a new ideology that has a vision powerful enough to generate passion and energy for progressive social change.

Already we can see some of the outlines of what this new ideology will contain, and there are strong signs that it will be very different from the protests and activism of the 1960s in the United States. This new social movement will be driven by the need to protect the environment and the urgency of ecological issues. Social problems will increasingly be defined globally (e.g., "What happens in the Brazilian rain forest or the Singapore job market also affects me"). Political and business decisions that put the world at risk while generating riches for the few will no longer be acceptable. The activism of the 1960s primarily focused on immediate goals, such as America pulling out of Vietnam or passing Civil Rights legislation, whereas this new social movement looks to challenge the basic assumptions of the world culture and the accepted practices it has developed over the past two hundred years. It looks to end oppressive business-as-usual policies that have put the planet on the brink of destruction.

Feminism has much to potentially offer here but some of its principles and objectives will have to be re-envisioned. Feminism has done a wonderful job of theoretically illuminating how gendered outlooks are used to create and sustain inequalities and oppression on all levels ranging from the individual to the global. Unfortunately, however, most of its activism has been focused on securing individual rights for women and not challenging the larger world structures that both reflect and sustain gender inequalities and women's oppression. Feminism needs to become more attuned and cooperatively active in social movements contesting environmentally harmful and oppressive practices on a worldwide level. The theoretical understandings of the gendered basis of all inequalities and forms of oppression provided by feminism will offer key insights into the causes and the possible solutions to environmentally destructive worldwide practices and how they are ultimately grounded in a worldview of male dominance that views Mother Earth as a woman, a rightful object for men to rape and pillage.

As we have consistently argued throughout this book, feminism also needs to redefine who is the enemy. White middle-class feminists in wealthy nations need to better recognize that their own countries are often the enemy and oppressor in the worldwide matrices of domination and subordination.[20] From these new insights will come many possibilities for radical alliances to be created across differences in the pursuit of an oppressive-free future.[21] (Pro)feminist men who are sincerely committed to ending oppression in all the gendered ways it manifests itself will be important allies in the quest for equality. Their demonstrated willingness to give up unearned male privilege and to cooperatively work with women will be a necessary step in undoing the harms of patriarchy. Other alliances across difference, some already occurring, will have to be created and sustained. Key to these efforts will be the recognition that oppressed and oppressor must join forces if the harms of inequality are ever to be undone and an oppression-free future made possible. This is the fourth wave of feminism that we have attempted to envision in this book.

Like the now obsolete idiom of communism, the term *feminism* has come to have a lot of negative connotations and itself may become more of a hindrance than a help in creating radical alliances to challenge and undo oppression in the twenty-first century. Perhaps what is needed is a new, gender-neutral term that is not associated with either the women's movement or men's movement. Such a term would make clear that *both* men and women must choose new ways of thinking and acting. It would also emphasize that true change to end inequality and oppression is not possible until alliances of people across difference are created and maintained. Such a term would have a global as well as local emphasis with a fundamental focus of transforming both our public and private lives. This new term would ultimately denote an inclusive stance against all of the harms from the multifarious forms of oppression.

Time will tell if a new, inclusive banner will be needed, but the gendered understandings of how oppression operates that feminism has made possible must never be lost if these new coalitions for social justice are to be successful. We believe that the time has come for women and men, oppressed and oppressors, to join forces as partners to not only create a new world outlook based on social justice but to ensure our survival as a species on planet earth. Only then will the present harms of doing "business as usual" be recognized, contested, and replaced. Only then will the concept of original sin, and all the various ways that it manifests itself, be undone and an egalitarian future be made possible. We sincerely hope that this book is a small, helpful step in the pursuit of an oppression-free future.

All people of conscience who occupy statuses of oppressor need to recognize the harms of their choices and ways. Sadly, for most people, both oppressor and oppressed, the pursuit of the good life seems more about finding ways to avoid being oppressed—often by seeking ways to oppress others. Is this a healthy approach to life? We think not! The only way for an egalitarian future to be realized is for the oppressed, and those who oppress them, to both acknowledge the unnecessary limits, pain, and suffering from inequality. Once this occurs, then truly radical alliances will be made possible where both the oppressed and the oppressors can enter into partnership to contest and dismantle the abject realities of today. Women and men must join together if this is ever to occur.

The very writing of this book has been the result of our efforts to dialogue and theorize across our disparate differences of gender and sexuality, across what are traditional categories of oppressor and oppressed. This has been a labor-intensive process where every word found on each page, in each paragraph, and even each sentence represent the very dialogue of our negotiations across these differences. The voice found throughout this book embodies our discussion as colleagues, comrades, and friends to live and envision new ways of viewing and being in the world. This book has very much been an inclusive project wherein each of us was accountable to the others perspective, a true partnership and praxis of equality in action. While the reader will ultimately determine how fruitful this approach has been, in our hearts we strongly believe that the sum of our voices is far more powerful than either of our individual utterances on the topics of feminism, men, women, and oppression could have been. Writing this book has been a growing experience for both of us and, much for the better, we are not the same people we were when we began this work.

At the individual, group, society, and international levels we believe that it is time for the oppressors to comprehend the historical moment—that present oppressive ways will very probably destroy the planet—and enter into radical alliances with the oppressed to challenge and end the unnecessary harms that result from any form of inequality. The oppressed alone cannot create an egalitarian future, nor can the oppressor do this for them because, viewed separately, both are necessary but insufficient for this to happen. Equality will only be realized when the oppressed and the oppressor enter into radical alliances and true partnerships are formed between them in pursuit of this long idealized goal of so many over the ages.

## Notes

1. Faludi 1999.
2. Connell 2000.
3. Connell 2000.
4. Messerschmidt 1993.
5. Kimmel 2002.
6. We thank Phyllis Elaine Liddell for this insight.
7. Connell 2000.
8. Ashley and Orenstein 2000.
9. Deckard 1983.
10. Daly with Caputi 1987.
11. Yamato 1998, 90.
12. Miller 1995.
13. Connell 2000.
14. McIntosh 2000; Schacht 2001a.
15. Deckard 1983.
16. Taylor 1989; Faludi 1991.
17. Even Karl Marx and Frederick Engels in the *Manifesto* grasped the significance of the bourgeoisie and proletariat, oppressor and oppressed, entering into alliance to make an egalitarian future possible.

Just as, therefore, at an earlier period, a section of the nobility went over to the bourgeoisie, so now a portion of the bourgeoisie goes over to the proletariat, and in particular, a portion of the bourgeoisie ideologists, who have raised themselves to a level of comprehending theoretically the historical moment as a whole. (1848 [1977], 46)

Engels and Marx's very working relationship—between have and have not, respectively—also attests to the power alliances between haves and have nots. Of course, significant numbers of bourgeoisie never did join the proletariat, and capitalist patriarchy prevailed. We believe, however, that the primary reasons that the communist revolution that they predicted never occurred was that their theoretical model for social change failed to recognize that oppression is multilayered and overemphasized economic forms of inequality while ignoring gender and ethnic inequalities, all of which are the basis of oppression. In short, all forms of oppression must be challenged to create a world where equality would be made possible.

18. Kimmel and Mosmiller 1992.
19. Bystydzienski and Schacht 2001.
20. Jordan 1985; Hagan 1998; McIntosh 2000.
21. Bystydzienski and Schacht 2001.

~

# Afterword

On November 21, 2003, Steven Philip Schacht left this world following a lengthy struggle with colon cancer. Steve was many things to many people, but will probably best be remembered as a truly gifted, passionate, and engaging teacher. Steve relied upon the wisdom and experiences of his students, rather than the teachings of "dead white men," and the classroom became an opportunity for consciousness raising and transformation. To Steve, teaching was an art form, a livelihood, and a way of practicing feminism through bringing a truly feminist pedagogical stance to the classroom discussion. Steve was like a bright shining light in a dark room. He actively challenged his students to look within themselves at those things they typically didn't want to acknowledge or bring to light—their internalized homophobia and oppressive beliefs. This was always balanced with humor, encouragement, love, and the deepest levels of compassion.

Steve's teaching was in no way limited to the classroom. Steve embodied and lived what I believe was a form of engaged feminism. He was a practitioner of feminism and consciously sought to engage with others in a way that emphasized his beliefs about being with others in a nonoppressive way. He was an advocate for marginalized groups, and transitioned easily from faculty meetings to an evening out at a drag show with his students. Steve believed that what he taught his students was only useful if they could find a way to practice the concepts, incorporating the teachings into their consciousness and transforming their interactions with others. And most who had the benefit of sitting in one of Steve's classes would say that the experience was radically transforming. Steve was always true to himself, and truthful with others. I have never met another human being who possessed such integrity, and this view is shared by most who knew him. Steve was continually evolving, embracing his limitations, and healing from his own (sometimes self imposed) patriarchal wounds. Steve showed us that it isn't simply enough to know and teach feminism—you have to become and be it. You have to embrace and live it.

Steve engaged passionately in the dying process, as he did in all matters of his life—with no apologies, and no regrets. He shared his painful journey with others, in vivid, colorful detail. Those of us who were privileged enough to have had the opportunity to travel this journey with him are forever changed as a result. And Steve gave until the end, of himself, and of his humanity. Steve didn't turn away from dying, rather he stepped fully into the process, as one would expect from an individual possessing such strength of character, determination, courage and compassion. What an honor . . . to bear witness to the passing of this great soul and to be fully present as he died. I can say that he died with the same passion and equanimity with which he lived. And I, and many others, will mourn this loss always.

Lisa Underwood

# References

Aronowitz, Stanley. 1992. *The Politics of Identity: Class, Culture and Social Movements*. New York: Routledge.

Ashley, David, and David Michael Orenstein. 2000. 5th ed. *Sociological Theory: Classical Statements*. Needham Heights, MA: Allyn & Bacon.

Baca Zinn, Maxine, Lynn Weber Canon, Elizabeth Higginbotham, and Bonnie Thorton Dill. 1986. "The Costs of Exclusionary Practices in Women's Studies." *Signs: Journal of Women in Culture and Society* 11:290–303.

Bart, Pauline B., Linda N. Freeman, and Peter Kimball. 1991. "The Different Worlds of Women and Men: Attitudes toward Pornography and Responses to *Not a Love Story*—A Film about Pornography." In *Beyond Methodology: Feminist Scholarship as Lived Research*, 172–96. Bloomington: Indiana University Press.

Bartky, Sandra L. 1990. *Femininity and Domination: Studies in the Phenomenology of Oppression*. New York: Routledge.

Bernard, Jessie. 1972. *The Future of Marriage*. New York: World.

Beauvoir, Simone de. 1953. *The Second Sex*. Middlesex, England: Penguin.

Bird, Caroline. 1979. *The Two-Paycheck Marriage*. New York: Simon & Schuster.

Bly, Robert. 1990. *Iron John: A Book about Men*. MA: Addison-Wesley.

Bonvillian, Nancy. 2001. 3rd ed. *Women and Men Cultural Constructions of Gender*. Upper Saddle River, NJ: Prentice-Hall.

The Boston Women's Health Book Collective. 1992. *The New Our Bodies, Ourselves: Updated and Expanded for the '90's*. New York: Touchstone.

Bradshaw, Jan. 1982. "Now What Are They Up To? Men in the 'Men's Movement'!" In *On the Problem of Men: Two Feminist Conferences*, edited by Scarlet Friedman and Elizabeth Sarah, 174–89. London: The Women's Press.

185

Brownmiller, Susan. 1975. *Against Our Will: Men, Women and Rape*. New York: Bantam Books.

Bullough, Bonnie, Vern L. Bullough, and James Ellias, eds. 1997. *Gender Blending*. New York: Prometheus Books.

Butler, Judith. 1990. *Gender Trouble: Feminism and the Subversion of Identity*. New York: Routledge.

———. 1991. "Imitation and Gender Insubordination." In *Inside/Out: Lesbian Theories, Gay Theories*, edited by Diana Fuss, 13–31. New York: Routledge.

———. 1993. *Bodies That Matter: On the Discursive Limits of Sex*. New York: Routledge.

Bystydzienski, Jill M., and Steven P. Schacht, eds. 2001. *Forging Radical Alliances across Difference: Coalition Politics for the New Millennium*. Lanham, MD: Rowman & Littlefield.

Bystydzienski, Jill M. and Joti Sekhon, eds. 1999. *Democratization and Women's Grassroots Movements*. Bloomington: Indiana University Press.

Canaan, Joyce E., and Christine Griffin. 1990. "The New Men's Studies: Part of the Problem or Part of the Solution?" In *Men, Masculinities, and Social Theory*, edited by Jeff Hearn and David Morgan, 206–14 . London: Unwin Hymna.

Carlin, Kathleen. 1992. "The Men's Movement of Choice." In *Women Respond to the Men's Movement: A Feminist Collection*, edited by Kay Leigh Hagan, 119–25. San Francisco: HarperSan Francisco.

Collins, Patricia Hill. 1991. *Black Feminist Thought: Knowledge, Consciousness, and the Politics of Empowerment*. New York: Routledge.

Connell, R.W. 1995. *Masculinities*. Berkeley: University of California Press.

———. 2000. *The Men and the Boys*. Berkeley: University of California Press.

Coontz, Stephanie. 1993. *The Way We Never Were: Families and the Nostalgia Trap*. New York: Basic Books.

Cromwell, Jason. 1999. *Transmen & FTMs: Identities, Bodies, Genders & Sexualities*. Chicago: University of Illinois Press.

Curry, Timothy Jon. 1991. "Fraternal Bonding in the Locker Room: A Pro-feminist Analysis of Talk about Competition and Women." *Sociology of Sport Journal* 8:119–35.

Daly, Mary. 1978. *Gyn/Ecology: The Metaethics of Radical Feminism*. Boston: Beacon Press.

Daly, Mary, with Jane Caputi. 1987. *Wickerdary: Websters' First New Intergalactic Wickendary of the English Language*. Boston: Beacon Press.

Deckard, Barbara Sinclair. 1983. 3rd ed. *The Women's Movement: Political, Socioeconomic, and Psychological Issues*. New York: Harper & Row.

Delphy, Christine. 1993. "Rethinking Sex and Gender." *Women's Studies International Forum* 16: 1–9.

duCille, Ann. 1994. "The Occult of True Black Womanhood: Critical Demeanor and Black Feminist Studies." *Signs: Journal of Women in Culture and Society* 19: 591–629.

Dworkin, Andrea. 1987. *Intercourse*. New York: The Free Press.

———. 1989. *Pornography: Men Possessing Women.* New York: E. P. Dutton.

———. 2000. "The Day I Was Drugged and Raped." *New Statesman* 13 (June 5): 13.

Eisler, Riane. 1987. *The Chalice and the Blade: Our History, Our Future.* San Francisco: Harper & Row.

———. 1995. *Sacred Pleasure: Sex, Myth, and the Politics of the Body.* San Francisco: HarperSan Francisco.

Ember, Carol R. 1983. "The Relative Decline in Women's Contribution to Agriculture with Intensification . . ." *American Anthropologist* 85: 286–93.

Ewing, Doris W., and Steven P. Schacht. 1998. "Introduction." In *Feminism and Men: Reconstructing Gender Relations,* edited by Steven P. Schacht and Doris W. Ewing, 1–17.. New York: New York University Press.

Ewing, Doris W., and Steven P. Schacht, eds. 2000. Special Issue on "Sexuality: Toward A Race, Gender, Class Perspective." *Race, Gender & Class* 7: 7–9.

Faludi, Susan. 1991. *Backlash: The Undeclared War against American Women.* New York: Crown Publishers.

———. 2000. *Stiffed: The Betrayal of the American Man.* New York: Perennial (HarperCollins).

Fausto-Sterling, Anne. 1985. *Myths of Gender: Biological Theories about Men and Women.* New York: Basic Books.

———. 2000. *Sexing the Body: Gender Politics and the Construction of Sexuality.* New York: Basic Books.

Feinberg, Leslie. 1996. *Transgender Warriors: Making History from Joan of Arc to Dennis Rodman.* Boston: Beacon Press.

Freire, Paulo. 2000[1970]. *Pedagogy of the Oppressed: 30th Anniversary Edition.* Translated by Myra Bergman Ramos. New York: Seabury Press.

Friedan, Betty. 1963. *The Feminine Mystique.* New York: Dell.

Friedl, Ernestine. 1975. *Women and Men: An Anthropologist's View.* Austin, TX: Holt, Rinehart, and Winston.

———. 2001[1978]. "Society and Sex Roles." In *Annual Editions Anthropology: 2002/2003,* edited by Elvio Angeloni, 127–32. Guilford, CT: McGraw-Hill/Dushkin.

Friedman, Scarlet and Elizabeth Sarah, eds. 1992. *On the Problem of Men: Feminist Conferences.* London: Women's Press.

Frye, Marilynn. 1998. "Oppression." In *Race, Class and Gender: An Anthology,* edited by Margaret L. Andersen and Patricia Hill Collins, 48–52. Belmont, CA: Wadsworth.

Gamson, Joshua. 1995. "Must Identity Movements Self Destruct? A Queer Dilemma." *Social Problems* 42: 390–406.

Garber, Marjorie. 1992. *Vested Interests: Cross-Dressing and Cultural Anxiety.* New York: Routledge.

Gerson, Kathleen. 1993. *No Man's Land: Men's Changing Commitments to Family and Work.* New York: Basic Books.

Gill, Harriet. 1992. "Men's Predicament: Male Supremacy." In *Women Respond to the Men's Movement: A Feminist Collection,* edited by Kay Leigh Hagan, 151–57. San Francisco: HarperSan Francisco.

Gitlin, Todd. 1993. "The Rise of 'Identity Politics': An Examination of a Critique." *Dissent* (Spring): 172–77.

Goffman, Erving. 1961. *Asylums*. New York: Anchor Books.

Hagan, Kay Leigh, ed. 1992. *Women Respond to the Men's Movement: A Feminist Collection*. San Francisco: HarperSan Francisco.

———. 1998. "A Good Man Is Hard to Bash: Confessions of an Ex-Man-Hater." In *Feminism and Men: Reconstructing Gender Relations*, edited by Steven P. Schacht and Doris W. Ewing, 161–70. New York: New York University Press.

Halberstam, Judith. 1998. *Female Masculinity*. Durham: Duke University Press.

Hanmer, Jalna, and Mary Maynard, eds. 1987. *Women, Violence and Social Control*. Atlantic Highlands, NJ: Humanities Press International.

Haraway, Donna. 1988. "Situated Knowledges: The Science Question in Feminism and the Privilege of a Partial Perspective." *Feminist Studies* 14: 533–57.

Hawkesworth, M. E. 1989. "Knowers, Knowing, Known: Feminist Theory and Claims of Truth." *Signs: Journal of Women in Culture and Society* 14: 533–57.

Heath, Stephen. 1987. "Male Feminism." In *Men in Feminism*, edited by Alice Jardine and Paul Smith, 1–32 . New York: Methuen.

Hekman, Susan. 1987. "The Feminization of Epistemology: Gender and the Social Sciences *Women and Politics* 7: 65–83.

Herdt, Gilbert, ed. 1994. *Third Sex, Third Gender: Beyond Sexual Dimorphism in Culture and History*. New York: Zone Books.

Hochschild, Arlie. 1990. *The Second Shift*. New York: Avon Books.

hooks, bell. 1984. *Feminist Theory: From Margin to Center*. Boston: South End Press.

———. 1992. "Men in Feminist Struggle: The Necessary Movement." In *Women Respond to the Men's Movement: A Feminist Collection*, edited by Kay Leigh Hagan, 111–17. San Francisco: Harper San Francisco.

———. 2000. *Feminism is for Everybody: Passionate Politics*. Cambridge, MA: South End Press.

Hughes, Donna M. 1995. "Significant Differences: The Construction of Knowledge, Objectivity, and Dominance." *Women's Studies International Forum* 18: 395–406.

Humphreys, Laud. 1975. *Tearoom Trade: Impersonal Sex in Public Places*. New York: Aldine de Gruyter.

Jardine, Alice, and Paul Smith, eds. 1987. *Men in Feminism*. New York: Methuen.

Jensen, Robert. 1998. "Patriarchal Sex." In *Feminism and Men: Reconstructing Gender Relations*, edited by Steven P. Schacht and Doris W. Ewing, 99–118. New York: New York University Press.

Johnson, Sonia. 1987. *Going Out of Our Minds: The Metaphysics of Liberation*. Freedom, CA: Crossing Press.

———. 1989. *Wildfire: Igniting the She/Volution*. Albuquerque, NM: Wildfire Books.

Jordan, June. 1985. *On Call: Political Essays*. Boston: South End.

*Journal of the Association for Research on Mothering*. 2000. Special issue on "Feminists Raising Sons." 2(1).

Keen, Sam. 1991. *Fire in the Belly: On Being a Man*. New York: Bantam Double Day Dell Publishing Group.

Kimmel, Michael S. 2002. "Gender, Class, and Terrorism." *The Chronicle of Higher Education*, February 8.

Kimmel, Michael S., and Michael A. Messner, eds. 2000. 5th ed. *Men's Lives*. Boston: Allyn and Bacon.

Kimmel, Michael S., and Thomas Mosmiller, eds. 1992. *Against the Tide: Pro-feminist Men in the United States: A Documentary History*. Boston: Beacon.

Leonard, Diana. 1982. "Male Feminists and Divided Women." In *On the Problem of Men: Two Feminist Conferences*, edited by Scarlet Friedman and Elizabeth Sarah, 157–75. London: The Women's Press.

Levine, Martin P. 1998. *Gay Macho: The Life and Death of the Homosexual Clone*. Edited by Michael S. Kimmel. New York: New York University Press.

Lorber, Judith. 1994. *Paradoxes of Gender*. New Haven: Yale University Press.

———. 2001. *Gender Inequality: Feminist Theories and Politics*. 2nd ed. Los Angeles: Roxbury Publishing Company.

Lorde, Audre. 1984. *Sister Outsider*. Freedom, CA: The Crossing Press.

Lyons, Lenore. 2001. "Negotiating Difference: Singaporean Women Building an Ethics of Respect." Pp. 177–190 In *Forging Radical Alliances Across Difference: Coalition Politics for the New Millennium*, edited by Jill M. Bystydzienski and Steven P. Schacht, 177–90. Lanham, MD: Rowman & Littlefield

MacKinnon, Catherine A. 1989. *Toward A Feminist Theory of the State*. Cambridge, MA: Harvard University Press.

Marti, Judith. 1993. "Economics, Power and Gender Relations." In *The Other Fifty Percent: Multicultural Perspectives on Gender Relations*, edited by Mari Womack and Judith Marti,Pp. ??-?? . Prospect Heights, IL: Waveland Press.

Martin, Biddy, and Chandra Talpade Mohanty. 1986. In *Feminist Studies/Critical Studies*, edited by Teresa de Lauretis, 191–212. Bloomington: Indiana University Press

Marx, Karl, and Frederick Engels. 1977[1848]. *Manifesto of the Communist Party*. Peking: Foreign Languages Press.

Messerschmidt, James W. 1993. *Masculinities and Crime: Critique and Reconceptualization of Theory*. Lanham, MD: Rowman & Littlefield.

McIntosh, Peggy. 2000. "White Privilege and Male Privilege: A Personal Account of Coming to See Correspondence through Work in Women's Studies." In *The Social Construction of Difference and Inequality: Race, Class, Gender, and Sexuality*, edited by Tracy E. Ore, 475–85. Mountain View, CA: Mayfield Publishing Company.

Messner, Michael A. 1997. *Politics of Masculinities: Men in Movements*. Thousand Oaks, CA: Sage Publications.

Miller, Jean Baker. 1995. "Domination and Subordiantion." In *Race, Class, & Gender*, edited by Paula S. Rothenberg, 57–63. St. Martin's Press: New York.

Mills, C. Wright. 1967. *The Sociological Imagination*. New York: Oxford University Press.

Moraga, Cherrie, and Gloria Anzaldua, eds. 1983. *This Bridge Called My Back: Writing by Radical Women of Color*. New York: Kitchen Table: Women of Color Press.

Morgan, Robin, ed. 1970. *Sisterhood is Powerful: An Anthology of Writings From the Women's Liberation Movement*. New York: Vintage Book.

———. 1978. *Going Too Far: The Personal Chronicle of a Feminist*. New York: Vintage Books.

Morris, Aldon, and Carol McClurg Mueller, eds. 1992. *Frontiers in Social Movement Theory*. New Haven: Yale University Press.

Murdoch, George P., and Caterina Provost. 1973. "Factors in the Division of Labor by Sex: A Cross-Cultural Analysis." *Ethnology* 12: 203–25.

Nelson, Mariah Burton. 1994. *The Stronger Women Get, The More Men Love Football: Sexism and the American Culture of Sports*. New York: Avon Books.

Newton, Esther, with Shirley Walton. 2000. "The Personal Is Political: Consciousness Raising and Personal Change in the Women's Liberation Movement. In Esther Newton, *Margaret Mead Made Me Gay: Personal Essays, Public Ideas*, 113–41. Durham: Duke University Press.

Offen, Karen. 1988. "Defining Feminism: A Comparative Historical Approach." *Signs: Journal of Women in Culture and Society* 14: 119–57.

Piercy, Marge. 1976. *Woman on the Edge of Time*. New York: Fawcett Books.

Ramazanoglu, Caroline. 1992. "What Can You Do with a Man? Feminism and the Critical Appraisal of Masculinity." *Women's Studies International Forum* 15: 339–50.

Rich, Adrienne. 1980. "Compulsory Heterosexuality and Lesbian Existence." *Signs: Journal of Women in Culture and Society* 5:631–60.

Rubin, Lillian B. 1992. *Worlds of Pain: Life in the Working-Class Family*. New York: Basic Books.

Rupp, Leila J., and Verta Taylor. 1999. "Forging a Collective Identity in a International Movement: A Collective Identity Approach to Twentieth-Century Feminism." *Signs: Journal of Women in Culture and Society* 24: 363–83.

Russell, Diana E. H. 1982. *Rape in Marriage*. New York: Macmillan.

Sanday, Peggy Reeves. 1981. *Female Power and Male Dominance: On the Origins of Sexual Inequality*. MA: Cambridge University Press.

Schacht, Steven P. 1996. "Misogyny on and off the Rugby "Pitch": The Gendered World of Male Rugby Players." *Gender & Society* 10: 550–65.

———. 1997. "Feminist Fieldwork in the Misogynist Setting of the Rugby Pitch: Becoming a Sylph to Survive and Personally Grow." *Journal of Contemporary Ethnography* 26: 338–63.

———. 1998. "The Multiple Genders of the Court: Issues of Identity and Performance in a Drag Setting." In *Feminism and Men: Reconstructing Gender Relations*, edited by Steven P. Schacht and Doris W. Ewing, 202–24 . New York: New York University Press.

———. 2000. "Paris Is Burning: How Society's Stratification Systems Make Drag Queens of Us All." *Race, Gender & Class* 7:147–66.

———. 2001. "Teaching about Being an Oppressor: Some Personal and Political Considerations." *Men and Masculinities* 4(2):201–8.

————. 2004. "Beyond the Boundaries of the Classroom: Teaching About Gender and Sexuality at a Drag Show." *Journal of Homosexuality* 46: 225–40.

Schacht, S. P., and Patricia H. Atchison. 1993. "Heterosexual Instrumentalism: Past and Future Directions." In *Heterosexuality: A Feminism & Psychology Reader*, edited by Sue Wilkinson and Celia Kitzinger, 120–35. Newbury Park, CA: Sage Publications.

Schacht, Steven P., and Doris W. Ewing. 1997a. "The Many Paths of Feminism: Can Men Travel Any of Them?" *Journal of Gender Studies* 6: 159–76.

————. 1997b. "Sharing Power: Entering Women's Space." *Achilles Heel* 22 (Summer/Autumn): 34–36.

Schacht, Steven P., and Doris W. Ewing, eds. 1997. Special Issue on "Feminism and Men: Towards a Relational Understanding of Patriarchy and Cooperative Social Change." *International Journal of Sociology and Social Policy* 17:1–7.

————.1998. *Feminism and Men: Reconstructing Gender Relations.* New York: New York University Press.

Schlegel, Alice, and Herbert Barry III. 1986. "The Cultural Consequences of Female Contribution to Subsistence." *American Anthropologist* 88:142–50.

Schwartz, Pepper. 1994. *Peer Marriage: How Love between Equals Really Works.* New York: Free Press.

Sharik, Lisa. 2000. *Feminism and Men: Exploring the Lived-Experiences of Men Involved in Feminism.* B.A. Honors Thesis. Brock University, St. Catharines, Ontario.

Showalter, Elaine. 1987. "Critical Cross-Dressing: Male Feminists and the Year of Women." In *Men in Feminism*, edited by Alice Jardine and Paul Smith, 116–32. New York: Methuen.

Sommers, Christina Hoff. 2000. *The War against Boys: How Misguided Feminism Is Harming Our Young Men.* New York: Simon & Schuster, 2000.

Spelman, Elizabeth. 1988. *Inessential Women: Problems of Exclusion in Feminist Thought.* Boston: Beacon Press.

Stanley, Liz. 1982. "'Male Needs': The Problems and Problems of Working with Men." In *On the Problem of Men: Two Feminist Conferences*, edited by Scarlet Friedman and Elizabeth Sarah, 190–213. London: The Women's Press.

Stanley, Liz, and Sue Wise. 1979. "Feminist Research, Feminist Consciousness, and Experiences with Sexism." *Women's Studies International Forum* 2:359–74.

Starhawk. 1992. "A Men's Movement I Can Trust." In *Women Respond to the Men's Movement: A Feminist Collection*, edited by Kay Leigh Hagan, 27–37. San Francisco: HarperSan Francisco.

Steinem, Gloria. 1992. *Revolution from Within: A Book of Self-Esteem.* Boston: Little, Brown.

Stoltenberg, John. 1990. *Refusing to Be a Man: Essays on Sex and Justice.* New York: Penguin.

————. 1993. *The End of Manhood: A Book for Men of Conscience.* New York: Dutton.

————. 1998. "Healing from Manhood: A Radical Mediation on the Movement from Gender Identity to Moral Identity." In *Feminism and Men: Reconstructing Gender*

*Relations*, edited by Steven P. Schacht and Doris W. Ewing, 146–60. New York: New York University Press.

Taylor, Verta. 1989. "Social Movement Continuity: The Women's Movement in Abeyance." *American Sociological Review* 54:761–74.

Thoreau, Henry David. 1997[1854]. *Economy*. Quality Paperback Book Club.

Thorne, Barrie, Cheris Kramarae, and Nancy Henley, eds. 1983. *Language, Gender, and Society*. New York: Newbury House.

Toffler, Alvin. 1981. *The Third Wave*. New York: Bantam Books.

Trigiani, Kathleen. n.d. [Discussion of how men overestimate the amount of housework they do]. http://web2.airmail.net/ktrig246/out_of_cave/gv_notes.html#133.

Walker, Alice. 1983. *In Search of Our Mothers' Gardens: Womanist Prose*. San Diego: A Harvest Book.

Ward, Martha Coonfield. 1999. 2nd ed. *A World Full of Women*. Boston: Allyn & Bacon.

Whyte, Martin K. 1978. *The Status of Women in Preindustrial Societies*. NJ: Princeton University Press.

Wikinson, Sue, and Celia Kitzinger. 1993. *Heterosexuality: A Feminism & Psychology Reader*. Newbury Park, CA: Sage Publications

Yamato, Gloria. 1998. "Something about This Subject Makes It Hard to Name." In *Race, Class and Gender: An Anthology*, edited by Margaret L. Andersen and Patricia Hill Collins, 89–93. Belmont, CA: Wadsworth.

Young, Iris. 1988. "The Five Faces of Oppression." *Philosophical Forum* 19:270–90.

# Index

abolitionist movement, 176, 177
abortion, 1, 23
abuse. *See* child abuse
academia, 50–52, 160
activism, 178
Addams, Jane, 176
adolescent males: feminist parenting and, 142; macho subculture of, 52, 67; socialization through video games of, 85; violence as proof of masculinity for, 77. *See also* boys
Afghanistan, 170
Africa, women's power in, 65–66
alcohol, 85–86
androgyny: as model for fatherhood, 136; as model for social relations, 14–15
anthropology, 9–10, 59
*Apocalypse Now* (film), 64
Atchison, Patricia, 27

backlash: against gender equality, 65; overview of, 2–3; persistence of, 35
Bart, Pauline B., 96
Beauvoir, Simone de, 96

Bible: Adam and Eve in, 172; and exploitation of earth, 173–74
binary categories, 11–12, 97, 152, 172
Bly, Robert, 64, 157
books, as sources for understanding women's oppression, 104
boys: and emotions, 88, 143; feminist parenting for, 140–43; girls versus, 16, 89; values taught to, 16, 87–88. *See also* adolescent males
Bush, George W., 168, 170
Butler, Judith, 4

Carey, Drew, 79
Carlin, Kathleen, 114
Carolla, Adam, 79
"Cat's in the Cradle" (Chapin), 136
Chapin, Harry, 136
child abuse, 36
children: boys versus girls, 16, 89; of feminist parenting, 135–48; gender role models for, 24–26, 42–43, 139, 141–42, 145–47; gender roles taught to, 89, 108, 141, 146; marital

relationships affected by, 70; power
and, 146–47; values taught to, 16
Civil Rights movement, 177–78
civilizations, cycle of, 8
class: gender relations and, 13; and
opposition to feminism, 153; women
of color and, 7
clothing, 46
coalition politics, 151–63; centrist
alliances, 160–63; frontier alliances,
163; for global activism, 179; history
of successful, 177–78; impediments
to, 151–53; male and female issues
in, 153–58; marginal alliances,
158–60; necessity of, 17, 163. See
also inclusion of men
Columbine school shootings, 170
communication, male-female behavior
in, 104–6, 130–31, 133, 147
compassion, 115, 129
competition: as essential to masculinity,
76, 77–80; in gambling, 84
computer games. See video games
Connell, R. W., 165, 166
conservative backlash. See backlash
conversations. See communication,
male-female behavior in
Cuba, 175
cultural imperialism: within feminism,
3; as oppression, 100

Daly, Mary, 46, 172
dating, 34
defense spending, 170
discrimination, 101
discussions. See communication, male-
female behavior in
divorce, 67, 68, 69, 137, 138
dominance. See male privilege;
oppression; patriarchy
Dorkin, Andrea, 46
double ontological bind, 102, 173
double shift. See second shift

double standard: in college, 44, 51;
concerning oppression, 155; at home
and work, 70, 102
drag queens, 29–30
Dworkin, Andrea, 106–7

Earth. See environment
Earth-based spirituality, 57, 159
emotions: of children, parenting and,
143–44; in conversation, 105; as
female trait, 12–13; of men, 30, 37,
78–79, 88, 92, 143–44; oppression
and, 103; self-transformation and,
92; women responsible for family,
108–9
employment. See work
empowerment, 48, 138–39
Engels, Frederick, 181n17
England, 175
environment: degradation of, 173–74,
179; Earth-based spirituality and, 57;
feminist values and preservation of,
37–38; global standards for, 175;
social movement to protect,
178–79
environmental movement, 17, 178–79
Equal Rights Amendment, 1–2, 176
equality. See inequality
Eskimos, women's lack of power among,
66
essentialism, 97
Ewing, Doris, 27–28
exploitation, 99

Faludi, Susan, 30
family, 64–70; equality in, 133;
individualism and, 67–68; money
and power in, 65–67; oppression of
women in, 108–10; two-earner,
69–70, 137; work balanced with,
146. See also parenting
fashion, 46
fatherhood, changing status of, 136–38

fear: of government authorities, 169;
     oppression of women through, 102,
     169; of terrorism, 169–70
female-headed households, 146
*Feminine Mystique* (Friedan), 43
feminism: achievements of, 7;
     androgyny versus complementary
     gender roles, 14–15, 18; backlash
     against (*see* backlash); cycle of, 8;
     debate over men in, 96–98; decline
     of, 1–5, 177; first wave, 176; fourth
     wave, 163, 176–81; fragmentation of,
     2; and global activism, 178–80; ideal
     model of, 7, 9, 15, 58, 139–40;
     inclusion of men in (*see* inclusion of
     men); margins of, 158–60;
     masculinity replaced by, 114–16; men
     excluded from, 5–7, 14, 55, 96–97,
     117n5, 130, 152–53, 154–56,
     157–58; and mother-daughter
     relationship, 138–40; and mother-son
     relationship, 140–43; opposition
     within, 3, 47–48, 155; and outreach,
     10, 17; paradigm shift in, 8–11;
     parenting and, 135–48; (pro)feminist
     men and, 133–34, 153–58, 161;
     realizing future based on, 19–20,
     176–81; rejection of, factors in, 6–8,
     14, 55; second wave (*see* second wave
     feminism); seeds of failure within,
     4–5; sexism in, 5–9, 29; socialist, 14;
     as source of understanding women's
     oppression, 104–6; and teaching by
     example, 145–47; and thinking like
     men, 16; third wave (*see* third wave
     feminism); values of (*see* feminist
     values); white, middle-class,
     heterosexual bias in, 2, 47, 153,
     154–55; women's path to, 96
feminist organizations, hierarchy in, 155
feminist values: efficacy of, 18; as
     human values, 15–16; traditional
     values as, 15–16, 18, 19

films, war represented in, 63–64
first wave feminism, 176
football, 82–83
fourth wave feminism, 163, 176–81
freedom, individualism and, 67–68
Freire, Paulo, 18, 111
Friedan, Betty, 43
Friedl, Ernestine, 65, 67

gambling, 83–84
gangs, 169–70
gay bars, 125–26
gays: drag queens, 29–30; female beauty
     determined by, 81; and multiple-
     gender groups, 158; oppression of,
     30; social progress for, 7; straights'
     friendship with, 125. *See also*
     homophobia
gender bending, 158–59
gender relations: androgyny and, 14–15;
     antagonism in, 152; binary basis of,
     11, 152, 172; changes in, 165;
     children inculcated in, 89, 108, 141,
     146; class and, 13; complementary
     gender roles, 14–15, 18; cross-
     cultural comparisons of, 59–60;
     model of, 15; mother-son, 89;
     personality traits and, 12–13, 44,
     115, 173 (*see also* emotions); and
     public versus private realms, 62–63,
     66; reconstruction of, 11–15; scarcity
     models of, 9, 14; sexuality and,
     106–8; transgendered individuals
     and, 13. *See also* marriage: roles and
     responsibilities in; social
     construction of gender
Genesis, Book of, 171
genetic engineering, 174
"gentle-men," 52–54, 56
Gill, Harriet, 106
girls: boys versus, 16, 89; and mother-
     daughter relationship, 138–40;
     values taught to, 16

glass ceiling, 7, 101
globalization: masculinity and, 165–81; social activism and, 178–81
God, as patriarch, 87
god/goddess traditions, 57
Goffman, Erving, 42
Green movement, 17
*Gyn/Ecology* (Daly), 46

Hawkesworth, M. E., 97
Hefner, Hugh, 79
heterosexuality: and gender inequality, 6–7; as oppressive, 106–8
high-risk behavior, 36
history, 100
Hollywood, war represented by, 63–64
home. *See* family
homophobia: avoidance of men's groups and, 92; conformity enforced through, 122–24; confronting, 124–27; masculinity and, 76, 77, 122–24
homosexuality. *See* gays; lesbians
*The Honeymooners* (television show), 66
hooks, bell, 5, 9, 56, 96, 140

"I Didn't Even Know Her Name" (Jaci), 31–33
identity politics: feminist groups and, 156; and gender antagonism, 152–53; of social movements, 4
inclusion of men: guidelines for, 131–32, 161–62; issues and questions about, 131, 153–58; need for, 55–58, 97–98, 163; pros and cons of, 54–55, 160–61. *See also* coalition politics
individualism: and changing family roles, 67–68; masculinity versus, 78, 87; (pro)feminism and, 115
inequality: Equal Rights Amendment, 1–2; of gender as fundamental, 171–72; gendered basis of global, 171–76; heterosexuality and, 6–7;

(pro)feminist men overcoming, 133; reluctance to confront, 10; in work assessment, 12. *See also* double standard
International Monetary Fund, 178
Iraq, 175
Iroquois, women's power among, 65–66

Jaci, 20, 31–33
Japan, 175
jobs. *See* work
Johnson, Sonia, 114–15, 116

Keen, Sam, 157
Kimmel, Jimmy, 79
Kyoto Agreement, 175

Lake, Meg "Nan," 24
leadership, bias toward males in, 12, 13
leisure, 110
lesbian separatists, 3, 6, 7
lesbians: and multiple-gender groups, 158; partner roles for, 48–50; social progress for, 7; straights' friendship with, 125
liberal humanism, 159
listening, women's oppression understood through, 104–6
Lorde, Audre, 17, 82, 108

male bonding, 33–34, 120–21
male dominance. *See* patriarchy
male privilege: alternatives to, 72–73; preserving, 33–34; reasons to abandon, 65; re-establishing, movements for, 157; revealing, 101–3; traditional sources of, 65–67, 69–70; using, for advantaged of the oppressed, 113. *See also* masculinity
*The Man Show* (television show), 79
manhood. *See* masculinity
Maples, Marla, 79

marginalization, 99–100
marriage: peer marriages, 110, 138; roles
    and responsibilities in, 49–50, 61,
    65–70, 71, 108–10, 136–38; sexism
    as cause of problems in, 71; as 60-40
    proposition, 45, 108–9. See also
    same-sex unions
*Married with Children* (television show),
    66
Martin, Biddy, 1
Marx, Karl, 181n17
masculinity: alcohol and, 85–86;
    components of, 76; costs of proving,
    35–37, 67, 75–92; empty promises of,
    86–89; fear of the feminine and,
    33–34, 76, 77, 88–89, 122–23;
    feminism as replacement for, 114–16;
    as fundamental in male socialization,
    71, 76–77; gambling and, 83–84;
    game of, 77–80; globalization of,
    165–81; hegemonic, 166–71;
    homophobia and, 76, 77, 122–24;
    misogyny and, 33–34, 76, 77, 89,
    122–24; pornography and, 81–82;
    promotion of, 77–86; role models for,
    79; social construction of, 89;
    television sports and, 82–83;
    varieties of, 75–76; vicarious
    experiences of, 81–86; video games
    and, 84–85; violence of
    subordinated, 167–70; warrior role
    and, 63–64. See also male privilege
*M.A.S.H.* (television show), 63–64
Masten, Ric, 53
masturbation, 107, 118n29
McGovern, George, 23
McIntosh, Peggy, 112
McVeigh, Timothy, 170
media: ethnic conflicts portrayed by,
    167; gender opposition promoted by,
    9, 14; misogyny of, 177; oppression
    as portrayed by, 99; power of, 46; war
    represented in, 63–64

men: anxiety and despair of, 86–89;
    bonding of, 33–34, 120–21; and
    compassion, 115; costs of male
    dominance for, 35–37, 61, 71–73,
    75; emotions of, 30, 37, 78–79, 88,
    92, 143–44; as equal partners in
    feminist reality, 9; equality promoted
    by, 35; healing journey for, 89–92;
    and incentives for social change,
    17–19, 72–73; inclusion of (see
    inclusion of men); listening as
    difficult for, 104–5; men's groups,
    91–92; moral self-examination
    needed by, 88; obstacles to feminism
    for, 6; oppression of women by, 33; as
    other for feminism, 5–7, 55, 96–97,
    117n5, 130, 152–53, 154–56,
    157–58; personality traits of, 12–13,
    30 (see also emotions of);
    (pro)feminist (see (pro)feminist
    men); reasons to abandon male
    privilege, 65; redefining relationships
    to, 52–55; rejection of oppressive
    values and behaviors by, 17; self-
    transformation of, 89–92; sexual
    attractiveness ideals of, 107–8;
    silence of, in presence of oppression,
    121–22; traditional sources of power
    for, 65–67, 69–70, 136–38; as victims
    of oppression, 29–30, 35–37;
    women's role in recognition of
    oppression, 34, 38. See also
    adolescent males; boys; male
    privilege; masculinity; patriarchy
men's groups, 91–92
Men's Rights Movement, 157
men's studies curriculum, 157
mentoring, 113–14
Miller, Jean Baker, 173
Million Man March, 157
minorities. See racism; women of color
misogyny: conformity enforced through,
    122–24; confronting, 124–27;

masculinity and, 33–34, 76, 77, 89, 122–24; of media and conservative right, 177; role models of, 79; in video games, 85; at work, 122. See also sexism

Mohanty, Chandra Talpade, 1

money: consumer spending and debt, 174–75; as essential to masculinity, 76; family and, 109; masculine perspective on, 79–80; power and, 65–67; two-earner families and, 69–70

morality, emotion prior to reason in acquiring, 87–88

mother-daughter relationship, 138–40

mothering, 143–45

mother-son relationship, 140–43

National Organization for Women (NOW), 23; achievements of, 7; criticisms of, 2; principles versus political expediency in, 47

National Women's Studies Association (NWSA): achievements of, 7; criticisms of, 2

nature. See environment

negative advantages, 112–13

Nineteenth Amendment, 177

objectification, 106–7, 132–33

oppression: alliances for overcoming, 180–81, 181n17; apparent naturalness of, 101; as basis of societies, 160; characteristics of, 99–101; defined, 99; emotions connected with, 103, 173; experiential recognition of, 96; global, 165–81; individual and structural means of, 106–11; internalized, 173; learning about women's, 104–6; male recognition of role in, 98–103; of men, 29–30, 35–37; multiple forms of, 7, 29, 153,

172, 181n17; revealing, 98–103; solidarity with victims of, 111–14, 124–27, 180–81; of Third World women, 7; by U.S., 167–68; of women of color, 7. See also patriarchy

organic model of history, 8

organizations, hierarchy in feminist, 155

original sin, patriarchy and, 172–73

other: cultural imperialism and, 100; as necessary to ideology, 4–5; stereotypes and, 125; video games and violence against the, 85

"Parable" (Jaci), 20

parenting, 135–48, 149n23; fatherhood changing, 136–38; mother-daughter relationship, 138–40; mothering, 145–47; power and, 146–47; role of emotions in, 143–44; sons and feminist, 140–43; teaching feminism by example, 145–47. See also children

patriarchy: alternatives to, 9–10, 59–60, 165; and binary categories, 97; breaking boundaries of, 116–17; as central issue in second wave feminism, 5; commercial reinforcement of, 81–86; environment threatened by, 37–38; ideology of, 62–63; objectification and, 107; persistence of, 10; personal problems resulting from, 61, 71–73, 75; reasons to abandon, 65; religion as support for, 62, 87–88, 171–72; and self-concept, 71–72; social conditions promoting, 10, 60; social ills resulting from, 19, 60–61, 71–73, 75; as target of feminism, 6; within women's rights movement, 48

peer marriages, 110, 138

Piercy, Marge, 149n23

Platoon (film), 64

Playstation II, 64
poor countries, exploitation of, 167–68,
174
population growth, 174
pornography, 33, 81–82, 100, 107,
118n29
positive advantages, 113
postindustrial society, 62–64
postmodernism, 12, 13
power: children and, 146–47; as
essential to masculinity, 76;
masculine perspective on, 80; money
as, 65–67; over, with, and under, 48,
129, 139, 142–43; in partnerships,
49–50; women and, 56, 65–67
powerlessness, 100
praxis, 119
(pro)feminist men: becoming, 55, 92,
95–117; being, 119–34; confidence
of, 127–29; feminism and, 114–16,
133–34, 153–58, 161; gay and
lesbian sympathies of, 126; groups
for, 151–52; and individual and
structural means of oppression,
106–11; and learning about women's
oppression, 104–6; mothering by,
143–45; parenting by, 135–48;
pathways to becoming, 103–16;; in
presence of men, 120–29; in
presence of women, 53, 129–33;
recognition of oppressor role by,
98–103; risks for, 115, 154; in
solidarity with women and the
oppressed, 111–14, 124–27; speaking
up for feminism by, 128–29; women
as equals for, 132–33
Promise Keepers, 65, 157
prostitutes, 33

queer politics, 158

racism, 7, 13
rape, 100, 101, 102, 112–13, 118n29

religion, patriarchy reinforced by, 62,
87–88, 171–72. See also Bible
Roe v. Wade (1973), 1

same-sex unions, 178
Sanger, Margaret, 176
Saving Private Ryan (film), 64
Schacht, Steve, 53–54
Schwartz, Pepper, 110
second shift, 108, 136
second wave feminism: identity politics
and, 152; men excluded from, 5; and
mother-daughter relationship, 139;
oppressive values identified by, 16;
summary of, 176; as unified, 2
self-concept: developing new, 89–92;
patriarchy and, 71–72; of
(pro)feminist men, 124, 126,
127–29; and response to slurs, 124,
126
September 11, 2001 terrorist attacks,
168–70
sex: as essential to masculinity, 76;
masculine perspective on, 78–79,
108; oppression through, 106–8
sexism: in college rules, 44; as enemy of
new feminism, 9; in feminism, 5–9,
29; gender antagonism and, 152;
marital problems caused by, 71;
societal awareness of, 7. See also
misogyny
sexual attractiveness, 107–8
The Simpsons (television show), 66
single mothers, 146
social activism, 178
social change: incentives for, 17–19,
72–73; necessity of, 19–20, 180; old
ideology versus, 71; readiness for, 10,
17, 178; recent, 165; responsibility
for, 162–63
social construction of gender: lesbian
relationships as revealing, 49;
masculinity, 89; in 1950s and 1960s,

41; in non-Western cultures, 52;
postmodern theory of, 12
social movements: coalitions in, 177–78;
exclusion as necessary to founding of,
4–5; marginalization of, 100
socialism: socialist feminism, 14;
socialist men, 159–60
solidarity with women and the
oppressed, 111–14, 124–27, 180–81
Sopranos (television show), 170
soul, as traditionally female, 57
Southwest Missouri State University,
27–28
spirit, as traditionally male, 57
spirituality: Earth-based, 57, 159; male
transformation through, 91
sports: gambling on, 83–84; masculine
violence in, 80; television, 82–83
stereotypes, 125
Stern, Howard, 35, 79
Stoltenberg, John, 75, 78, 114, 123
strength, emotional, 145
strip shows, 33
subordinated masculinities, 169–70
suicide, 37

Taliban, 170
Tao, 58
technology: alteration of environment
through, 174; relation to patriarchy
of, 59–61
television sports, 82–83
terrorism, 168, 170
therapy, 91
The Thin Red Line (film), 64
"thinking like men," 16
third wave feminism: and mother-
daughter relationship, 138, 139;
summary of, 176–77; variety within,
2–3, 152–53
The Third Wave (Toffler), 62
Third World women: complementary
gender roles promoted by, 14, 153;

multiple oppressions of, 7; opposition
to feminism of, 7, 153
Title IX (1972), 1
Toffler, Alvin, 62
transgendered individuals, 13
transsexuals, 13
Trump, Donald, 79
Trump, Ivana, 79
Truth, Sojourner, 7
two-earner families, 69–70, 137

Underwood, Lisa, 34
United Nations, 175
United Nations Convention on the
Elimination of All Forms of
Discrimination against Women, 175
United States: global exploitation by,
167–68, 175–76; and international
agreements, 175; worldwide hatred
of, 176

values. See feminist values
Veblen, Thorstein, 172
Victoria, queen of England, 68
video games: masculinity and, 84–85,
93n14; moral character of, 64
violence: as essential to masculinity, 76,
80; global, masculinity and, 167–68;
males as perpetrators and victims of,
36; masculinity proved through, 64,
77, 80, 167–68; as oppression,
100–101; of subordinated
masculinities, 169–70
voting rights, 176, 177

Walker, Alice, 97–98, 153
war: hegemonic masculinity and,
166–67, 171; masculine role in, 63;
moral character of, 63–64; U.S. and,
170–71
The Warriors (film), 170
Wayne, John, 63
West Side Story (musical), 170

*Woman on the Edge of Time* (Piercy), 149n23
womanism, 153
women. *See* feminism; girls; Third World women; women of color
women of color: complementary gender roles promoted by, 14; multiple oppressions of, 7; opposition to feminism of, 7, 153; social progress for, 7
Women's Art Registry Movement (WARM), 23
women's athletics, 1
women's issues, 9, 51, 159
women's liberation, 47
women's movement. *See* feminism
women's rights movement, 47–48

women's studies curriculum, 104
work: balanced with family, 146; equality at, 133; gender roles in, 12, 63, 66–67, 69; men and, 79–80; misogyny at, 122; oppression of women at, 110–11; powerlessness at, 100; two-earner families and, 69–70; unpaid, 99; white male privilege at, 101; women's power and, 65–67
World Bank, 167, 178
World Trade Organization, 178

XBox, 64, 85

Yamato, Gloria, 172
Young, Iris Marion, 99

# About the Author

Steven P. Schacht (1960–2003) served as professor in the Department of Sociology at Plattsburgh State University of New York. The bulk of his research over the past 10 years was ethnographic in approach, exploring issues of gender identity and gender construction. He also served as coeditor of *Feminism and Men: Reconstructing Gender Relations* with Doris Ewing, and *Forging Radical Alliances Across Difference: Coalition Politics for a New Millennium* with Jill Bystydzienski. Steve openly and honestly battled colon cancer for five years, dying in 2003 with the same passion and equanimity with which he lived.

Doris W. Ewing is a professor emeritus of sociology at Southwest Missouri State University. Her primary areas of research and teaching are race, class, gender, and disability. She has been active in community organizing and has previously coauthored a book and several articles on men and feminism with Steven P. Schacht.